Tocqueville's Nightmare

Tocqueville's Nightmare

The Administrative State Emerges in America, 1900–1940

DANIEL R. ERNST

OXFORD
UNIVERSITY PRESS

OXFORD
UNIVERSITY PRESS

Oxford University Press is a department of the University of Oxford. It furthers the University's objective of excellence in research, scholarship, and education by publishing worldwide.

Oxford New York
Auckland Cape Town Dar es Salaam Hong Kong Karachi
Kuala Lumpur Madrid Melbourne Mexico City Nairobi
New Delhi Shanghai Taipei Toronto

With offices in
Argentina Austria Brazil Chile Czech Republic France Greece
Guatemala Hungary Italy Japan Poland Portugal Singapore
South Korea Switzerland Thailand Turkey Ukraine Vietnam

Published in the United States of America by
Oxford University Press
198 Madison Avenue, New York, NY 10016

Library of Congress Cataloging-in-Publication Data
Ernst, Daniel R.
Tocqueville's nightmare : the administrative state emerges in America, 1900–1940 / Daniel R. Ernst.
pages cm
ISBN 978–0–19–992086–0 (hardback : alk. paper) 1. Public administration—United States—History. 2. Administrative agencies—United States—History. 3. Bureaucracy—United States—History. 4. Rule of law—United States—History. 5. United States—Politics and government—1901–1953. I. Title.
JK411.E76 2014
320.97309'041—dc23
2013039989

1 3 5 7 9 8 6 4 2
Printed in the United States of America
on acid-free paper

For Joy

Contents

Acronyms Used in Text

AAA	Agricultural Adjustment Administration
AALS	Association of American Law Schools
ABA	American Bar Association
AFL	American Federation of Labor
ALP	American Labor Party
APA	Administrative Procedure Act
BCLB	Bituminous Coal Labor Board
CIO	Congress of Industrial Organizations
ECC	Employees Compensation Commission
FTC	Federal Trade Commission
ICC	Interstate Commerce Commission
NBCC	National Bituminous Coal Commission
NIRA	National Industrial Recovery Act
NLRA	National Labor Relations Act
NLRB	National Labor Relations Board
NRA	National Recovery Administration
NYSBA	New York State Bar Association
OIRA	Office of Information and Regulatory Affairs
OPA	Office of Price Administration
PAB	Petroleum Administrative Board
SEC	Securities and Exchange Commission
TVA	Tennessee Valley Authority
USDA	United States Department of Agriculture

Tocqueville's Nightmare

Introduction

TOCQUEVILLE'S NIGHTMARE

WHEN THE FRENCH aristocrat Alexis de Tocqueville visited America in the 1830s, he discovered that although the United States had "centralized government," it had little in the way of "centralized administration," bureaucracies through which federal officials could impose their will on a dispersed and factious people. This seeming shortcoming, Tocqueville decided, was a very good thing. If the populace of a democratic republic like the United States ever habituated itself to centralized administration, he warned, "in that country a more insufferable despotism would prevail than any which now exists in the monarchical states of Europe; or indeed than any which could be found on this side of the confines of Asia."[1] Fifty years later, an Englishman retraced Tocqueville's steps and reached a similar conclusion. "That which Europeans call the machinery of government is in America conspicuous chiefly by its absence," James Bryce reported in 1885.[2]

By 1940, America was still not Europe, but it had acquired a great deal of centralized administration.[3] Teams of administrators resolved disputes; regulated agriculture and industry; collected taxes; and distributed grants, loans, and other benefits. Although some grumbled that Americans had thrown off "the despotism of a *supreme* autocrat" only to succumb to "the *petty* despotism which may come from vesting final discretion to regulate individual conduct in the hands of lesser officials," others countered that the new agencies made individual freedom possible in an age of industrial concentration, national markets, and sweeping social change.[4] The contrast with the dictatorships of Mussolini, Hitler, and Stalin made the liberal and democratic nature of the American state all the more apparent.[5] Something about the "machinery of government" that Americans had built for themselves had confounded Tocqueville's expectations.

That something was the rule of law. The term, which dates at least to Aristotle, has had many meanings over the centuries, several of which were available to Americans when, around 1900, they started building their new administrative state.[6] In the nineteenth century, German liberals had developed the notion of the *Rechtsstaat*, a state bound by rules clearly specifying where the sovereign's will prevailed and where it yielded to the will of the individual. Although the *Rechtsstaat* had a great champion, Ernst Freund, a leader of Chicago's progressives, it fell before a rival approach with deep roots in the Anglo-American legal tradition: the rule of law as an appeal from government officials to independent, common-law courts. Invented to keep Stuart kings from importing absolutism to England, this court-centered notion of the rule of law found devotees in the United States, as elites sharing Tocqueville's anxiety over "the tyranny of the majority" sought to keep government from being put to partisan use. It envisioned courts of general jurisdiction as being above the state, staffed by judges whose "artificial reason," acquired through mastery of the common law, enabled them to resolve fairly "causes which concern the life, or inheritance, or goods, or fortunes" of a people.[7] Even after a transformation in legal thought brought the judiciary down to the level of the rest of the state, the common-law court continued to serve as the ideal against which administrative agencies were judged.

Americans' belief that courts might deliver them from Tocqueville's nightmare gave a distinctly legalistic cast to the administrative state they created after 1900. Although courts accorded administrators great freedom when acting within their legislative and constitutional limits, they insisted on retaining the power to call wayward administrators to account, much as they would farmers who let their cattle forage on the land of others.[8] Further, the agencies themselves usually acted by deciding individual cases rather than making rules and regulations, their most controversial activity today.[9] Even when engaged in the "legislative" act of prospectively setting rates for public utilities, administrators proceeded case by case. Judges readily assumed that norms of due process that had been worked out in the courts ought also to govern the "quasi-adjudication" of administrative agencies, and they condemned administrators who violated these norms. In particular, they expected administrators to maintain a judicial aloofness from subordinates presenting the government's case against a respondent. To do otherwise would violate the ancient maxim that no man should be the judge in his own cause. It would also mix powers that, as Montesquieu and John Adams had insisted, must be kept separate if a government were to be one "of laws and not of men."[10]

The courts' influence went beyond the structure of an agency; it reached deep into the thought processes of administrators and taught them to justify their actions in a peculiarly legalistic way. To keep tabs on agencies, courts had to be able to see what administrators had done and understand why they had done it. Whenever some statute or constitution required agencies to hold a hearing, the courts required administrators to compile a record of the testimony they heard, including the findings of fact supporting their order. The requirement of findings may seem arcane to readers without legal training or to the many lawyers who found their administrative law course less than enthralling. Nonetheless, it is the key to understanding the twentieth-century origins of the administrative state in America.

In legal parlance, to find a fact is not to record evidence but to conclude from evidence that some condition existed or had transpired. As a Chicago lawyer explained in 1940, fact-finding "entails the exercise of experienced and expert discretion."[11] Sometimes statutes expressly stated the facts administrators had to find. The National Industrial Recovery Act, for example, required administrators to find that a group proposing a Code of Fair Competition was "truly representative" of the industry it was to govern.[12] Other facts were implicit. The preamble or declaration of policy of a statute, for example, did not just empower agencies to act for certain ends; it implicitly limited the agency to act only for those ends. The careful agency thus found facts showing that it acted within its statutorily prescribed jurisdiction, and not beyond it. A constitution might also require factual findings. For example, during the New Deal, Congress enacted much legislation under the Commerce Clause. Mindful of the judiciary's superintendence, administrators learned to show that the activities they regulated fell within the prevailing interpretations of that provision. The syllogism of fact-finding was not, of course, the only logic that governed administrators' thinking. Secretaries of agriculture regarded the dictates of nature and the predilections of farmers; public utility commissioners looked to costs or capital markets in determining the reasonableness of a railroad or electric company's rates. Still, legalism pervaded the administrative state, and at times an agency's life or death turned on whether it had observed its niceties.

Just as important as the requirement that administrative agencies find facts were the legal doctrines governing how aggressively courts reviewed the facts agencies found. Should judges accept an agency's findings, even when they would have found otherwise, if the record contained evidence upon which a reasonable person could have reached the agency's conclusion? If so, the agency acquired something like a ticket of leave, freeing it, in the usual case, from the prison of close judicial scrutiny. This deferential approach became known as "substantial evidence" review. The alternative was "weight of the evidence" review, in which judges made up their own minds about disputed questions of fact. When applying it, they confronted a further issue: should they determine where the weight of the evidence lay on the record made by the agency or should they compile their own record de novo, in keeping with the common law of evidence? De novo review effectively transferred decision-making from agencies to the courts and turned independent administrators into judicial underlings whose suggestions judges were free to heed or ignore.

Not surprisingly, the standard of review of findings of fact was the most contested issue of administrative law in the early twentieth century. "The power of administrative bodies to make findings of fact which may be treated as conclusive, if there is evidence both ways, is a power of enormous consequence," Chief Justice Charles Evans Hughes declared in 1931. "An unscrupulous administrator might be tempted to say 'Let me find the facts for the people of my country, and I care little who lays down the general principles.' "[13] Yet if courts reviewed findings strictly, it would practically destroy the usefulness of agencies needed to address the social and economic ills of modern times. Further, the courts' victory over the agencies might be pyrrhic. As Hughes observed, when judges attempted to resolve matters not susceptible to principled reasoning, they stepped into the political arena and jeopardized the neutrality upon which the rule of law itself depended.

From 1900 to 1940, judges struggled with this dilemma. One solution was to distinguish between classes of facts. Courts would review most facts deferentially and cede a large realm to the discretion of administrators, but they would review facts aggressively in fields "peculiarly exposed to political demands."[14] For example, courts could determine for themselves whether a public service commission had set rates so low as to deny utilities an adequate return on their investment, whether a state's regulators had shifted costs from their consumers onto those of other states, or whether federal regulators had usurped the jurisdiction of their state-level counterparts. Further, judges could draw upon a repertoire of techniques to fine-tune the exercise of their tutelary power. When finding a fact de novo, for example, they could put the burden of proof on one party or the other. They could define the category of facts subject to heightened review broadly or narrowly or the elements of a particular fact, such as the reasonableness of rates, in terms of vague concepts, such as reproduction cost, that administrators could never quite determine to the satisfaction of a hostile judiciary. Judges could even transmute a seeming question of fact into a question of law and decide it de novo.[15]

From the welter of closely reasoned opinions, a trend emerged. By the end of the 1930s, even judges who believed that the US Constitution obligated the federal courts to determine some facts de novo thought it did so only infrequently. The old doctrines became "ghosts" of their former selves.[16] The courts continued to hold agencies accountable to a notion of the rule of law inspired by the common-law courts, but increasingly, court review was procedural rather than substantive. Courts insisted that agencies apprise parties of the reasoning underlying decisions, prevent their adjudicators from conferring with their "prosecutors" ex parte (outside the private party's presence), and generally observe fundamental notions of fair play as developed in the common-law courts. By 1940, the rule of law no longer required that individuals subject to economic regulation receive a "day in court" as long as administrators had given them a "day in commission." Thus, Americans decided they could avoid Tocqueville's nightmare if administration approximated the structure, procedures, and logic of the judiciary.[17]

To prevail, the courts' vision of a liberal administrative state needed allies among the members of a powerful profession. Tocqueville considered lawyers an aristocratic counterpoise to democracy in the United States; more recently, the political scientist Stephen Skowronek identified them as the "special intellectual cadre" that provided continuity to the American "state of courts and parties" during the nineteenth century.[18] Well into the twentieth century, most lawyers practiced before or in the shadow of the common-law courts. They closely identified with the judiciary, as guardians of civil liberty and out of self-interest. The American version of the "government of law," observed the progressive reformer Herbert Croly, "is not only a government by lawyers, but is a government by litigation. It makes legal advice more constantly essential to the corporation and the individual than any European political system."[19]

In contests with the new administrative agencies, most lawyers at first took the courts' side and equated the rule of law with aggressive judicial review. They pressed bar associations to criticize New Deal agencies and, after President Franklin D. Roosevelt's failed attempt to pack the US Supreme Court, acquired an ally in the nation's most eminent legal scholar, Roscoe Pound, dean of the Harvard Law School from 1916 to 1936.[20] Their updating of the rule of law concept was a lawyerly contribution to an antistatist body of thought that conservatives could draw upon whenever attacks on big government came into fashion.[21]

At the same time, other lawyers came to value administration as an expert and nonpartisan vehicle of governance. Specialized bars had already coalesced around patent, customs, land, and pension agencies; but of more general influence were the members of the great metropolitan law firms founded in the first years of the twentieth century. Although their litigation partners could be as vehemently anti-administration as any country lawyer, these firms' more influential members had traded courtroom forensics for law-office negotiations. In their dealings with public officials, they much preferred expert administrators to generalist judges or partisan legislators. Once they realized that the new administrative agencies meant more work for their firms, they were willing to trade their traditional status as "officers of the court" for a more expansive one, "officers of the state."[22]

Two early landmarks of Franklin D. Roosevelt's New Deal, the Agricultural Adjustment Act and the National Industrial Recovery Act, severely tested the courts' and lawyers' acceptance of the administrative state. Hurriedly drafted and incautiously implemented, the two statutes ignored or slighted the courts' requirement that administrators make their own findings of fact and observe the basics of due process. By delegating to agricultural and industrial concerns the power to legislate for their own industries, the new laws also violated a crucial tenet of the liberal state, and seemingly set the United States on a path leading to the corporatist governments of Europe.[23] In a series of decisions in 1935–36, Chief Justice Hughes united a fractured Supreme Court to quash the corporatist démarche and reassert the liberal principle of "popular rule carried on through the instrumentalities of responsible legislators and administrators."[24] The New Deal's lawyers got the message. They revised most of the items on Roosevelt's legislative agenda for 1935 to meet the Court's specifications. When their handiwork came before the justices in 1937—as it happened, in the midst of the furor over FDR's attempt to pack the Court—the new statutes passed muster where other measures had failed.[25]

Historians, focusing on constitutional doctrine, have long debated whether politics or law best accounts for the Supreme Court's response to the New Deal. Did moderate justices change their positions on crucial constitutional doctrines in response to the Court-packing plan or to Roosevelt's landslide reelection in 1936, or because some process internal to the law had made the doctrines unstable? Historians have also differed over whether the Court's decisions in 1937 amounted to an abrupt watershed—a "constitutional revolution"—or merely steps in a longer and more gradual process of legal change.[26] Viewed from the vantage point of administrative law and procedure, the crucial factor—the proper design of the administrative state—combined politics and law, and the decisions of 1937 seem less a revolution than a reconciliation between the judicial and executive branches. Administrators would have great autonomy so long as they observed due process and developed the particular content of their statutorily conferred mission in dialogue with an adverse but not implacably hostile bar.

Probably the most important consequence of the Court-packing plan was unintended. Professional politicians in Congress concluded from Roosevelt's all-out campaign to pass the measure and from a series of other moves in its wake that FDR wanted to convert administrative agencies into an independent source of presidential power and to change the rules of the political game.[27] During most of the 1930s, Congress showed little interest in the reform of federal administrative procedure. After the Court fight, however, it took up a proposal of the American Bar Association to heighten judicial review of agencies' fact-finding, to alter agencies' internal procedures, and to give more people standing to challenge administrative decisions. Supporters of the legislation, known as the Walter-Logan bill, claimed that it would keep the United States from devolving into Nazi Germany or Stalinist Russia, but their more likely purpose was to make it easier for Roosevelt's corporate enemies to harass the New Deal in court. From 1938 through 1940, legislators, journalists, and law professors quarreled over such arcane matters as the standard of review and the structure and procedures of administrative agencies; but when the impending entry of the United States into World War II finally quieted the debate, the entente between the courts and the agencies was still the one the Hughes Court had fashioned. Administrators exercised great discretionary power but only if they treated individuals fairly and kept within limits imposed by Congress and the Constitution.

The story of how Americans faced down Tocqueville's nightmare still matters, but not because the solution they settled on by the end of the 1930s can or should be ours today. New forms of governance have emerged since 1940, in response, in part, to problems, such as expense, delay, and the "capture" of regulators, that resulted after the rule of law became a rule of lawyers.[28] Even so, the story told here answers a complaint that has gained in popularity since the eruption of the Tea Party movement in 2009: the statebuilders of the early twentieth century abandoned an American tradition of individualism in what amounted to "the decisive wrong turn in the nation's history."[29] This claim overlooks a crucial fact: the reformers who supposedly sent the

Constitution into exile, actually designed the principles of individual rights, limited government, and due process into the administrative state.[30]

The story of how they did this begins with two great legal progressives. Both championed the new administrative agencies of the twentieth century. But they differed sharply over how to bring them within the rule of law.

I

Freund and Frankfurter

ALTHOUGH HE IS little remembered today, Ernst Freund was a hero to reformers at the turn of the twentieth century. His great treatise *The Police Power* (1904) was a favorite counter to any conservative who insisted that "constitutional limitations" prevented effective regulation of the American economy and society.[1] Like the other "transatlantic" reformers the historian Daniel T. Rodgers studied in his magisterial *Atlantic Crossings,* Freund believed that Europe's city planning, social insurance, rural cooperatives, and other attempts "to limit the social costs of aggressive market capitalism" were presumptively appropriate models for the United States.[2] He felt the same way about European approaches to implementing those programs. Above all, he expected to see the United States, like other modernizing countries, follow Germany in establishing a *Rechtsstaat,* that is, a state bound by fixed and certain rules that demarcate spheres of legitimate state action and of individual liberty.[3] Despite Freund's best efforts, however, the *Rechtsstaat* was one European import that never established itself on American soil.

We can see why the *Rechtsstaat* was shipwrecked by observing the quarrel that broke out between Freund and the Harvard law professor Felix Frankfurter in the years 1921 to 1932, as the two jointly directed a foundation-supported research program on administrative law. The two men had much in common. Both had lived in Europe before taking up residence in the United States. Freund was born in the United States to German parents in 1864, educated in Germany, and emigrated in 1884, settling in New York City.[4] Frankfurter was born eighteen years after Freund and emigrated with his family from Austria to New York's Lower East Side in 1894. Both were active in the reform movements of the Progressive Era. Jane Addams eulogized Freund as "the finest exponent in all Chicago of the conviction that as our sense of justice widens it must be applied to new areas of human relationships or it will become stifled and corrupt." Frankfurter labored tirelessly on behalf of the National Consumers League and progressive industrial unions. Both protested the deportation of suspected radicals arrested in the Palmer Raids of 1919.[5] Each haled the other's scholarly accomplishments. Frankfurter dedicated his casebook on administrative law to "Ernst Freund, Pioneer in Scholarship." Freund repaid the compliment by placing Frankfurter "at the forefront of the field of administrative law in this country."[6]

For all that, the two disagreed fundamentally on how law could both empower and constrain the administrative state. Freund hoped to bring the *Rechtsstaat* to America. Nineteenth-century German liberals had developed the concept to constrain the discretion of revanchist, aristocratic bureaucrats, but Freund found it no less serviceable in an American polity dominated by political machines. For Freund, administrative discretion was an evil, tolerable only until experience under an open-ended "standard" suggested the content of a bright-line "rule." Frankfurter's outlook was quite different. He had been a government lawyer in the presidential administrations of Theodore Roosevelt and William Howard Taft, when the need for trained administrators was, as he put it, "becoming a more accepted commonplace of statecraft."[7] He thought that the governance of modern societies required more subtle adjustments of social interests than any simple rule could anticipate.

The Rechtsstaat's American Advocate

We do not know all that Roscoe Pound wrote to provoke Ernst Freund in October 1913, but we do know that he made a slighting reference to "administrative law people." "I can assure you that there are mighty few of us and of a very different type from what you imagine," Freund protested in reply. "*Administrative Law* stands not for administrative power but for control of administrative power, and if I favor delegation [of legislative power to administrators] it is only because I believe that control of delegated power is more capable of development than control of legislation." Evidently, when Pound read the words "administrative law," he focused on the word "administrative" and associated it with unbridled discretion. Freund focused on the word "law" and associated it with the constraint of arbitrary power. He defined administrative law as "the system of legal principles which settle the conflicting claims of executive or administrative authority on the one side, and of individual or private right on the other."[8]

Freund grounded his definition of administrative law in the German ideal of the *Rechtsstaat*. "In order to secure with certainty and predictability a sphere in which the citizen could act free from the interference of the state," writes the historian Kenneth Ledford, "*Rechtsstaat* doctrine sought to replace both unwritten customary law and arbitrary bureaucratic law with a system of law that was general and autonomous, public and positive, aiming at generality in legislation and uniformity in adjudication."[9] The ideal was given an institutional dimension in the mid-nineteenth century by Rudolph von Gneist, a Prussian jurist and statesman who taught at the University of Berlin. Turning to English constitutional history for inspiration, he found in the eighteenth-century justice of the peace a model civil servant—a member of the gentry, to be sure, but one "purged of...selfish class interests" by his voluntary and uncompensated governance of the locale for the good of the nation.[10] From the English case Gneist developed a proposal for an independent administrative judiciary consisting of mixed bodies of administrators and judges drawn from the ordinary law courts. Between 1872 and 1883—that is, while Freund was studying law in Germany—Prussia established administrative courts more or less along the lines Gneist proposed. These courts soon established their independence from the bureaucracy in a series of notable cases. As Ledford has argued, they "brought into being a meaningful rule of law in Germany," albeit one of a procedural nature that was vulnerable to "the strongly formalist notions of German positivist legal theory."[11]

While studying at the University of Berlin, Freund must have heard Gneist speak; but he did not write about administrative law until 1893, after he had taught the subject himself at Columbia University, where he studied with the political scientist Frank J. Goodnow. (Goodnow had attended Gneist's lectures and acknowledged him in his *Comparative Administrative Law* [1893].)[12] Soon Freund was praising Gneist's history of the English constitution, deploring the American doctrine of sovereign immunity for putting officials "beyond the pale of those principles which constitute what the Germans call the *Rechtsstaat*," and applauding Gneist's administrative courts as "the most ingenious solution of the problem how to combine bureaucracy and self-government."[13]

Freund followed Tocqueville in seeing a fundamental difference between the European and American states, which he encapsulated in a distinction between "bureaucratic government" and "self-government." In Europe, the chief executive was "the head of an army of officials who derive their function and duties directly or indirectly from him, whose hierarchical organization culminates in his person, who have received a special training, who serve the state for life, and whose interests are therefore to a large extent identified with those of the government, and somewhat dissociated from those of the people." In contrast, "self-government" prevailed in the United States. "Not only are the people the source of governmental power," Freund wrote, but they kept the power to themselves by staffing public offices with amateurs who stayed at their post only briefly. Because public offices were not joined in a hierarchy of authority and control, some other means of keeping them in check had to be found. Freund thought that those means were specific statutory delegations to officials, coupled with review of their actions in courts of general jurisdiction. He was convinced that most executive functions were so minutely regulated that they had become ministerial acts. "We may truly speak of a government by law and not by men," Freund maintained, for the "officer has no one to look to for instruction and guidance, except the letter of the statute."[14]

That is, in theory the officer did not look beyond the statute. Freund, however, feared that in practice America's administrators took their lead from political bosses. Andrew Jackson intended his principle of rotation of office to replace aristocratic government with rule by the people, but it had become "an instrument for partisan purposes." "Professional office-seekers" had become "a separate class of the community, just like the bureaucracy in Europe," Freund complained, "only without the same training and expertise."[15]

German jurists developed the idea of the *Rechtsstaat* to keep a royal government from playing favorites; in the United States, Freund invoked it to constrain "the shady and corrupt aspects" of patronage politics.[16] Where questions of fact and law in matters of private right were at stake, he looked to the judiciary to keep administrators within the bounds of the law. On one score, he preferred the American system of review by courts of general jurisdiction to the German administrative courts: the latter, he observed, were "not entirely independent," because administrators served on them alongside ordinary judges. On balance, though, Freund believed that the German system better protected private rights. Its procedures were simpler, and it gave individuals the option of appealing upward through a bureaucratic hierarchy as well as laterally into the administrative courts. His preference grew stronger in the early twentieth century as American courts started to defer to the findings of fact of administrative agencies rather than decide factual questions de novo.[17]

In 1894 Freund still hoped for "an infusion of bureaucratic or professional elements" into the American system of self-government. In the interim, he looked to legislatures to "narrow as much as possible the sphere of discretionary action" by fixing "precisely and completely" how and when administrators should act. "Compliance with these conditions will place all individuals upon a basis of equality, and the administration is bound by fixed rules which are controllable and enforceable by the courts." The *Rechtsstaat* would come to America, Freund predicted, in the guise of detailed delegations of legislative power that banished unreviewable discretion from the administrative state.[18]

He could hardly have been more wrong. For some years Freund took comfort from New York's passage of the Raines liquor law in 1896. Under earlier law, the decision to award or revoke a liquor license to persons of "good moral character" had been committed to the discretion of local officials. Although New York's judges had professed to see little to fear from an abuse of this discretion, Freund believed that machine politicians had used it to reward friends and punish enemies and that a statute was needed to "take liquor licenses out of politics." The Raines Law substituted rule for discretion by detailing the factors left unspecified in the old, open-ended standard. Henceforth, the applicant who made an adequate showing of compliance with these requirements received the requisite certificate as a matter of course.[19]

Freund would invoke the Raines Law in all his major writings on administrative law. He soon realized, however, that whatever it heralded for licensing, it was not typical of a growing number of delegations of legislative power to independent regulatory agencies in statutes that revitalized the Interstate Commerce Commission (ICC), established state public utility commissions, and created the Federal Trade Commission (FTC).[20] If, as Freund insisted, "the progress of law should be away from discretion toward definite rule," if "all discretion in administration . . . is an anomaly and the modern tendency is to reduce it to a minimum," had America turned its back on history?[21]

Freund persuaded himself that it had not and that in fact "the gradual and rather unconscious drift" of American public policy was "toward the displacement of discretion" in administrative power over private rights.[22] First, he believed that legislation could provide administrators with clearer principles if legislators would draw upon legal and social expertise. In Europe, Freund noted, important legislation was almost always drafted by the ministries. "It is prepared by high officials, trained and experienced jurists and economists, who work under the guidance and advice of practical administrators with all the official information of a centralized bureaucracy at their command." In the United States, statutes had long been the product of "a large political body possessing no particular qualifications," yet Freund saw signs that an era of "intelligent legislation based upon expert advice" had at last arrived. He could point to his own service as Illinois's delegate to the

FIGURE 1.1 Ernst Freund, 1903.
Source: Courtesy of the Special Collections Research Center, University of Chicago Library, Law School Records, Addenda. Box 220.

National Conference of Commissioners on Uniform State Laws, the enactment of his bills on illegitimacy and divorce, the creation of legislative reference bureaus in Illinois and Wisconsin, and the American Bar Association's establishment of a special committee on legislative drafting.[23] Although few schools took up his suggestion that graduate study in law be devoted to "discovering definite and demonstrable working principles of legislation," Harvard had seemingly endorsed his call for law professors to frame legislation by awarding him the James Barr Ames Prize for his treatise *Standards of American Legislation* (1917).[24]

Freund also looked to the agencies to develop principles themselves. In a lecture first delivered in 1914, Freund denied that recent delegations of legislative powers to administrative agencies amounted to "a shifting from judicial rule to administrative discretion." Before the rise of administration, the courts had been the nation's de facto regulators, and they had left to juries the work of applying vague standards of "reasonableness, safety and adequacy." In criminal trials, jurors sympathized with and favored the accused; in civil ones, they favored plaintiffs, especially in suits in which the defendant was a corporation. An administrative agency, in contrast, was responsible to "the force of circumstances" and "surrounded by procedural guaranties and other inherent checks." Much more so than legislators and jurors, administrators were obliged to defend their decisions. For this reason, they tended to respect precedent and expert opinion and to "evolve principle out of constantly recurrent action."[25]

When Freund predicted in 1914 that American administration would transform itself into the *Rechtsstaat*, he had to concede that the matter was still in doubt. "The next ten or twenty years," he thought, would be decisive."[26] One can imagine, then, his excitement six years later, when a private foundation suddenly materialized with funds for a study of "administrative law and practice in the United States." Freund still believed that "unstandardized power" over private rights was "undesirable *per se*" and "hardly conformable to the 'Rule of Law'"; now he would have the chance to see whether the *Rechtsstaat* had in fact come to America.[27]

The "Constructive Study" of the Administrative State

The Commonwealth Fund was founded in October 1918 by the widow of Stephen V. Harkness, John D. Rockefeller's silent partner, with an endowment of $10 million. Its president was Edward Harkness, Stephen's only surviving son. The other members of the board of directors were Edward's law partner and fellow Yale alumnus Samuel H. Fisher; the president of a trust company, who served as treasurer; and George Welwood Murray, John D. Rockefeller's favorite lawyer and a member of the New York City law firm Milbank, Tweed.[28] In 1919, Max Farrand, a historian at Yale University, became general director. He oversaw the Fund's portfolio of scholarly research, including the administrative law project, until his departure in 1927 to run the Huntington Library.[29]

Although the Fund's first grants supported research on child welfare, public health, and medicine, it soon added legal research. Probably at the urging of Murray, an alumnus and booster of the Columbia Law School, Farrand turned to its dean, Harlan Fiske Stone, for suggestions. Having two experts on his faculty—Thomas Reed Powell and Thomas Parkinson—Stone suggested administrative law.[30] Farrand may also have consulted Roscoe Pound, dean of the Harvard Law School, who had recently written on the place of administration in a common-law system.[31]

In any event, Stone's and Pound's ideas appeared prominently in the proposal for a legal research committee that Farrand submitted to the board of directors. In 1916, Stone had warned that "the entire legal system is in the process of undergoing re-examination in the supposed interest of reform" and argued that university-based scholars ought to take the lead. In 1920, Farrand quoted Stone in arguing to the Commonwealth Fund's directors that professors, rather than practitioners or judges, were the proper people to conduct "scientific" investigations of the law.[32] To convey the urgency of the moment, Farrand employed a theme that Pound had sounded earlier that summer.[33] In "the critical period of American legal history" after the Revolutionary War, Farrand explained, "all sorts of crude projects" threatened to replace the English common law. Just in time, however, James Kent, Joseph Story, and other treatise writers did "what no one else could": they stated the common law in a form that judges could easily understand and use in their decisions. In 1920 law teachers had a "somewhat similar" job. Once again, the common law was confusing, uncertain, and unpopular. Once again, it lagged behind "rapidly changing economic and industrial conditions." And, once again, "we must rely upon legal scholars, especially in the Law School, to do the constructive work necessary."[34]

But just *what* constructive juristic work were the law professors to undertake? From the start, it seems, the Commonwealth Fund took a cosmopolitan approach to administrative law. Farrand told its board of directors that the study of American legal institutions ought to be conducted "in comparison with other legal systems."[35] Sometime between July 1920, when the board voted to create the Legal Research Committee with an annual budget of $50,000, and July 1921, when the committee finally convened and approved "an inquiry into administrative practices affecting private right," Farrand had settled on Freund to chair the project and asked him for a research agenda. Not surprisingly, judicial review of administrative decisions figured in Freund's plans; he had been teaching that subject since 1904, and his casebook, published in 1911, covered it at length.[36] But Freund recognized that law could arise outside the courts. He proposed that the statutes of Congress and a few state legislatures be studied to "segregate, systematize, and analyze" the provisions that kept administrators in check and that "actual administrative practices" be investigated to make clear the informal norms and routines that protected private interests. Freund acknowledged that English legislation and practices were relevant, but he also said that those of the civil law countries France and Germany were too.[37]

A more parochial oversight committee might have balked at an approach that looked beyond common-law countries for inspiration, but the

Commonwealth Fund's Legal Research Committee included some of the most thoughtful and wide-ranging jurists of the day. Three law deans signed up: Stone, Pound, and the University of Chicago's James Parker Hall, who served as chair. Benjamin Cardozo of the New York Court of Appeals also served, as did the patrician New York City lawyers C. C. Burlingham and John G. Milburn.[38] Cardozo, at least, felt that the law deans held "the balance of power."[39] The Legal Research Committee insisted that the subcommittee overseeing the administrative law project include a practicing lawyer. The one obtained, Walter Fisher, was known for his public service. William Howard Taft had appointed him to clean up a scandal-plagued Department of the Interior, and Freund had labored beside him in the campaign for a municipal charter for Chicago.[40]

The Legal Research Committee approved Freund's preliminary program for research and even swallowed Farrand's recommendation that Felix Frankfurter be recruited to the project. Initially, George Welwood Murray balked at the Harvard law professor, who had acquired a reputation as a dangerous radical by harshly criticizing the trial of the labor organizer Tom Mooney and the mass deportations following the Palmer Raids of 1919 and 1920. Murray explained that he hesitated "not because [Frankfurter's] point of view is apt to differ from mine, but because he seems so ill-balanced in any point of view." But Farrand was persistent and persuasive: the Commonwealth Fund project "would be liable to serious criticism" should it omit so prominent an expert, and other members of the administrative law and legal research committees could be counted on to veto "any radical conclusions" he might advance. Besides, Farrand argued, "it would be safer to have Frankfurter on the committee than it would be to have him criticize it from the outside." In the end, Murray acquiesced and assured Farrand that he would object only "in a very glaring case."[41]

Although Goodnow would ultimately join Freund, Frankfurter, and Walter Fisher on the letterhead of the "Administrative Law and Practices Project," leadership of the enterprise fell to Freund and Frankfurter. That they thought very differently about the administrative state soon became apparent.

Freund's Fall and Frankfurter's Rise

Felix Frankfurter came of age as a lawyer in the new politics of the administrative state. After graduating from the Harvard Law School and working briefly at a Wall Street firm, he joined the legal staff of Henry Stimson, a corporation lawyer who, at Theodore Roosevelt's request, served as United States Attorney in New York City. From 1906 to 1909, Frankfurter helped Stimson defend the ICC, the Bureau of Immigration, and other federal agencies. When his mentor became the secretary of war, Frankfurter accompanied Stimson as his special counsel and the law officer of the Bureau of Insular Affairs. In 1914, Frankfurter joined Harvard's law faculty, but he returned to Washington for the war, during which he exerted an outsized influence within the Wilson Administration. "Mr. Wilson has charge of foreign policy and Felix seems to sponsor the rest of the government," marveled his friend, the English intellectual Harold Laski.[42]

Freund met Frankfurter for the first time in October 1921 and was impressed by his command of administrative law. "I found him keenly alive to the importance of the work, fully familiar with every problem I touched upon, and generally admirable in his attitude," Freund reported to Farrand. The Harvard law professor was also "eager to help," albeit "mainly through assistants."[43] Despite Frankfurter's suggestion that only the national government be studied, Freund proceeded with his original plans and prepared a lengthy prospectus that projected studies of the states of Massachusetts, New York, and Wisconsin and the City of Chicago, as well as the federal government. The main object of the inquiry, as Freund saw it, was "to ascertain whether private interests are adequately safeguarded under delegated administrative action." To this end, investigators would take up six principal problems: "(1) the legitimate province of delegated legislation or rule making power; (2) the legitimate sphere and extent of administrative discretion; (3) the problem of separating incompatible functions; (4) what constitutes due process, in an equitable, not merely constitutional sense, in administrative procedure; (5) a clear theory of judicial relief; and (6) simplification of remedies."[44]

Freund explained the need for "a reasonably complete survey" of several jurisdictions in straightforward terms. "In that way alone is it possible to get a view of the growth and extent of administrative power, and the legislative practice in regulating or not regulating it," he told Farrand. "Upon the basis of a few selected subjects you cannot form a general judgment."[45] Left unsaid were his methodological assumptions. In Germany, Freund had been taught to see the material world as the manifestation of the spirit of an age, which would be revealed if studied "systematically." To study "law as a system," he had written in 1904, was to see it as "a body of reasoned principles," of rules "consciously founded in principle" and of principles embodying a "common purpose."[46] Thus, Freund, in the philosopher Morris Cohen's judgment, "always sought to find a genuinely rational pattern" in the law he studied. For administrative law, the pattern he hoped to discern was a trend away from discretion.[47] Only a comprehensive study could reveal whether Americans had embraced the *Rechtsstaat*.

Felix Frankfurter had his own notion of the scientific method. "Much of research," he wrote to Freund, "is a painful process of proving what you already know, or at least feel." Yes, the "objective demonstration of a scientific study" was called for, but studies of a handful of agencies would suffice, at least initially. "The generalizations, the philosophizing, the ultimate answers" would emerge in due course. Frankfurter also questioned Freund's formulation of the object of the inquiry as "whether private interests are adequately safeguarded." Would it not be more accurate to ask whether administrative law afforded "substantive justice both to public and private interests"? he asked. "After all, we *can't* consider whether private interests are safeguarded without equally considering the public interests that are asserted against them." The younger scholar concluded deferentially. "The field needs your leadership, for no one has so deeply and comprehensively made the field his own. To whatever extent I can—if you think me of use—I should deem it a real privilege to work with you."[48]

Frankfurter shared his views with Farrand, who found them to be in line with Stone's complaint that Freund ought to get "down to a concrete practical job" of proposing specific reforms. Farrand told Freund that he would have to confine himself to "a very limited field so that we can be sure of concrete results." After all, the Chicago professor had to "convince the Directors of the Commonwealth Fund that their expenditures have not been misused."[49]

Farrand proposed that the interested parties confer after the annual meeting of the Association of American Law Schools (AALS) in Chicago in late December 1921. Farrand, Freund, Frankfurter, and other scholars of administrative law met over three days. When the meeting broke up on January 1, Freund's unified research project was abandoned. Instead, Freund was to prepare his own survey of statutes creating administrative power over private rights in the United States, New York state, England, and Germany. Frankfurter was to oversee a series of "intensive" studies, mostly of federal agencies.[50]

These turned out to be elaborations of papers written by students in Frankfurter's graduate seminar on administrative law.[51] In the wake of the Chicago meeting, he pushed for a greater share of Commonwealth Fund largess and went out of his way to puncture Freund's claim that rule was replacing discretion in administrative law. "I wonder if you weren't struck by the recurrence by Freund to several instances that seemed to him very interesting, the existence of which he didn't want 'lost,' but which, under questioning (like the N.Y. liquor license cases) turned out to be merely instances, and frankly admitted to be such by him," he wrote to Farrand. A "comprehensive" volume was too great a task to expect "even from Freund in two or three years." Although scholars would value such a treatise, its effect "on professional opinion and on the stimulation of research in general" would be "very slight." Freund thought "in terms of German philosophic *Grundrisse*," Frankfurter complained, when what was needed were "the necessary factual demonstrations out of which the general problems and the unifying elements will emerge." As he later put it, administrative law had to be studied "functionally, and not analytically." Whatever typology Freund came up with would be no more deserving of the Commonwealth Fund's endorsement than anyone else's "pet schemes."[52]

Frankfurter's opposition at the Chicago meeting had left Freund shaken. Not only had the younger man insisted on "the paramount importance of the intensive studies" and dismissed "the present value of anything like a comprehensive survey," Frankfurter had rejected as "mere examples" the evidence upon which Freund had based his entire understanding of the field. Freund considered Frankfurter's own notion of empirical research inadequate. "It may be that a mass of statistical and factual material will result in scientific demonstration of the merits or demerits of administrative practices and of the legislation underlying them, but it may also be that the material will be inadequate to support 'scientific' generalizations."[53]

For the rest of the twenties, the two scholars proceeded on separate tracks.[54] Frankfurter paired present or former students with various topics: Eleanor Bontecou with federal rule-making, John Cheadle with the US Customs Service, William McCurdy with the US Post Office, Edwin Patterson with state insurance commissioners, I. L. Sharfman with the ICC, William Van Vleck with immigration. Bontecou, Cheadle, and McCurdy never completed their manuscripts; the others proceeded at a glacial pace. Patterson's book, well underway when the administrative law project was organized in 1921, did not appear until 1927. Van Vleck published his study in 1932.[55] Sharfman's aspirations for his ICC study proved so burdensome that he suffered a nervous breakdown, after which the Commonwealth Fund decided to publish the work piecemeal. The first volume appeared in 1931; the last, in 1937.[56]

The book that made good on Frankfurter's claims for the intensive study of administrative law was Gerard Carl Henderson's *Federal Trade Commission* (1924). Henderson had graduated from the Harvard Law School in 1916, having served as president of the law review. He was the rare top graduate who went into government service, as a lawyer at the FTC, the War Shipping Board, and the War Finance Corporation. Along the way he wrote for the

New Republic, economic journals, and law reviews; ghostwrote portions of the report of Woodrow Wilson's Second Industrial Conference; and remained close to Frankfurter, who persuaded his colleagues to hire the young lawyer in 1919, only to see the Harvard Corporation veto the appointment.[57]

The offer to write a study of the FTC reached Henderson in July 1922, when he was in private practice in New York City. He plunged in and, with his sterling legal pedigree and former service at the commission, gained access to its files, lawyers, and economists. The draft he completed in September 1923 thrilled his mentor. "I knew that if we got Henderson to do the Trade Commission we'd get an outstanding piece of work," Frankfurter enthused to Farrand. "But he has exceeded even my expectations—he has dug out unexpectedly rich material from the records of the Commission, which bears on our main problem, namely, the nature of administrative procedure and the dependability of its process in accomplishing the ends for which it was established, and at the same time protecting individual interests affected by its action."[58]

A work that better confirmed what Frankfurter already "knew, or at least felt," about the FTC could scarcely have been written. By 1922, that flower of progressive reform, while not yet blasted by the chairmanship of William Humphrey, had wilted considerably. The federal courts trusted neither its findings of fact nor its conclusions of law, because they appeared in lifeless, formulaic opinions rather than compelling narratives.[59] Even before examining the commission's files, Henderson had reached "one tentative, but fairly well defined conclusion—namely, that the practice of the Commission in failing to file and publish written opinions, including dissenting opinions, if any, is fundamentally vicious, and impairs considerably the value of the work that the Commission has done from a juristic standpoint." Although he later claimed to have had "not the slightest idea" what he would conclude, his original, "tentative" conclusion would become the book's principal finding. According to Henderson, the problem with the FTC was not Congress's vague delegation of power or the substance of its policies but its failure to buttress its orders with findings of fact that conscientiously resolved conflicting evidence. Until the FTC demonstrated that it had made "an expert judgment of a practical nature," courts would substitute their own judgments for those of the commission.[60]

The book was exactly the kind of narrowly focused, concrete, and reformist work that Stone and Farrand had envisioned for the administrative law project. Walter Fisher, the practitioner on its oversight committee, asked that a copy be sent to the official responsible for administering the Packers and

Stockyards Act (under which Fisher frequently litigated). Every federal judge received a copy, as did leading Wall Street lawyers and scholars of administrative law from New Haven to Calcutta.[61] FTC chairman Huston Thompson groused about the book but revised the commission's rules to meet its criticisms. Pound called it "a great contribution"; Stone offered Henderson a job at Columbia on "handsome terms." Former commissioner George Rublee, among other reviewers, joined Henderson in blaming the agency's decline upon "its failure to convince the courts that it has exercised an expert judgment in making its decisions."[62] And when another Frankfurter protégé, James Landis, was appointed to the FTC in 1933 to implement a new securities law, he followed Henderson in vowing to write "full opinions as distinguished from mere formal findings of fact" prepared by a subordinate. "If we can show to the courts and the country at large that we are a competent body," he told a congressional ally, "we are likely to have the same force and respect attach [to] our opinions as is now true of the Interstate Commerce Commission."[63]

Frankfurter seized upon Henderson's success to renew his argument that "intensive studies" were far preferable to studies "unnourished by the realities of 'law in action.'" He lectured Farrand that judicial review and discretion had to be studied "organically," in light of "the specific interests entrusted to a particular administrative organ," the history of an agency, its structure, and its "enveloping environment." "Only such a physiological study of Federal Trade Commission administrative law and practice *in action* as Mr. Henderson has attempted could have possibly disclosed the processes, the practices, the influential factors which *make* Federal Trade Commission rulings," Frankfurter crowed.[64]

While the Commonwealth Fund basked in the praise lavished on Henderson's book, Freund soldiered on with his statutory survey, plagued by illness and staggered by the enormity of the task.[65] At last. the massive manuscript of *Administrative Powers over Persons and Property* arrived at the Commonwealth Fund, in two parts, in the summer of 1926. The first, "analytical" part, Freund explained, gave "what the Germans call a system of administrative law." It was a painstaking, elaborate taxonomy of the forms and methods of administrative power over private rights, as revealed in the legislation of New York state, the United States, England, and Germany. The second, "descriptive" part grounded the first in specific legislation under sixteen headings: public utilities, shipping, banking, insurance, trade, labor, the professions, religion, education, political action, safety, health, morals, personal status, land use, and revenue. Freund conceded that the second part was "somewhat repellent in form" and "a laborious piece of work which few persons will care to read through"; but he insisted it was necessary to "lend weight and support to the exposition" of the first part.[66] The style was aptly, if delicately, characterized by an English scholar. "The author's Teutonic education produced an inexhaustible industry, a remarkable capacity for inventive classification, and a power of subtle and penetrating analysis," William Robson wrote, but "one sometimes wished Freund had attempted to formulate some body of conclusions at the end of his fine-spun web of conceptual exposition."[67]

Farrand was dismayed and turned to Pound for help. The Harvard law school dean reported that although the manuscript contained "a great deal of good material," it was "so written as to make the reading of it indescribably tedious. I thought for a while that possibly bad eyes had something to do with my difficulty in reading it, but I find I can read other things quite as technical and still keep awake, while the labor of working out exactly what Freund means thoroughly, phrase by phrase, sentence by sentence, and paragraph by paragraph, puts me to sleep."[68]

Attempts to persuade Freund to revise the manuscript proved unsuccessful. "My experience with Freund," Farrand complained, "has been that he is so sensitive that when I offer anything that might be interpreted as a criticism, he closes up his shell and you might as well pour water on an oyster for all the effect it has." Pound urged Farrand to publish the book as it was. "A man of Freund's calibre has some rights," Pound advised, "and one of them is to put things as he wants them. We ought to be glad to have so monumental a work on almost any terms."[69] Frankfurter agreed. Although the book would "not commend itself even to the 'learned members' of the teaching or the legal profession," it would serve as "a rather recondite source for the few specialists who are ready to quarry into it." Putting the best face on the situation, Farrand told his board of directors that although Freund's monograph was "not as interesting reading as the Henderson study of the Federal Trade Commission," it was "a perfectly impartial analysis of an unbelievable amount of detail" and would "reflect credit on the author and upon those who have sponsored it."[70]

Unacknowledged in these assessments was Freund's conclusion: Americans had embraced the *Rechtsstaat*. Freund distinguished between two devices administrators used to resolve private rights: (1) "the advance checks" of licenses, permits, or certificates; and (2) the "corrective intervention" of administrative orders or directives. He was most confident of the "trend toward the reduction of discretion in the grant of licensing powers." With a mental glance over his shoulder at Frankfurter, he insisted that his conclusion was "not based on so unique an instance as the New York Raines Liquor Tax Law of 1896 with its absolute elimination of all discretion." Even the Transportation Act of 1920, which seemingly endowed the ICC with "the widest type of discretion" in deciding whether to grant certificates of convenience and necessity to railroads, also required hearings. It thereby set in motion a process of official justification that would "inevitably tend to check and reduce discretion."[71]

The case of administrative orders was more doubtful. The FTC Act was the most prominent example of a grant of discretion "as a means of finally evolving a definite rule." The decision to leave "the indeterminate concept of unfair competition" to the commission to define through an accumulating body of precedents was "an admissible, if novel, method of dealing with practices which appear detrimental to the public when it is difficult to formulate with clearness either the evil or the remedy." The setting of rates for regulated industries was harder to account for. "The whole course of rate legislation and action under it has been an effort to discover some principle of rate control." Regulators, it was apparently assumed, would ultimately hit upon the true principle, which they could then apply with only the same "margin of discretion" that judges exercised in resolving questions of fact. Freund doubted that they would ever find one. Ratemaking, he strongly implied, was a matter of "expediency"; the discretion of ratemakers was "not displaceable by rule." As conducted in the United States, rate making was "a legislative makeshift to appease the demand for public control" and a "claim on the part of the state to be recognized as a quasi-partner with paramount powers unattended by obligation or liability." "In a sense," Freund concluded, it was "a negation of law."[72]

No economic issue was of greater concern to Frankfurter and other legal progressives in the 1920s than the regulation of public utilities.[73] Any generalization that failed to account for such an important case was, to their mind, not worth entertaining. Freund countered that a systematic study of administration ought to account for the entire statute book, and not just legislation creating the most controversial agencies. His survey revealed that American legislation used the license-granting power more than the order-issuing power and that "licenses tend to become ministerial acts." Still, Freund could not quite dismiss the possibility that he had only discovered what he had set out to find. "In ascertaining tendencies it is not easy to divest the mind of bias or prejudice," he confessed. "Evidence of a development that seems desirable easily appears persuasive or convincing."[74] Could the obscurity of Freund's *Administrative Powers* have been the result not simply of his scholarly caution and "Teutonic" style but of his doubt that the book really documented the existence of an American *Rechtsstaat*?[75]

Certainly, the few legal scholars who read the book were unconvinced. Freund's focus on private right to the exclusion of public policy and the social interest was "one-sided," Edwin Patterson complained. "A Martian reading this book would wonder why one group of humans ('officials') were taking so much trouble to trouble another group of humans ('private individuals')." Freund's fear of discretion was the product of his "fundamentally conservative point of view." If discretion was always an evil, Patterson demanded, what "becomes of Mr. Justice Holmes' 'intuitions too subtle for any articulate major premise'?"[76] John Dickinson, a lawyer and quondam law professor, took issue with Freund's claim that discretion as other than a prelude to a rule was an "anomaly." Freund evidently believed that only legislatures should exercise the "political" function of discretion and that rules could be developed for all matters properly the subject of regulation by an administrative agency, Dickinson observed. These a priori assumptions were at least dubious and probably wrong.[77]

FIGURE 1.2 Felix Frankfurter in a classroom at the Harvard law school.
Source: Courtesy of the Library of Congress, LC-USZ62-111157.

If Freund required further evidence that his star had fallen and Frankfurter's was ascendant, he need only have considered the Commonwealth Fund's actions in March 1927. After reluctantly authorizing the publication of *Administrative Powers*, the Legal Research Committee enthusiastically invited Frankfurter to write the readable, synthetic account it had hoped for from Freund.[78] The Harvard law professor declined the challenge, but a few years later he delivered a set of lectures, published as *The Public and Its Government* (1930), that called for government by expert administrators free to act as their scientific "temper of mind" led them. (As he told his students, public utility regulation had to be "flexible enough to meet the flexibilities of life," and securities laws should enact only broad "standards of fair dealing," as no "legislative net" could anticipate the multifarious schemes of stock swindlers.) Although administrative discretion "opened the doors to arbitrariness," the remedy was not a rule-bound officialdom but a professional civil service, fair procedures, public scrutiny, and the criticism of "an informed and spirited bar." He would restate his views in the preface to his casebook on administrative law, published in 1932.[79]

In his review of Frankfurter's casebook for the November 1932 issue of the *Harvard Law Review*, Freund acknowledged that his attempt to transplant the *Rechtsstaat* in American soil had failed. "The reviewer's own ideas about administrative law were undoubtedly influenced by Goodnow, who in his turn was influenced by continental jurists and treatises," Freund wrote, "but the process of transmission brought eliminations and substitutions; and now the presentation of an entirely new plan appears to break the old tradition completely." The concession was all the more poignant for being posthumous: Freund had died of a heart attack on October 20. He was spared seeing the New Deal's vast expansion of administrative discretion and the Nazis' perversion of the *Rechtsstaat*.

The Politics of Administrative Discretion

The obscurity of Freund's prose cannot be the only reason why the *Rechtsstaat* failed to take root in the United States. After all, Woodrow Wilson, a gifted stylist, also feared that, without "precise terms of regulation," administration was a turn "from law to personal power."[80] Far more important was the openness of administration in the United States, relative to its aristocratic counterparts in, say, England and Germany, to a wide variety of politically active groups. Although championed as a way to take government "out of politics," in fact administration offered a new field of political influence to those who thought legislatures hopelessly mired in the corrupt bargains of party bosses and business interests.[81]

Nonpartisan interest groups, which had emerged in great variety by the early twentieth century, were the greatest enthusiasts for "commission government." After his election as governor of New York in 1906, Charles Evans Hughes, a corporation lawyer appalled by the corruption of public officials by utility and insurance companies, won much recognition for his program of transferring authority over complex economic matters from the legislature to administrative agencies. Yet even those with a stake in older systems of governance warmed to administration. As early as 1892, a railroad lawyer advised his client that over time the ICC would "take the business and railroad view of things" and become "a sort of barrier between railroad corporations and the people and a sort protection against hasty and crude legislation hostile to railroad interests."[82] Once they overcame their reflexive identification with the courts, other lawyers found a remunerative role for themselves in administration and saw it as a way of extending their influence to new realms of decision-making. Legislators found that they could pass politically divisive decisions to administrators, and party bosses sometimes discovered that they could turn some agencies to their own ends. In the process, however, the reformers' ideal of administration as a "rational, monocratic system of firmly arranged levels of hierarchical authority flowing from superior to inferior roles" dissolved into a welter of heterogeneous, internally conflicted, and poorly coordinated fiefdoms.[83]

As various actors acclimated themselves to administrative discretion, Freund's insistence on formal rules seemed to permit only "a laissez faire role for government." His scholarship was forgotten or, if remembered, dismissed as "of little usefulness on current problems."[84] But if the *Rechtsstaat* was not the way to prevent "those abuses of caprice and oppression" that even Frankfurter conceded administrative discretion made possible, what was?[85]

America's judges provided an answer, and the answer they provided gave the American administrative state its distinctively legalistic cast. If Freund had looked to continental Europe for his version of the rule of law, the judges found one within the more familiar confines of the Anglo-American common law. A classic formulation by a great English scholar provided a point of departure, but judges had to translate it into legal doctrines that gave administrators the freedom to perform their mission without allowing them to exceed their mandate or violate constitutional rights. From his initial appointment to the US Supreme Court in 1910 until his resignation as chief justice in 1941, no one did more to make administration over in the image of the courts than Charles Evans Hughes.

2

Hughes

WHEN, IN HIS memoirs, Charles Evans Hughes reached his campaign as governor of New York to create a state public utility commission, he paused to reflect on its significance to himself and to the nation. The episode, he recalled, "brought me at the beginning of my public career to the close study of administrative agencies, their necessity and appropriate sphere of action. We were then . . . at the threshold of the extraordinary development which for the past twenty-five years has been the most important feature of the political history of the nation and the States."[1]

In fact, Hughes had been puzzling over what he once called "the severest test of the Republic" ever since he first achieved public notice in 1905.[2] With others trained in the common law, Hughes looked to the courts to serve as "the final safeguard of our liberties" by reprimanding administrators *after* they had violated someone's rights.[3] A commission that confiscated a railroad's property by setting its rates too low was no different from a cattle rustler who stole a rancher's livestock; in both cases, the court's job was to do corrective justice and restore property to its rightful owner. The rule of law required that both the railroad and the rancher have their day in court. Yet Hughes also appreciated the limits of the analogy between the commission and the cattle rustler: the legislature had delegated its lawmaking authority to the former but not the latter. If a railroad could go to court every time it plausibly alleged a commission had erred, say, by getting the facts wrong, the court, and not the commission, would become the de facto rate setter, contrary to the will of the people, who had entrusted the matter to administrative experts.

As governor of New York (1907–1910) and as an associate justice of the US Supreme Court (1910–1916), Hughes helped articulate an "after the fact" method of holding administrators accountable. Because the agencies of his day typically acted on a case-by-case basis, rather than by promulgating rules, the medium in which the judges worked was a body of legal doctrines governing how courts reviewed agencies' determination of the facts of a dispute. A strict version of the rule of law would require judges to find the facts themselves, either on the record before the agency or even de novo on a new record created in their court. Because this would make generalist courts rather than expert administrators the ultimate arbiters of contested cases, Hughes and his fellow justices developed a less exacting approach. Courts were to engage in only a minimal review of most facts; they could make their own determinations only when they suspected administrators of violating constitutional rights or grasping for power not conferred on them by the legislature. This framework, fully articulated before Hughes left the Court in 1916 to make an unsuccessful presidential bid, gave the courts the freedom to correct agencies (such as the FTC) that failed to show the reasoned basis for their orders or assumed arbitrary power but also to give them free rein when they displayed the comprehensive knowledge, technical skill, and rationality behind their decisions.

Of course, this doctrinal framework also assumed that judges could distinguish on a principled basis between facts that could be safely committed to the discretion of administrators and those that courts had to determine for themselves. During the twenties, when Hughes was in private practice, the Supreme Court aggressively asserted the judiciary's power to second-guess ratemaking by public utility commissions. Lawyers, law professors, and even a handful of judges objected that these judicial decisions had thrown courts into the political arena and made judges the champions of big business.

Hughes, it seems, never doubted that he could distinguish between "matters of detail," which could be left to the discretion of administrators, and "real" judicial questions, such as when rate regulation became confiscatory.[4] But, although he never renounced courts' power to reprimand administrators after the fact, well before his return to the Supreme Court, Hughes saw that judicial intervention would be unnecessary if agencies were structured so as to make them unlikely to abuse their power in the first place. The primarily responsibility for constituting agencies was the legislature's, but if the legislature stumbled, the courts could step in and instruct agencies on the proper way to decide cases. As Gerard Henderson concluded from his study of the FTC, the more the agencies followed the procedures and reasoning of the courts, the more the courts would leave them alone.

The Rule of Law

As Rudolph von Gneist institutionalized the *Rechtsstaat* on the European Continent, an Englishman was developing an alternative notion of the rule of law for the common-law world. Albert Venn Dicey was the Vinerian Professor of Common Law at Oxford University from 1882 to 1909. His *Introduction to the Study of the Law of the Constitution* (1885) was hailed as "one of the great law books of all time." Its influence on American lawyers was enormous. "Generations of judges and lawyers," Felix Frankfurter observed, "were brought up in the mental climate of Dicey."[5]

Dicey's rule of law was a composite of three principles. The first was that "no man is punishable or can be lawfully made to suffer in body or goods except for a distinct breach of law established in the ordinary legal manner before the ordinary Courts of the land." The second was that "no man is above the law" but that "every man, whatever be his rank or condition, is subject to the ordinary law of the realm and amenable to the jurisdiction of ordinary tribunals." Every English official, Dicey maintained, "from the Prime Minister down to a constable or a collector of taxes," was answerable in court for acts done without legal justification. The third principle was that constitutional liberty was not defined in some extraordinary act of law-giving but emerged gradually as common-law judges determined "the rights of private persons in particular cases brought before the Courts." In resolving everyday disputes over contracts, property, and torts, the judges of the "ordinary Courts" defined freedom for Englishmen. "The constitution," Dicey argued, "is the result of the ordinary law of the land."[6]

The great contrast to Dicey's rule of law was France's *droit administratif*. France firmly denied its "ordinary tribunals" any jurisdiction over the acts of "any official, high or low, *bonâ fide* in his official character," Dicey claimed. In England, a police officer was answerable for his trespasses in the ordinary courts of the land; in France, he could only be called to account before a tribunal staffed by administrators rather than "ordinary judges." Unlike ordinary judges, devoted to the principles of individual liberty embodied in the common law, the members of administrative tribunals regarded disputes "from a government point of view." The special rules they developed to define the relationship between government and the citizenry—the *droit administratif*—had an "official bias." With great relief, but in seeming ignorance of the practice of English local government and the unlikelihood of prevailing in a suit against Crown officials, Dicey declared the *droit administratif* "all but unknown" in his country. He could find "very few traces indeed" of the notion that, in disputes between government officials and private parties, "the interests of the government should be in any sense preferred or the acts of its agents claim any special protection."[7]

Dicey gave his distinction between the rule of law and the *droit administratif* a heroic cast by invoking the successful defense by common-law judges of the "ancient constitution" from Tudor and Stuart kings who sought to bring absolute monarchy to England. All English lawyers knew the story of how their seventeenth-century counterparts had resisted attempts by these grasping monarchs to collect revenue and suppress opposition through prosecutions conducted in the Star Chamber and other prerogative courts. The climactic moment was Sir Edward Coke's stand against King James I, memorialized in Coke's posthumously published *Prohibitions del Roy*. James I had presumed to settle a jurisdictional dispute between the church and the common-law courts. James believed he had acted appropriately. As Coke summarized James's view, "He thought the law was founded on reason, and that he and others had reason, as well as the judges." Coke's reply was that "causes which concern the life, or inheritance, or goods, or fortunes of subjects are not to be decided by natural reason but by the artificial reason and judgment of law," acquired through years of study. This greatly offended the king, who accused Coke of asserting that "he [James] should be under the law, which was treason to affirm." The doughty judge was said to have responded with a quote from a medieval legal treatise: "The King ought not to be under any man but under God and the law."[8]

Dicey depicted this era as a death struggle between the *droit administratif* and the rule of law. "From the accession of the Tudors till the final expulsion of the Stuarts," he wrote, "the Crown and its servants maintained and put into practice, with more or less success and with varying degrees of popular approval, views of government essentially similar to the theories which under different forms have been accepted by the French people." The gist of the matter was "whether a strong administration of the continental type should or should not be permanently established in England." Every feature of the *droit administratif* had its "curious analogy either in the claims put forward or in the institutions favoured by the Crown lawyers of the seventeenth century." The king's men failed chiefly because "the whole scheme of administrative law was opposed to those habits of equality before the law which had long been essential characteristics of English institutions."[9]

Although, as Frankfurter wrote, "America had no Dicey," American lawyers found his ideas "congenial" to their own notions of the rule of law.[10] Dicey's influence could bubble up unexpectedly in their speeches and writings, as when the great corporation lawyer Elihu Root warned that recent immigrants from southern and central Europe threatened American institutions because they came from communities in which courts were "part of the administrative system of the government, not independent tribunals to do justice between the individual and the government," and because in Europe laws took the form of codes rather than case law "made by the people, through their own recognition of their needs."[11] In 1914, George Sutherland, a learned member of the Utah bar and the US Senate, likened the proposed Federal Trade Commission to the bloodthirsty tribunals of revolutionary France. Two years later, as president of the American Bar Association (ABA), Sutherland charged that the FTC's vague mandate to punish unfair methods of competition substituted "the shifting frontiers of personal command for the definite boundaries of general, impersonal law."[12]

Well into the twentieth century, American lawyers usually followed Dicey in believing that the rule of law required that judges "take the whole case" when administrative agencies determined private rights. In particular, they believed that judges ought not to be bound by an agency's finding of the facts of a dispute, which so often proved dispositive. Rather, they should find the facts themselves on a new record created in their own court. Nothing less, they believed, would ensure that matters of private right were ultimately determined "in the ordinary legal manner before the ordinary Courts of the land." Thus, Dean Acheson, at the start of a long and eminent legal career, wrote that under Dicey's conception of "a government of laws and not of men," judges were to regard proceedings before commissions "with cold aloofness" and insist on trying cases de novo.[13]

Robert H. Jackson, who, from his practice in western New York, understood the biases of trial lawyers but, from his service in the New Deal, also appreciated the case for administration, understood why Dicey appealed to most American lawyers. "The lawyer is inclined by habit and training to prefer the court over the administrative tribunal," he wrote in 1940. "Lawyers only preside, and lawyers alone address it." Further, "most lawyers like court procedure, which is somewhat ceremonial and moves according to a prescribed ritual." Administrative tribunals, in contrast, were "not as dependent as the ordinary court upon the arguments of partisan counsel to get at the truth. Skilled advocacy is neither so necessary to keep such a body informed nor is stupid or cute advocacy so apt to blur the merits of a controversy."[14]

In time, however, thoughtful lawyers like Jackson came to see weight-of-the-evidence review, whether on a record created by the agency or on a new one created in court, as impractical or undesirable. First, public utility commissions, worker's compensation tribunals, and other administrative agencies acquired enormous caseloads; weight-of-the-evidence review of more than a tiny fraction of their decisions would swamp the courts. Second, they came to see that many social problems were best addressed by officials who, through repeated encounters with a particular class of disputes, understood their origins.[15] Increasingly, they tolerated departures from a strict version of Dicey's rule of law, but they were most likely to do so when agencies' procedures approximated "the ordinary legal manner" of the courts. If individuals had their "day in Commission," they were not owed a further "day in court."[16]

At times, Charles Evans Hughes spoke of the rule of law in language that would satisfy the most fervent of Dicey's American apostles. During the ABA's meeting in London in 1924, for example, Hughes spoke of "the law of a free people, springing from custom, responsive to their sense of justice," and "opposed to those insidious encroachments upon liberty which take the form of an uncontrolled administrative authority." The "ancient right . . . to be governed by law and not by officials—the right to reasonable, definite and proclaimed standards which citizens can invoke against both malevolence and caprice"—was as necessary as ever.[17] But he was too great an advocate of the expert regulatory commission to see it throttled by unrelenting, after-the-fact judicial review. Over his long public career, he devoted his remarkable talents to adjusting both judicial doctrine and the design of administrative agencies so that the liberal state might survive in illiberal times.[18]

"A Chance to Go to the Courts"

Hughes was the kind of lawyer other lawyers regarded with awe. Born in 1862 in upstate New York to a Baptist minister and his devout wife, Hughes began to read at the age of three-and-a-half, to study French and German at six, to learn Greek at seven, and to read Bunyan and Shakespeare by the age of nine. At nine, too, he was admitted into his family's strict church after amazing the deacons with his mastery of the denomination's doctrines. He graduated from Brown University and, in 1884, from the Columbia Law School. Walter Carter, who pioneered the practice of employing the top graduates of case-method law schools, hired Hughes as his associate, blessed his daughter's marriage to him, and made him his partner. Hughes's clients included brokerage houses, stock exchanges, railroads, and other large business concerns, but he would sooner take a seemingly intractable case than a more remunerative but tedious corporate matter.[19] He lived more simply than his peers and charged less than he was worth. And he was worth a great deal, thanks to a mind a subordinate once called "the most perfect mental machine in the whole world." It was said that he could read "a paragraph at a glance, a treatise in an evening, a roomful of papers in a week." If a case proved too complicated for other corporation lawyers, at length one of them would sigh, "I guess we'd better take that to Hughes."[20]

A profound sense of obligation and duty, grounded in classical study and religious faith, could make Hughes seem austere and self-righteous. One of his favorite quotations was from George Santayana: "what truly matters is that 'we should carry on perpetually, if possibly with a *crescendo*, the strenuous experience of living in a gloriously bad world, and always working to reform it.'" Hughes thought we should do so even though we could never make "reform less necessary, or life happier," and even if our efforts sowed "'the seeds of new and higher evils to keep the edge of virtue keen.'"[21]

In 1905, Hughes placed himself in the midst of the gloriously bad world of gaslight franchises in New York City as the chief counsel of an investigating committee of the state legislature. His methodical cross-examination revealed that the Consolidated Gas Company had grossly exaggerated the value of its assets in calculating rates for its service. He then drafted a bill, passed by the legislature, that created a commission to limit gas and electric utility companies to a fair return upon the capital actually invested in their enterprises. A still more sensational investigation of New York–based insurance companies won him national acclaim. "Hughes pried open strongboxes by sheer force of intellectual power," one reporter marveled.[22]

In September 1906, New York City's Democratic bosses pushed through the nomination of newspaper publisher William Randolph Hearst as the party's gubernatorial candidate. Hearst's call for government ownership of the city's street railways alarmed President Theodore Roosevelt and other patricians in the liberal branch of New York's Republican Party, who feared that Tammany Democrats would convert them into a source of patronage and influence. Over the objections of Republican stalwarts, they persuaded Hughes to run against Hearst on the platform that regulation by commission was the safe alternative to government ownership.[23]

Hughes defeated Hearst, but Republican politicos still loathed the aloof and uncompromising newcomer, whom they dubbed "Charles the Baptist." In contrast, reformers and professionals thrilled to Hughes's gubernatorial exploits. "It is impossible to reproduce for the present generation the aggressive personality, the seemingly inexhaustible energy, the unrelenting insistence of Governor Hughes," a lawyer later wrote. He "took his appeals on nearly every issue direct to the people, usually disregarding political advice;

always fighting against the power of patronage and invariably disdaining considerations of political expediency."[24]

The first great battle of Hughes's governorship was the passage of the Public Service Commissions law in 1907, which extended the state regulation of public utilities to railroads. Hughes stumped for the measure in a series of speeches to local chambers of commerce. The railroad companies believed they had laid a trap for him by arranging for John B. Stanchfield to argue against the commission bill at a widely heralded stop in Elmira. Stanchfield, an eminent railroad lawyer, spoke first and assured a huge throng that he did so from personal conviction. "I stand before you with no man's retainer in my pocket. I represent no corporation or combination of men, but appear simply as a citizen interested in the growth and prosperity of Elmira."[25]

Hughes replied with a devastating riposte. "In distinction from my learned friend," he declared,

> I *am* here on a retainer. I am here retained by the people of the State of New York, to see that justice is done, and with no disposition to injure any investment, but with every desire to give the fullest opportunity to enterprise, and with every purpose to shield and protect every just property interest. I stand for the people of the State of New York against extortion, against favoritism, against financial scandal, and against everything that goes to corrupt our politics by interference with the freedom of our Legislature and administration. I stand for honest government and effective regulation by the State of public-service corporations.[26]

Many in the audience would have interpreted Hughes's mention of the corruption of the legislature as a reference to "strike bills," legislation introduced solely to extort contributions to the party's coffers.[27] A commission promised to deliver the railroad men from this nightmare, but would it subject them to a new one, particularly when some less obviously incorruptible person sat in the governor's chair? At Elmira, Hughes recounted the moment when he realized what the railroad executives felt was needed to prevent the politicization of the rate-setting process. "What you really want," he had exclaimed during a conversation with one of them, "is a chance to go to the courts." The executive's reply? "Yes, that is all there is about it."

Hughes declared that he had "the highest regard for the courts" and revered them as "the safeguard of our liberty," but he also warned that judicial review would transfer the ultimate responsibility for a regulatory decision from administrators, who could devote "their entire attention" to the subject, to generalist judges. Moreover, weight-of-the-evidence review of the many mundane questions that arose in the running of a utility or a railroad would be disastrous for the judiciary. Not only would appeals swamp the courts; the "independence and public esteem" of the judges would be imperiled. Regulatory matters, the governor explained, "lie close to the public impatience." If courts were to render a series of unpopular decisions, the public would subject them to "hostile and perhaps violent criticism" and reduce judges' terms to keep them on a short leash. "You must have administration," Hughes insisted, "and you must have administration by administrative officers."[28]

At Elmira and at an earlier stop in Utica, Hughes modified Dicey's rule of law by employing a distinction that he would later help enshrine in case law. Courts should leave "matters of detail" to commissions. "To provide a right of appeal to the courts from every order of the commission not only invites delay and an unnecessary multiplicity of proceedings, but has for its object the substitution of the judgment of the court for the action of the commission." Courts should only hear "real" judicial questions. First, judges should determine whether an agency's order violated constitutional rights, especially by violating "the constitutional right to hold property and not be deprived of it without due process of law." Jurists would refer later to this as the *constitutional fact* doctrine. Second, judges should determine whether, "under the guise of regulation," commissioners had exceeded their statutory authority and assumed "arbitrary power not related to public convenience." Jurists would later refer to this as the *jurisdictional fact* doctrine. Hughes believed that the two doctrines gave courts sufficient power to keep agencies from invading property rights or roaming beyond their legislative mandate.[29]

In May 1910, Governor Hughes became Mr. Justice Hughes, a member of the United States Supreme Court. His fellow justices had already begun to build a framework of legal doctrines that ceded considerable discretion to a newly powerful ICC and other agencies without relinquishing the judicial oversight needed if the United States was to have a government of laws.

Accommodating Administration

Before 1900, it seems, if courts decided to review the decisions of executive officials at all, they followed Dicey strictly and determined both the law and the facts de novo.[30] For much of the nineteenth century, for example, an importer wishing to overturn a customs officer's valuation of his goods would bring an action in a trial court, where a jury would decide where the weight of the evidence lay, as in any other common-law action.[31] Litigants could also obtain a de novo judicial hearing under a prerogative writ, such as prohibition, mandamus, and habeas corpus. Finally, they could ask a court to exercise its equitable power and, after a juryless hearing, enjoin an administrative officer or body from enforcing an order. By the end of the nineteenth century, judges used injunctions to have the last word on a host of regulatory matters.[32]

Statutes could also provide for judicial review by not permitting an agency's order to become binding until a court agreed to enforce it. When the ICC went to court to enforce its orders, it found that judges insisted on determining the facts of the case themselves on evidence that need not have been heard by the commission. Railroads often postponed revealing some or all of their evidence until they reached the more hospitable confines of the judiciary. As the ICC complained, "the case made before the circuit court may be entirely different from the case made before the Commission." A survey compiled in 1906 found that courts had considered new evidence in twenty-six of thirty-two decisions reversing the ICC. In one case, the judicial hearing lasted thirty days and produced 3,000 pages of new testimony. Under the circumstances, the ICC warned, "the people should no longer look to this Commission for a protection which it is powerless to extend." A dissenting Supreme Court justice agreed. De novo review of factual findings made the ICC "a useless body, for all practical purposes."[33]

Congress freed the ICC from its judicial bondage with the Hepburn Act of 1906. Among other things, the statute provided that the commission's orders would become effective thirty days after their issuance unless or until they were overturned in the courts.[34] No longer could a railroad wait to comply until the ICC persuaded a court to enforce its order; now a railroad had to comply until it persuaded a court to order the ICC not to enforce its order. Of course, the change would make little practical difference if the courts still found facts without regard for the record before the commission. Not surprisingly, the issue of judicial review prompted sharp disagreement in Congress. The railroads' principal advocate in the Senate called for broad review by the courts, which, he intoned, had "been from the beginning of the common law the sure bulwark of the liberties and rights of the Anglo-Saxon race."[35] The railroads' critics replied that broad review would let judges proceed "as if no such body as the Interstate Commerce Commission had ever existed upon the face of the earth." They wanted weight-of-the-evidence review limited to constitutional or jurisdictional facts. After extensive debate, Congress adopted ambiguous language that left the question to the courts.[36]

An initial response came shortly before Hughes joined the Supreme Court. In *Illinois Central* (1910), a railroad company that also owned coal mines satisfied its own needs for coal cars before allocating the remainder to other shippers. The ICC ordered the railroad to stop. After a lower federal court enjoined the commission from enforcing its order, the Supreme Court reversed. Justice Edward Douglass White announced that when reviewing the ICC, a court should consider (1) "all relevant questions of constitutional power or right", and (2) "all pertinent questions as to whether the administrative order is within the scope of the delegated authority under which it purports to have been made," for these were "of the essence of judicial authority." Yet under the guise of reviewing facts on constitutional or jurisdictional grounds, the courts must not "usurp merely administrative functions by setting aside a lawful administrative order upon our conception as to whether the administrative power has been wisely exercised." White thus read the distinction Hughes made at Elmira between "real" judicial questions and "matters of detail" into the Hepburn Act.[37]

Two later opinions, written by Joseph Lamar, set out the framework for judicial review of the ICC more systematically. As White did in *Illinois Central*, Lamar instructed lower courts to reprimand the ICC when it set rates "so low as to be confiscatory and in violation of the constitutional prohibition against taking property without due process of law" or when it strayed "beyond its statutory power." Courts could also intervene when the ICC misinterpreted the meaning of a section of the Interstate Commerce Act, made some other mistake of law, or failed to disclose the evidence supporting its findings of fact.[38]

Finally, the courts should step in to correct procedural missteps whenever a statute or the "quasi-judicial" character of a dispute require that a commission grant interested parties a hearing.[39] Commissioners had to reveal to the parties the evidence on which they acted and to provide them with the chance to cross-examine witnesses, inspect documents, and offer their own evidence. Lamar did not insist that the ICC follow the ordinary legal manner of the ordinary courts of the land in every respect. For example, the commission need not follow precisely the law of evidence as developed in the common-law courts. Still, it seems, the justices' paradigm of due process was the procedure of the nation's courts.[40]

In time, legal reformers would criticize the constitutional fact and jurisdictional fact doctrines as judicial intrusions into the domain of administrative discretion, but the Supreme Court's application of them in the ICC cases was remarkable less for what the Court preserved of Dicey's rule of law than for the terrain it ceded to the *droit administratif.* Although courts were to determine for themselves facts going to the constitutionality of the ICC's order or to whether the commission had acted within its jurisdiction, they were to defer to the commissioners on such vital matters as the reasonableness of the railroad rates. Lamar explained that whenever a record contained "substantial evidence" supporting the order, a court should not decide "whether, on like testimony, it would have made a similar ruling." He did not define "substantial evidence," other than to say that it was more than "a mere scintilla of proof," but the deferential way he applied the standard implicitly instructed lower courts to accept even doubtful findings if the record contained evidence to support them.[41]

Hughes joined in Lamar's decisions and summarized them for New York's lawyers in January 1916. He still believed that the social and economic problems of the new century required "the continuous and expert attention" of agencies "removed so far as possible from the blandishments and intrigues of politics." If administrators kept faith with "the ideal of special knowledge, flexibility, disinterestedness, and sound judgment," judges should defer to their resolution of "the details of administrative problems." But should administrators ever indulge in "mere bureaucracy—narrow, partisan, or inexpert"—judges should make them respect constitutional rights and limitations, stay within their statutorily defined jurisdiction, and observe "the requirement of a fair hearing, of action upon evidence, of a disclosure of the basis of action that all parties interested may have suitable opportunity to challenge it."[42]

Judging from his own opinions as an associate justice, Hughes believed that administrators were, by and large, doing their job. A complicated series of appeals from state railroad commissions that reached the Court in 1912 gave him his first chance to write in a rate case. Argued over two weeks, the appeals came from several states, including Arkansas, Kentucky, Missouri, and West Virginia, but the most important dispute was the combined appeal of three railroads operating within Minnesota. The *Minnesota Rate Cases* raised two main issues. First, did the Commerce Clause prevent state railroad commissions from setting rates on the intrastate transport of people and goods when the rates practically forced railroads to charge less for interstate shipping over the same lines, even though Congress had not yet expressly addressed the problem? Second, were the intrastate rates so low as to be confiscatory and therefore a violation of the railroads' right not to have their property taken without due process of law? Both issues led into an impenetrable thicket of precedents and factual determinations, including the value of the railroads' property in Minnesota and how to apportion their expenses and income between intra- and interstate traffic. The record was enormous; the briefs, voluminous. One, filed by a team of railroad lawyers including the future Supreme Court justice Pierce Butler, totaled nearly 900 pages.[43]

Appalled by the task confronting his Court, Chief Justice White did what New York's corporation lawyers had done with intractable matters a decade earlier: he gave it to Hughes. The associate justice worked on the decision over the summer of 1912 and throughout the next term, during which he wrote in more than twenty other cases. At last, in June 1913, Hughes produced an opinion for a unanimous Court.[44] It was a triumph of intellect in the public service comparable to his investigations of skullduggery in New York's gaslight and insurance industries. As Hughes read his lengthy opinion, his brethren sent notes to his wife, who had come to the Court for the occasion, praising her husband's "great work" in producing "as able and important" an opinion as any in the history of that august body. Justice Mahlon Pitney assured Hughes that the results of his efforts "far outclass any of the previous opinions of the Court on subjects of this character."[45]

In the *Minnesota Rate Cases,* Hughes affirmed the principle of judicial deference to ratemaking commissions that he had insisted upon in Elmira. "We do not sit as a board of revision to substitute our judgment for that of the legislature, or of the commission lawfully constituted by it, as to matters within the province of either," he wrote. Only in clear cases, when a complaining party had proven certain invalidating facts, such as the confiscatory nature of a rate, should the Court act.[46] After citing a long line of precedents, Hughes announced that the proper standard was whether the railroad had received "a fair return upon the reasonable value of the property at the time it is being used for the public." Since *Smyth v. Ames* (1898), the Supreme Court had struggled to provide workable principles for determining a fair return. Much of the controversy turned on the proper definition of the "rate base," the valuation of assets upon which a fair return would be calculated. In the late nineteenth century, as prices fell, railroads argued for "investment costs," that is, the sum actually spent to acquire each asset. As prices rose after the turn of the century, they switched to "reproduction costs," the sum that would have been needed to replace the whole concern when the rate proceedings commenced. The latter formulation was particularly difficult to estimate. "The ideas underlying the cost of reproduction are so hypothetical, the mutually diverse approaches of the carriers and public servants, respectively are so contradictory," a pair of experts confessed, "that we do not even find common grounds from which to proceed, let alone arriving at similar conclusions."[47]

In his brief in the *Minnesota Rate Cases*, Butler concocted a version of reproduction costs variously known as "real" or "railway" value. The rate base included not only physical property but also such intangibles as good will, going concern value, contracts, investments, and franchises. Further, land holdings should be valued at a premium to capture what the owners would have extracted from the railroads as they attempted to assemble a continuous right of way or a complete parcel for terminals and switching yards.[48]

Hughes routed the railroads' contentions. Valuation for ratemaking purposes was "not a matter of formulas" or "artificial rules" but of "reasonable judgment," he declared. Butler's "railway value" turned not on fact but "mere conjecture." It would require commissioners and judges first to value property as it was, having benefited from the existence of the railroad, and then, in calculating the premium, imagine what the property owners might have held out for if the railroad were still to be built. "The assumption of [the railroad's] existence, and at the same time that the values that rest upon it remain unchanged," Hughes wrote, "is impossible and cannot be entertained." It turned on speculations that were "wholly beyond [the] reach of any process of rational determination." Besides, Minnesota had given railroads the power of eminent domain, so they could take the property of any would-be holdouts at market value. Hughes then embarked on his own review of the record to determine the fair value of the railroads' property and to apportion this value and the railroads' expenses between their intra- and interstate traffic. He concluded that the rate allowed for one railroad was too low but that the other two railroads had not shown that theirs were confiscatory.[49]

In the *Minnesota Rate Cases*, Hughes applied the constitutional fact doctrine but refused to use it to shift responsibility for most fact-finding from commissions to the courts. He displayed a similar wariness with the jurisdictional fact doctrine. On an extreme view, *every* material fact found by an agency was jurisdictional, because the legislature had authorized the agency to act only when certain conditions existed, such as when a rate charged by a railroad was unreasonable. But if every fact was jurisdictional, a party could always force a court to take the whole case, contrary to the Supreme Court's position that weight-of the-evidence review ought to be the exception and not the rule.[50]

In a case decided shortly before Hughes joined the Court, Justice Oliver Wendell Holmes acknowledged the difficulty of distinguishing between jurisdictional and garden-variety facts but invoked the jurisdictional fact doctrine anyway to overturn an ICC finding that no "reasonable or satisfactory through route" existed between two points.[51] In contrast, Hughes brushed aside the argument that the unreasonableness of a rate was "the essential jurisdictional fact" when raised in a later case. "The ratemaking power necessarily implies a range of legislative discretion," he explained, "and, so long as the legislative action is within its proper sphere, the courts are not entitled to interpose and upon their own investigation of traffic conditions and transportation problems to substitute their judgment with respect to the reasonableness of rates for that of the legislature or of the Railroad Commission exercising its delegated power."[52]

But Hughes apparently felt that "the blandishments and intrigues of politics" had fatally infected the setting of rates in a case that reached the Court in 1915. One of the few natural resources frontier North Dakota possessed, besides clay and prairie sod, was lignite coal. Although wetter, more fibrous, and less efficient than anthracite and bituminous coal, lignite was easily mined, because its seams started at or near the surface and were widespread across the sparsely populated western half of the state. Homesteaders settling in that largely treeless region counted on lignite as a source of fuel. When commercial mining began in the late nineteenth century, the state geologists bravely predicted that "this abundant and cheap supply of fuel" would attract new industries to North Dakota.[53] Less often acknowledged was that, given lignite's thermal shortcomings, the state's own industrialists preferred coal from other regions, if it was competitively priced. North Dakota's mine operators could not tell the ICC how to fix rates for shipments of coal to their state, but they could persuade their own legislators to set low rates for the intrastate shipment of lignite. A 1907 statute set those rates so low that one railroad cleared only $828 on a year's carriage, and another operated at a loss, once any of the railroad's fixed costs incurred in carrying freight within the state were charged against its receipts from carrying lignite.

North Dakota's attorney general argued before the US Supreme Court that the promotion of the state's lignite industry was a permissible end of rate regulation and that the rate benefited not just the mine operators but also the state's consumers, who would otherwise "pay the freight" for eastern coal. Besides, even if the railroads made no money on shipments of lignite, they received an adequate return on the rest of their intrastate business. Under the circumstances, the lawyer argued, the rate was not confiscatory.[54]

Hughes disagreed. As governor of New York, he had vetoed a bill adopted elsewhere in 1907 that limited the intrastate rate for carrying passengers to two cents a mile. He had done so not because he was convinced that the rate was unreasonable but because the legislature had enacted it without making a case for its reasonableness. True to his word, Hughes upheld a comparable two-cent-fare law when it had come before him with a proper supporting record in one of the companions to the *Minnesota Rate Cases*.[55] The defenders of North Dakota's lignite law, however, offered no standard whatever under which the rate could be deemed reasonable, and no prior experience of rate setting afforded "any semblance of support to a rate so low."[56]

"We do not sit as a revisory board to substitute our judgment for that of the legislature, or its administrative agent, as to matters within its province," Hughes wrote. Courts ought not to concern themselves "with mere details of a schedule" or "review a particular tariff or schedule which yields substantial compensation for the services it embraces." But the presumption of reasonableness that normally attached to a statutory rate was rebutted when a legislature singled out a particular commodity and compelled railroads to transport it at a loss or without substantial compensation. After his own review of the record, Hughes concluded that, by compelling railroads to carry lignite "gratuitously, in order to build up a local enterprise," North Dakota had appropriated their property to public use on terms they had never agreed to.[57]

In sum, when Hughes left the Court in 1916 to accept the Republican nomination to campaign against Woodrow Wilson, he and his fellow justices had fashioned a doctrinal framework that revised Dicey's strict understanding of the rule of law to make room for expert administrators. Although Hughes never disclaimed the courts' power to decide where the weight of the evidence lay when reviewing the finding of constitutional and jurisdictional facts, he generally resolved close questions in favor of administrators. (Even in the lignite coal case, the rate he struck down was set by legislators, not administrators.) During the twenties, he continued to believe that judges could distinguish applications of administrative expertise from partisan confiscations of the investments of public utilities and bureaucratic overreaching. But as the focus of rate regulation shifted from a stable network of intercity railroads to increasingly powerful utility companies serving masses of city dwellers, the politics of judicial review changed.[58] Influential critics ridiculed the Supreme Court's attempts to value a utility's rate base and argued that, whether they knew it or not, the justices were taking business's side in commission-mediated struggles between capital and the consuming public. Even Hughes, the architect of public utility regulation in New York, would not escape unscathed.

The Barrister and the "Little Bureaucrats"

"The core Progressive sequence," writes the historian Morton Keller, was "a sharp increase in the range of what was politically possible, and then an equally sharp reminder of what was *not* politically possible." After Congress declared war in April 1917, the politically possible soared to its apogee. As Keller observes, the mobilization of the American economy was the "ultimate application of the Progressive belief in forceful, active government." A War Industries Board coordinated the nation's industrial output, a Food Administration did the same for agriculture, and a National War Labor Board resolved labor disputes. A War Shipping Board oversaw the nation's merchant marine; railroads and telegraph and telephone lines were nationalized; the federal government vastly expanded its ability to tax and issue public debt.[59]

Citizen Hughes applauded these developments. "War demands the highest degree of efficient organization," he told the members of the ABA in September 1917. Activities that in peacetime could be left to individual volition became affected with a public interest and subject to regulation during wartime. Food, natural resources, and other "articles of prime necessity" all fell within this category. Moreover, because Congress could not "prescribe many important details as it legislates for the purpose of meeting the exigencies of war," it had to set out broad principles in statutes and leave to the president the work of deciding when and how they applied. But if war had brought "a vast increase of administrative authority," it had not required the suspension of constitutional principles. "While we are at war, we are not in revolution," Hughes declared. "We are making war as a nation organized under a Constitution."[60]

After the Armistice, however, Hughes thought that that same Constitution demanded an end to "the astounding spectacle of centralized control."[61] His investigation, at President Woodrow Wilson's request, of the government-run aircraft industry left him fuming over "the stupid arbitrariness and partiality of little bureaucrats selected in the course of payment of political debts."[62] Hughes still believed that Congress had to delegate legislative power to administrators, but now he saw that broad delegations could be "an instrument of legislative evasion" and permit "incompetency, ignorance and petty tyrannies" to flourish. Increasingly, the personal will of these "little chieftains" determined "for practical purposes the rights of American citizens."[63]

He still considered judicial review one way to check administrators' abuse of discretion. "Liberty in the long run cannot be secured," he wrote, without "recourse to impartial and independent tribunals where the announced common understandings which we call laws are enforced." Yet if "ordinary courts of justice" regularly made their own determinations of the factual bases of administrators' decisions, "dilatory litigation will leave vast activities to the mercy of the cunning, selfish and avaricious, and the means designed for protection will defeat their own purpose." "The dilemma," he observed, "is apparent."[64]

The way out, Hughes decided, was to design agencies so as to minimize the need for judicial review. Long before critics arraigned New Deal agencies for combining powers that should be kept separate, Hughes urged that "the different functions of prosecutor and judge" be vested in different officials.[65] The ICC did this by organizing its quasi-judicial officers, called trial examiners, into their own bureau within the commission.[66] Another approach, employed by the Customs Service, was to constitute the quasi-judicial officers as a distinct agency, the Board of General Assessors, with its own staff and appropriations. Hughes thought that its officers were likely to develop "the same detachment and standards of impartial judgment which have made our courts, after proper allowance for all just criticism, the most successful in their working of all the departments of free government." Other liberal Republicans, including Learned Hand, Henry Stimson, and Thomas Thacher, shared Hughes's preference for independent administrative "courts," including especially the Board of Tax Appeals, created in 1924.[67]

Hughes also urged agencies to make their procedures more closely approximate those of the courts. If we are to have agencies that "conduct investigations, ascertain facts, and judge conditions," he wrote, "we must have, in

FIGURE 2.1 Charles Evans Hughes, sometime between 1921 and 1923.
Source: Courtesy of the Library of Congress, LC-H27-A-2576.

substance, judicial standards; otherwise we shall not be able to safeguard the essentials of liberty." And this was true whether an administrative proceeding was formally classed as quasi-legislative, such as ratemaking, or quasi-judicial, such as the determination of a worker's compensation claim.[68]

Hughes served as US Secretary of State from 1921 to 1925 and during the rest of the twenties occasionally made time for lesser acts of public service, including membership on the committee that oversaw the Commonwealth Fund's monographs on administrative law and practice. He found these "especially valuable" and called for studies of worker's compensation commissions and the regulatory programs of the US Department of Agriculture.[69] Otherwise, he devoted himself to his lucrative practice of law. "I maintained a position of complete independence at the bar," he later claimed, "taking cases which I thought should be argued, regardless of popular feeling, and refusing those in which for one reason or another I did not care to appear."[70]

Rate cases bulked large in his docket. In 1918, he served as referee in a dispute involving a small natural gas company in Brooklyn after the state legislature fixed its rates at an amount 16 percent lower than the state's public utility commission had set only a few years earlier.[71] In 1919, he volunteered his services to a committee created by the Merchants Association to help a local judge value the assets, costs, and revenue of New York City's transit companies.[72] In 1926, he appeared before the ICC to seek a 5 percent rate increase for one railroad and to dispute the commission's valuation of the assets of another. Among his many appearances before the US Supreme Court were a broad challenge to the ICC's valuation procedures and an appeal of an allegedly confiscatory rate set for a New York street railway decided shortly before his nomination as Chief Justice.[73]

In none of these cases did Hughes fundamentally rethink his views on judicial review of rate-setting commissions. In particular, he continued to believe that courts could and should objectively determine that a rate was confiscatory under *Smyth v. Ames*'s standard of a "fair return" on the "fair value of the property used for the public."[74] Yet as Hughes stood his ground, a growing body of legal opinion held that the *Smyth* doctrine turned on inherently speculative and subjective factors and that in attempting to apply it judges were actually picking favorites from among the many interests affected by utility rates. Hughes still thought that "courts of justice were organized 'with peculiar advantages to exempt them from the baleful influence of factions.'" The new critics set out to show that judges were not in fact above the fray.[75]

The most persistent and prominent critic was the lawyer and economist Robert Lee Hale, who taught at the Columbia Law School.[76] Hale noted that judges' notion of "value" in applying the *Smyth* doctrine differed from economists' definition of the term. Economists equated the value of an asset with the capitalization of its anticipated earnings, he observed. This definition was no help to rate regulators, however, because a utility's anticipated earnings were nothing other than the rate set by the commission. *Any* order that reduced its rates reduced the value of its property and to that extent confiscated it. Hale argued that the Supreme Court had attempted to construct its own notion of value from the *cost* of a utility's property, a bewilderingly complex and elusive matter. The Court had shifted ground on which assets counted as property under the *Smyth* doctrine. That tangible assets counted was clear from the case law, but the status of intangible assets was less certain. Good will and going concern value were at first excluded but gradually found their way into the rate base.[77] Further, the Court's precedents left in doubt whether reproduction cost was the only way to value the relevant assets and how to define that vexing concept. In the *Minnesota Rate Cases*, Hughes allowed that reproduction cost was some evidence of fair value, but he rejected Pierce Butler's position that it should be the sole measure. After the railroad lawyer joined the Court, Butler won a majority for his view in *Southwestern Bell Telephone Company v. Public Service Commission* (1923).[78]

As early as 1914, Hale pronounced the Supreme Court's decisions under the *Smyth* doctrine "confused and unsatisfactory" and blamed the justices for not acknowledging that they were "performing the legislative function of determining a policy." In 1916 he urged Louis Brandeis, newly confirmed as a Supreme Court justice, to drop the "metaphysics" of "Justice Harlan's meaningless but much-quoted paragraph in Smyth v. Ames." In its place he proposed what became known as the "prudent investor" rule. "We want people to invest in railroads and the like," Hale lectured Brandeis. "They will not do so unless they expect earnings sufficient to give their stock (considering all risks etc.) a value at least equal to what was put in; most of the excess earnings which give property a value greater than it cost might just as well be diverted from the owners, either to their own employees, or to the consumers in the form of lower rates, or to a broader public in the form of a payment to the public treasury." The proper inquiry, as Hale later formulated it, was whether a rate gave utilities "the amount of return necessary to secure the needed capital and efficient management."[79]

Ohio Valley Water Company v. Borough of Ben Avon (1920), in which the Supreme Court insisted that courts determine for themselves whether a rate was confiscatory, galvanized Hale and others to mount a broad attack on the *Smyth* doctrine.[80] Hale complained that the doctrine placed an "important policy question" in "the hands of small bodies of men not chosen primarily because of their views on policy."[81] Gerard C. Henderson denied that the fair value of a utility's property was "a simple, quantitatively ascertainable fact" or that it could "be scientifically ascertained by observation and induction." To pretend otherwise was to propagate "a gigantic illusion." Ernst Freund declared the line between confiscatory and nonconfiscatory rates "arbitrary" and beyond the capacity of judges to draw.[82] The Chicago lawyer Donald Richberg called *Smyth v. Ames* "a will-o-the-wisp leading the explorer into a morass of shifting, uncertain 'valuations.'" John Dickinson claimed that judges were acting "on no more accurate grounds than their own private opinions." The law professor Thomas Reed Powell scoffed that, "notwithstanding occasional lapses into common sense," the Supreme Court's standard of fair value was a "compound of contradictory considerations concocted by the alchemy of uncontrolled and changeful compromise."[83] Felix Frankfurter considered the Court's reasoning in *Ben Avon* "appalling," encouraged his graduate students to attack the *Smyth* doctrine, and finally published his own assault in 1930.[84]

Three highly regarded judges joined the protest. A few months after the Supreme Court decided *Ben Avon*, the federal district judge Learned Hand claimed that the prevailing case law amounted to "an abandonment of any attempt to deal intelligently" with the valuation of the rate base. He proposed that "fair return" be defined as "such a profit as would induce the venture originally," that is, Hale's prudent investor standard.[85] Then, dissenting in *Southwestern Bell*, Brandeis wrote for himself and Holmes that the "wild uncertainties" of the "shifting and treacherous" *Smyth* doctrine had saddled courts with a "laborious and baffling task." Like Hand, Brandeis and Holmes preferred the prudent investor standard.[86]

The uncertainty of the *Smyth* doctrine allowed utilities to mire regulators in interminable and costly litigation. Recall that the Supreme Court's earlier ICC decisions had signaled that weight-of-the-evidence review was supposed to be the exception and substantial evidence review the norm in rate cases. Because estimates of the "fair value of the property used for the public" varied so widely and because state regulators tended to set rates as low as possible, lawyers for utilities often could credibly allege that a rate was confiscatory and require reviewing courts to determine themselves where the weight of the evidence lay. The "original salutary rule limiting the scope of judicial review" might soon become extinct, warned a commentator in the wake of *Southwestern Bell*.[87]

Further, the utilities' lawyers often brought rate cases before federal judges, who tended to be more solicitous of the utilities' interests than elected state judges.[88] Litigation over rates became appallingly long. Consider, for example, the case of the Indianapolis Water Company. In December 1923 it asked a federal judge to enjoin Indiana's public utility commission from enforcing a rate for its services. In subsequent hearings, estimates of the company's "fair value" ranged from $8.6 to $25.5 million. Almost three-and-a-half years later, the US Supreme Court upheld the injunction and told the commission to start over. Ratemaking for the New York Telephone Company was begun in 1919 and still not concluded in 1930, when an exasperated Governor Franklin D. Roosevelt accused the federal courts of making rate regulation "a mere legal fantasy." Frankfurter blamed the "present enfeeblement of utility administration by the states" on federal judges, and a bill to deny them jurisdiction in challenges to state ratemaking was introduced in 1928. A version finally became law in 1934.[89]

Thus, the same views that made Hughes appear progressive when William Howard Taft nominated him to the Supreme Court in 1910 made him seem conservative when Herbert Hoover named him to replace Taft as Chief Justice on February 3, 1930. During the surprisingly heated debate on his confirmation, senators objected to Hughes's age (he would turn sixty-eight in April), his upholding of the ICC in a clash with a state railroad commission in 1914, his leaving the Court to run for president in 1916, and his stumping on behalf of Republicans in later presidential campaigns. Several dwelt upon his clients, "corporations of almost untold wealth," in whose service Hughes had denounced the antitrust laws, federal control of oil production, and public ownership of the air waves.[90]

But the objection the Senate's progressive Republicans and Democrats voiced most frequently was that Hughes would solidify a majority bent on crippling rate setting by state commissions. William Borah predicted that if Hughes became Chief Justice, the Court's rate decisions would "result in great economic oppression to the people of the United States." Carter Glass seconded a newspaper's prediction that Hughes, like Butler, would read a pro-business interpretation of the *Smyth* doctrine into the Constitution. Robert La Follette, Jr., declared a vote for Hughes a vote to ratify the Supreme Court's "usurpation" of state utility commissions. Walter George, George Norris, and Burton Wheeler concurred.[91]

Hughes's opponents knew that they could not block his appointment—the vote to confirm was 52 to 26—but they hoped that their opposition would make him circumspect in deciding rate cases.[92] For a time, it seemed to have had the opposite effect, as Hughes asserted the judiciary's supremacy over administrative agencies in controversial applications of the jurisdictional and constitutional fact doctrines. His point made, he then pulled the Court back from the extreme positions it had taken under the *Smyth* doctrine during his absence. He might well have kept a majority of the justices on this accommodating trajectory had the New Deal's first state builders, acting at the urging not of half-baked reformers but hardheaded businessmen, not ignored the Court's position that findings of fact backed by substantial evidence were indispensable in a government of laws. When challenges reached the Supreme Court, Hughes and his justices firmly instructed the other branches on the proper design of the administrative state.

3

Chief Justice Hughes

DURING HIS YEARS of public service and private practice, Hughes had many opportunities to observe bureaucracy in its American setting, but as a former secretary of state who frequently summered abroad, he also thought of administration in transatlantic terms. After a visit to Mussolini's Italy in 1931, for example, he warned that popular rule through responsible legislators and administrators was under attack. Whether acting in the name of an all-encompassing state or from class consciousness, "self-constituted authorities assume the responsibility of supplying the intelligence which government by the people is said to lack." In June 1937, as European dictatorships grew in power and the United States economy stagnated, Hughes feared that Americans, too, might succumb to the attractions of official discretion unsubdued by law. "Are our democratic impulses growing weaker?" he wondered. "Under the pressure of economic forces and the insidious teachings of an alien philosophy, will our democracy be able to survive?"[1]

When Hughes began his work as chief justice, the arbitrariness of often obscure bureaucrats was his biggest concern. Then the first fruits of President Franklin D. Roosevelt's "bold, persistent experimentation" reached the Supreme Court, alarming Hughes with their indifference to what he considered a prerequisite for a government of laws, the discipline of findings of fact on a record.[2] He massed the justices in opposition to the New Deal, not in a last ditch defense of a dying constitutional order, but to keep the federal government from abandoning liberal principles for the corporatism of Europe. With that peril and the unexpected threat of the FDR's "Court-packing" plan averted, he turned to the less sensational but no less vital task of instructing the New Dealers on the fundamentals of administrative procedure, which, if observed, reduced the need for judicial review in the first place.

"A Government of a Bureaucratic Character Alien to Our System"

In February 1931, Chief Justice Hughes warned a group of government lawyers to be on guard against "unscrupulous" administrators who, shielded by the substantial evidence rule, found facts so as to evade inconvenient legal principles.[3] Seven months later, the Supreme Court heard oral argument in *Crowell v. Benson*, a case that seemingly instantiated Hughes's fear. On the Fourth of July, 1927, a maritime worker named Joe Knudson was injured while attempting to splice a cable on board a derrick barge tied to the dock of one Beauregard Roberts, located in the navigable waters of Alabama's Mobile River. Some time earlier, Charles Benson, the owner of the barge, had hired Knudson to rig it with an expensive steel cable. Thereafter, Benson lent the barge to Roberts, a friend of his with whom Knudson happened to lodge. Knudson went out on the barge to help Roberts raise a sunken vessel. While on that trip, Knudson cut the cable, even though Benson had told him not to. Benson fired Knudson when he discovered what he had done. In an attempt to make amends, Roberts told Knudson to go onto the barge and splice the cable. Knudson was injured while following Roberts's order.[4]

Because Knudson's injury occurred on a navigable waterway, he filed a claim against Benson under the Longshoremen's and Harbor Workers' Compensation Act. Letus Crowell, a deputy commissioner of the Employees Compensation Commission (ECC), heard much testimony—not all of it admissible in a court of law—on whether Knudson was Benson's employee at the time of the accident. Although the relevant statute did not expressly require Crowell to make findings in support of his decision, he nonetheless produced a document headed "Findings of Fact." It simply announced that Knudson was "in the employ of the employer above named"—that is, Benson—without providing any evidence supporting this conclusion.[5]

Benson challenged the award in federal court. Crowell's handling of the case so troubled the presiding judge that he insisted on having the dispute retried before him and refused to enter the transcript of the ECC hearing into the record. In the retrial, he found that Knudson was not Benson's employee at the time of the accident and set aside the award. The Fifth Circuit affirmed.[6]

By a 5–3 vote, so did the Supreme Court. Hughes's majority opinion commenced deferentially enough. For most facts, he wrote, judges should only review the record before the deputy commissioner to determine that it contains substantial evidence in support of his findings. Thus, on such matters as "the circumstances, nature, extent, and consequences of the employee's injuries and the amount of compensation that should be awarded," courts should defer to the agency, lest a "prompt, continuous, expert and inexpensive method" of addressing workplace injuries be destroyed. But, Hughes continued, judges should make their own determination of facts that are "fundamental or 'jurisdictional,' in the sense that their existence is a condition precedent to the operation of the statutory scheme." Not only should judges decide where the weight of the evidence lay in considering a jurisdictional fact, they should make that determination de novo on a record compiled before them. Anything less, Hughes maintained, would "sap the judicial power as it exists under the Federal Constitution" and "establish a government of a bureaucratic character alien to our system wherever fundamental rights depend, as not infrequently they do depend, upon the facts." In such cases, "finality as to facts becomes in effect finality in law."[7]

Which facts were "condition[s] precedent to the operation of a statutory scheme" was open to interpretation.[8] If every significant fact in a statute was, then all could be retried, and, as the solicitor general objected, the ECC hearing would become "a mere rehearsal for a trial de novo in the District Court."[9] But de novo review had crippled the ICC before the passage of the Hepburn Act, and Hughes, who had rejected broad applications of the jurisdictional fact doctrine as an associate justice, did so again in *Crowell*. He identified only two facts as jurisdictional: (1) whether the injury had occurred upon "the navigable waters of the United States", and (2) whether the respondent and claimant had been master and servant at the time of the injury. Felix Frankfurter objected that "to make the issue of employment more jurisdictional than any other fact upon which liability depends is to turn these matters into a game much more sterile than the speculations of the Schoolmen." But Hughes did have a limiting principle: jurisdictional facts were the ones that determined whether the authority under which an agency acted was authority that was in fact Congress's to confer.[10] As Mark Tushnet has noted, under prevailing doctrine, congressional power turned on both of the facts Hughes identified. If an injury did not occur on a navigable waterway, the dispute was a matter for the states, not the federal government. If it did not occur in the course of employment, forcing a business owner to compensate the injured person was an unconstitutional taking of the property of A and giving of it to B. Far from expanding the category of jurisdictional facts, Hughes's approach collapsed it into the category of constitutional facts.[11]

Two other phases of Hughes's opinion indicated that he was far from calling for a general revival of Dicey's rule of law. First, Hughes limited the de novo trial in federal court to jurisdictional facts; courts were to review other facts on the record before the commission. Parties still had to prove the bulk of their cases in an administrative hearing. Having done so, some and perhaps most would not wish to incur the additional expense of relitigating a jurisdictional fact.[12] Second, Hughes limited *Crowell's* holding to agencies that resolved matters of "private right, that is, of the liability of one individual to another under the law as defined." It did not apply to "public rights," which grew out of exercises of "the congressional power as to interstate and foreign commerce, taxation, immigration, the public lands, public health, the facilities of the post office, and payments to veterans." The FTC and the ICC were thus beyond *Crowell's* reach.[13]

In Hughes's first rate case as chief justice, he also asserted the power of federal courts to review facts aggressively; then he reverted to a deferential understanding of the *Smyth* doctrine. *Smith v. Illinois Bell Telephone Company* (1930) began when Illinois's public utility commission set rates for Chicagoans in 1923. When a three-judge federal district court temporarily enjoined the order, the commission appealed directly to the Supreme Court, which issued an opinion and remanded. Further delays ensued until January 1930, when the district court permanently enjoined the rates. Hughes wrote the Court's opinion in the ensuing appeal. He faulted the commission for, among other things, not distinguishing between intrastate and interstate traffic when estimating Illinois Bell's property, revenue, and expenses. This was the same issue he had tackled in the *Minnesota Rate Cases*, and it went not simply to whether the commission had denied AT&T a reasonable return on its investment but also to whether the state commission was exceeding its jurisdiction. The Supreme Court remanded the case, even though doing so prolonged an already lengthy dispute.[14]

When rate regulators did not stray across the boundary between state and federal power, Hughes applied the *Smyth* doctrine more deferentially than had the Taft Court.[15] Recall that in the *Minnesota Rate Cases* Hughes rejected a version of reproduction costs propounded by the then-lawyer Pierce Butler. Recall, too, that, after joining the Court, Butler persuaded a majority to adopt reproduction costs as the measure of fair value in *Southwestern Bell* (1923). In 1926, he scored another victory by committing the Court to a definition of going-concern value that promised to inflate utilities' rate bases. Robert Lee Hale complained that these decisions required regulators and judges to guess at a cost that "nobody concerned ever had to incur, or ever will have to," namely, the cost of reproducing in the present a concern that had been built up gradually over time.[16]

In two opinions, Hughes demoted reproduction costs to only one of several factors regulators could consider and rejected speculative estimates of going-concern value. In *Los Angeles Gas & Electric Corporation v. Railroad Commission* (1933), Hughes went back to basics. "We do not sit as a board of revision," he wrote, "but to enforce constitutional rights." Courts were simply to determine whether a utility had clearly established that a rate was confiscatory. In valuing rate bases, the Supreme Court had "refused to be bound by any artificial rule or formula" and had considered "all relevant facts." Reproduction cost was one factor, but it had never been the exclusive test of fair value. Indeed, the Court had "emphasized the danger in resting conclusions upon estimates of a conjectural character." To illustrate the point, Hughes cited his own rejection of Butler's valuation in the *Minnesota Rate Cases*![17]

Hughes renewed his campaign when the Illinois Bell case returned to the Supreme Court as *Lindheimer v. Illinois Bell Telephone Company* (1934). After reviewing the record, Hughes concluded that the state commission had properly valued Illinois Bell's property. While the rates were in effect, he observed, the company's capital stock had more than doubled, it had met all its interest payments, and it had never missed a dividend of 8 percent. "Elaborate calculations which are at war with realities are of no avail," Hughes announced. "The actual results of the company's business makes it impossible to accept [the trial court's valuation] as a basis of decision."[18]

Hale was elated. "The rule of Smyth v. Ames no longer prevails," the professor exulted to Hughes. At last, rate setting could "be faced with a view to the realities brought out so clearly by you."[19] *Lindheimer* and another decision that term, *Nebbia v. New York*, in which a five-justice majority discarded the hallowed category of "businesses affected with a public interest" as the test for determining which industries could be subjected to price-and-entry regulation, convinced Hale that the Court had embarked on a new era of deference to rate regulators.[20]

Other decisions during Herbert Hoover's final years in office were just as deferential. The justices did nothing to correct the lower federal courts as they limited *Crowell* to the ECC and the particular jurisdictional facts Hughes had discussed. The chief justice himself wrote that, under the substantial evidence standard, courts were "not concerned with the weight of the evidence or with the expediency of the administrative action." In February 1933, he practiced what he preached by upholding an order of the ECC.[21] Thus, as the New Deal commenced, a majority consisting of Hughes, Owen Roberts (appointed in 1930), Louis D. Brandeis, Harlan Fiske Stone, and Benjamin N. Cardozo (appointed to Holmes's seat in 1932) had returned the Supreme Court to the accommodating trajectory it had been on when Hughes left it in 1916.

The New Deal's Corporatist Adventure

That changed at the end of 1934, when the first challenges to agencies created during Roosevelt's Hundred Days reached the Court. At their birth, the new agencies were ambiguous affairs, hastily created to save an economy that had ground to a halt. The National Industrial Recovery Act (NIRA) delegated to the president the power to regulate industries through "codes of fair competition." Roosevelt, in turn, delegated the authority to draft the codes to the National Recovery Administration (NRA) and, for the oil industry, to the Petroleum Administrative Board (PAB), located within the Department of the Interior. Another statute created the Agricultural Adjustment Administration (AAA) to control agricultural prices through licenses, marketing agreements, and production control orders.

Although Frankfurter and other experts had attempted to advise the drafters, neither NIRA nor the Agricultural Adjustment Act consistently required findings of fact backed with substantial evidence in support of their orders.[22] In addition, NIRA delegated to the president sweeping power to set the terms of business competition in an industry. Charles E. Wyzanski, Jr., Frankfurter's protégé and the top lawyer at the US Department of Labor, thought NIRA "a most unbelievably sloppy piece of work" that no amount of rewriting was likely to save.[23] NIRA's proponents ignored such criticism, convinced that it would save the economy or fail to do so well before any rendezvous with the Supreme Court.[24]

Since early in the Depression, Hughes had watched for signs that Americans might join Europe in abandoning responsible government for some "form of autocracy, whether contrived to promote efficiency or to establish class rule."[25] Whether NIRA and the Agricultural Adjustment Act amounted to such a departure would depend on their administration. If the NRA's administrators fashioned a standard from NIRA's miscellaneous declaration of policy, held formal hearings, and buttressed their orders with findings of fact, they would be meeting the Court's requirements for responsible government.[26] If the administrators imposed their own codes on industry (as NIRA allowed) without much regard for statutory policy or the evidence, the NRA would be on the path to fascism.[27] And if the administrators simply promulgated whatever the "code authority" for an industry proposed, the NRA would be practicing a business variant of European corporatism, the delegation of public power to private bodies to govern whole industries or sectors.[28]

Although some detected "an unpleasant whiff of Hitlerism" in the first speeches of administrator Hugh Johnson and his general counsel, the NRA soon set a corporatist course.[29] "The idea is that industry shall govern itself," Johnson explained. "Through its trade associations and similar organizations, it and not the NRA shall enforce compliance with the rules."[30] Critics charged that an NRA code was little more than "a bargain between business leaders on the one hand and businessmen in the guise of government officials on the other." Even one of the AAA's own lawyers thought that "in essence we're creating gigantic trusts in all the food industries."[31] Lawyers at both agencies often called for careful hearings and detailed records but rarely got them. The NRA's top administrators decided that findings were unnecessary because the issuance of a code was a "quasi-legislative" task. NIRA may have made "a noise like a dictatorship," Wyzanski remarked, but it was really "the beginning of cartels without much government supervision."[32]

The first case arising under NIRA reached the Supreme Court in December 1934. In *Panama Refining*, an oil refiner and several oil producers sought injunctions to prevent the enforcement of bans on the sale of "hot oil," petroleum produced in excess of state quotas, adopted under two different sections of NIRA. The first was the section of the statute that generally empowered the president to approve and enforce codes of fair competition. A petroleum code had been adopted under that section and its enforcement given to Harold Ickes, the secretary of the interior, and the PAB. Among the code's provisions was a ban on sales in excess of production quotas.

Soon after its adoption, Ickes's lawyers decided to revise the code slightly. An executive order made the intended change but also an unintended one: it deleted the section of the code that established criminal penalties for the interstate shipment of hot oil. Although junior lawyers at the PAB soon spotted the mistake, Chairman Charles Fahy regarded it as "purely a clerical error" without legal effect. Apparently, Fahy lacked the courage of his convictions, however, because he did not send the executive order to the State Department, the usual custodian of such documents, or to the Department of Justice. Not until a Department of Justice lawyer tracked down the order while preparing for the appeal of *Panama Refining* did it become clear that the PAB could not prosecute the oil men under the code. The Department of Justice promptly disclosed the mistake to the Supreme Court and abandoned this branch of the case.[33]

That still left a second section of NIRA, section 9 (c), which independently empowered the president to prohibit sales of hot oil by issuing regulations of his own. The section did not expressly state when the president should exercise this delegated legislative power, and it did not require him to make a finding of fact before acting. The unintended repeal of the enforcement provision of the petroleum code did not affect the PAB's regulation of the industry under section 9 (c), and the Justice Department decided to proceed on that ground in the Supreme Court.[34]

Although the justices acknowledged that the government had abandoned the prosecution under the petroleum code, they grilled Assistant Attorney General Harold M. Stephens about that branch of the case anyway.[35] When Brandeis complained that the executive order promulgating the code lacked findings of fact, Stephens lamely replied that the supporting evidence was in the files of the Interior Department. Hughes rejoined that the evidence ought to have been on a public record, and Brandeis agreed. A reviewing court should be able to verify all the facts justifying a code, he said.[36]

When the justices finally turned to section 9 (c), they also complained that it did not require the president to make findings of fact when criminalizing the sale or receipt of hot oil. Whether and when to so act, the justices complained, was left to his complete discretion. The justices were "really concerned with the fundamentals of representative and responsible government, not with the ills of the oil industry," a knowledgeable observer reported to Frankfurter. "All in all, a salutary approach, I think, though the oil boys and the Department of Justice are sorrowful."[37]

In an opinion for the Court, issued in January 1935, Hughes struck down section 9 (c), albeit on grounds easily remedied with new legislation. First, he revived the nondelegation doctrine, a moribund body of law that prohibited Congress from granting its legislative power without providing an adequate standard to guide its use. The Supreme Court had long undermined the doctrine by treating even vague statutory language as a suitable standard. Cardozo, the lone dissenter, was prepared to follow suit, but Hughes argued that neither section 9 (c) nor NIRA's declaration of purposes nor any other part of the statute articulated a policy, standard, or rule that allowed judges to determine whether the president was following Congress's wishes in deciding whether to ban the sale of hot oil. Second, Hughes argued that the Due Process Clause required executive officials to find that the factual circumstances Congress contemplated for the exercise of legislative power were actually present. Commission government was one thing, Hughes implied. "Uncontrolled legislative power" vested in the president was quite another.[38]

Commentators ventured that the justices had used *Panama Refining* "to lay down further principles as a guidance" for new legislation.[39] Privately,

Justice Roberts said as much. At an embassy dinner he assured Ickes "that he was entirely sympathetic with what we are trying to do in the oil matter and that he hoped we would pass a statute that would enable us to carry out our policy."[40] The New Deal lawyers got the message. The decision's "requirement of findings, if complied with," an NRA lawyer observed, "goes a long way toward justifying delegation."[41] Legal divisions at the NRA and the AAA identified scores of codes and licenses that lacked the required findings.[42] This was not exactly a surprise: an NRA lawyer reminded his superior that, despite their counsel, administrators had approved codes "without much concern about the facts relating to the subject of regulation." The NRA could "derive a good lesson" from *Panama Refining*, the lawyer decided.[43] The AAA's and NRA's legal divisions quickly prepared legislation "to make careful findings based on [a] proper record mandatory" in the future.[44]

The Supreme Court delivered a harsher lesson in May by unanimously striking down NIRA in *Schechter Poultry Corporation v. United States*, a challenge to New York City's Live Poultry Code. At oral argument, the justices had returned to the issues that dominated the argument of *Panama Refining*: the delegation of legislative power and inadequate findings of fact. Solicitor General Stanley Reed wrote to Frankfurter that the justices "made my life miserable by demanding to have pointed out to them the lines of the Act which laid down the definite standards for Presidential action." After this "bombardment," Butler loosed "a barrage on Presidential findings. He wanted to know what facts the President or his delegated officers found and how they had determined the necessity of wage and hour limitation."[45]

Frankfurter had speculated that the justices would decide the case on the ground that NIRA's code-making provisions had impermissibly delegated legislative power to the president, who was not statutorily obligated to conduct formal hearings and make findings of fact. This approach, Frankfurter told Reed, would permit the Court "to avoid knotty problems of interstate commerce."[46] Yet when Hughes read his decision for a unanimous Court on Black Monday (May 27, 1935), he delivered two death blows. After striking down NIRA as an undue delegation of legislative power, he killed it again with the Commerce Clause.

Hughes commenced with the delegation issue. When Congress created the ICC and FTC, it established standards which, if vague, acquired content as those expert bodies justified their orders and regulations with findings of fact that were sustained by evidence produced at hearings.[47] In contrast, the diverse collection of policies mentioned in NIRA's preamble amounted not to a standard but "a wide field of legislative possibilities" in which the president could "roam at will." The government's suggestion that the industry would guide the president horrified Hughes. "Such a delegation of legislative power is unknown to our law, and is utterly inconsistent with the constitutional prerogatives and duties of Congress," he wrote.[48]

Hughes might have stopped there, but FDR had already asked Congress to pass a new NIRA, and the NRA was prepared to tell Congress that with adequately drafted standards, "all could go on as before." The justices thought otherwise and decided to say so.[49] Under even the most promising branch of the Court's Commerce Clause doctrine, the effect on interstate commerce of the company's violations of the Live Poultry Code was, on the record before the Court, too indirect to permit federal regulation. If such violations sufficed, Hughes wrote, so would the violation of provisions regulating how many employees Schechter could hire, what rents it should pay, and whether it should advertise its wares. "There would be virtually no limit to the federal power," he warned. "For all practical purposes we should have a completely centralized government."[50]

To make sure that Roosevelt and "the men Felix brought into the Government" understood the depth of the Court's opposition to the New Deal's corporatist adventure, after the reading of the day's opinions, Brandeis immediately summoned two of FDR's most trusted lawyers, Benjamin Cohen and Thomas Corcoran. "The President has been living in a fool's paradise," the justice thundered at the pair, as an assistant helped him off with his robe. Everything that the administration had done or would do had to be "considered most carefully in light of these decisions by a unanimous court."[51]

Roosevelt did not take the rebuke well. *Schechter* and a second decision announced on Black Monday declaring his removal of a Republican FTC chairman unlawful, convinced him that the justices had acted on their "partisan political views."[52] Before the week was out, FDR called a news conference to attack *Schechter*. The justices' understanding of the Commerce Clause might have worked in "the horse-and-buggy age," he declared, but it did not meet the needs of "present-day civilization."[53]

Message Received

While Roosevelt criticized the Supreme Court, his best lawyers were already revising New Deal legislation to comply with the justices' instructions. Their efforts would ultimately reassure Hughes that the New Deal had learned its lesson. Not only would the new statutes create the legal infrastructure of the liberal state; the improved drafting and advocacy before the Supreme Court would assure Hughes that the New Deal lawyers were at last behaving as the "protectors of society from bureaucratic excesses" he expected them to be.[54]

Three centers of legal expertise were most important. The first was the two-man team Brandeis had summoned on Black Monday, Benjamin V. Cohen and Thomas G. Corcoran. Together with James Landis they had drafted the Securities Act of 1933 in a single weekend; and, over a much longer period, the Securities Exchange Act of 1934.[55] Thereafter, Cohen and Corcoran, assisted after hours by some of the New Deal's best young lawyers, wrote the Public Utility Holding Company Act of 1935 and early drafts of the Fair Labor Standards Act of 1938. They also advised agency lawyers on countless other bills, regulations, and other matters.[56]

A second center of legal expertise was the office of Senator Robert F. Wagner, over which Leon Keyserling, a 1931 graduate of the Harvard Law School, presided. Unlike other legislators, Wagner insisted on having tight control over the drafting of the bills he introduced, including the National Labor Relations Act (NLRA), enacted in July 1935. For help with the procedural aspects of that statute, Keyserling turned to Milton Handler, a Columbia law professor who had been general counsel to the NRA's first labor board, and especially to Handler's protégé Philip Levy, a former law review editor at Columbia who worked at the NRA's second labor board.[57]

Down to 1935, a third potential center, the Department of Justice, contributed little expertise on administrative law to the New Deal. The Office of the Solicitor General was hardly devoid of legal talent, as Erwin Griswold, a former president of the *Harvard Law Review* and a coauthor of the government's brief in *Crowell*, had stayed on after the Hoover administration. Yet Griswold and another *Harvard Law Review* man found that covering for their chief, J. Crawford Biggs, a country lawyer from North Carolina, was a full-time job.[58] The head of the Antitrust Division, which handled the court work of the federal regulatory agencies, was Harold Stephens. Stephens inherited two honors graduates of the Harvard Law School and added a third, but his excessive caution, mistrust of young liberal lawyers, and jealous defense of the prerogatives of the attorney general limited his staff's impact.[59]

After Stephens's embarrassing argument of *Panama Refining*, Attorney General Homer Cummings finally conceded the need to hire lawyers with a sophisticated understanding of administrative law and procedure. Abe Feller, a brilliant 1928 graduate of the Harvard Law School, joined the Antitrust Division, where he would write penetrating analyses of *Panama Refining* and *Schechter*. From the PAB, Stephens hired Robert L. Stern, who had graduated magna cum laude from Harvard in 1932. Stern would become Justice's expert on findings of fact and the Commerce Clause.[60]

Still more important was the appointment of Stanley Reed as solicitor general in March 1935.[61] Reed, a Kentucky lawyer trained in part at the Columbia Law School, had been serving as general counsel of the Reconstruction Finance Corporation. He had the intelligence, judgment, and courtroom presence to win the respect of judges and the bonhomie to get along with key congressional leaders. He had also won Frankfurter's approval by hiring and relying upon the law professor's students. The best of these was Paul Freund. During the Hundred Days, Frankfurter had tried and failed to inject Freund, then serving as Justice Brandeis's legal secretary, into the drafting of NIRA. Two years later, Freund oversaw efforts to replace that ill-conceived piece of legislation.[62] As Reed's top assistant, Freund surrounded himself with unusually talented graduates of elite law schools to form "the best law office in the world." At various times, Warner W. Gardner, Henry Hart, Alger Hiss, Charles Horsky, Harold Leventhal, Arnold Raum, and Charles E. Wyzanski, Jr., were assistant solicitors. They joined the office to a larger network of New Deal lawyers, who, Wyzanski recalled, "ate, slept, and constantly talked the topics of their jobs."[63]

Three statutes showed the difference legal talent (or its absence) could make. Two were carefully designed to accord with administrative law and the liberal model of regulation. The first was the handiwork of Cohen, Corcoran, and Landis, the Securities Act of 1933, which became a model for the New Deal drafters. It required the FTC (and later the Securities and Exchange Commission [SEC]) to give parties notice and a hearing before issuing a stop order, which temporarily blocked the issuance of a security. The drafters of the NIRA and Agricultural Adjustment Act had not been so punctilious; not until the amendment of the Agricultural Adjustment Act in 1935 were proper hearings and findings of fact required before the AAA issued a license. Second, the Securities Act provided that the FTC's findings, "if supported by evidence, shall be conclusive" in any judicial review of its orders. That language, sometimes rendered as "substantial evidence," appeared in almost every major piece of New Deal legislation.[64] Thus, the New Dealers wrote into their legislation the principle of judicial deference to administrative findings of fact developed during Hughes's first stint on the Supreme Court.

Keyserling, Levy, and the other drafters of a second measure, the NLRA, followed the Securities Act in these and other ways.[65] Further, they decisively rejected the corporatist approach of the NRA's early labor policy. The NRA's first labor board consisted of an impartial chairperson and representatives of business and labor and attempted merely to mediate disputes. In time, however, Handler and his successors recast the resolution of labor disputes in liberal terms, as a quasi-judicial vindication of a worker's right to organize and to bargain collectively. The FTC Act provided a model. If the FTC could defend competitors and consumers from "unfair methods of competition," why could not a labor board defend workers from the "unfair labor practices" of employers?[66] Judges had already dismissed as "too unsubstantial to justify discussion" the objection that the FTC impermissibly combined prosecutorial and judicial functions; surely the National Labor Relations Board (NLRB) would receive the same protection if it observed the fundamentals of due process?.[67]

The NLRA drafters also appreciated the FTC's enforcement procedures. To enforce its codes, the NRA had to persuade the Department of Justice to bring a civil or criminal proceeding in federal court, in which the law of evidence prevailed. The department lawyers frequently declined because the evidence the NRA had collected did not suffice. In contrast, the NLRA followed the FTC Act in providing for the agency to issue cease and desist orders after hearings in which the rules of evidence were not strictly followed. The NLRB's lawyers still had to persuade a court to enforce the order, but in that proceeding judges were to defer to the board's findings of fact.[68] "We had control of the fact-finding process, the initial decision was made by us," an NLRB lawyer recalled. "The Department of Justice wouldn't have gotten involved until we held the hearing, made the record, made the decision and were attempting to go to the court to enforce it. The court would be bound to enforce our decision if it were supported by substantial evidence."[69]

A third statute fell short of the new standard of draftsmanship. Prepared not by New Dealers but by Henry Warrum, general counsel for the United Mine Workers, the Bituminous Coal Conservation Act of 1935 created a National Bituminous Coal Commission (NBCC) to set prices and a Bituminous Coal Labor Board (BCLB) to enforce labor provisions. The price provisions of the Guffey Act (as the law was known) set out extensive criteria that fully met *Panama Refining*'s strictures against uncabined discretion. The labor provisions, in contrast, continued the corporatist approach of the early NRA. Rather than arrive at wages and hours for the coal industry, the BCLB was simply to enforce upon the entire industry whatever a certain percentage of coal operators and miners had agreed to in bargaining with each other.[70]

Robert Stern was one of several New Deal lawyers who thought the Guffey Act unconstitutional. The labor provisions, he decided, were particularly dubious. The act did not contain findings that showed how the nonrecognition of unions and poor labor conditions obstructed interstate commerce. Further, it delegated the setting of wages and hours to labor and capital "without any standards whatever."[71] Stern drafted a substitute that, as he later put it, showed that the New Deal had "learned its lesson on the delegation of legislative power," but John L. Lewis, president of the United Mine Workers, insisted on Warrum's version and threatened a national strike. Roosevelt and Attorney General Cummings conceded that the Guffey Act might be unconstitutional but asked Congress to pass it anyway. The day after FDR signed it into law, the lawyer who had argued *Schechter* in the Supreme Court asked a federal judge to enjoin a coal company from complying with its terms. *Carter v. Carter Coal Company* would arrive at the Supreme Court seven months later.[72]

Hughes Agonistes

In the 1934 term, Hughes massed large majorities for his reprimands of the New Deal. The 1935 term was altogether different. "He is deeply unhappy," Brandeis wrote to Frankfurter in May 1936. "He has no control over the Court."[73] Butler, James McReynolds, George Sutherland, and Willis Van Devanter, dubbed "the mastiffs" by Judge Learned Hand, had shown themselves willing to use even quite implausible arguments to strike down legislation until the nation came to its senses and elected a Republican president.[74] Sometimes Hughes joined Roberts and the mastiffs in opinions that may well have struck him as dubious rather than have them go out as the statement of a bare majority.[75] For example, in a decision attacking a minor procedural misstep of the SEC, Hughes switched his vote rather than produce a 5–4 decision and joined Sutherland's opinion, even though its likening of the facts to the "intolerable abuses of the Star Chamber" read, as Frankfurter observed, as if Sutherland "were still a United States senator, making a partisan speech." But sometimes the majority's position was more than Hughes could bear, and he wrote separately.[76]

Twice Hughes wanted to dispatch New Deal agencies on the ground that a vague delegation of legislative power had left administrators unconstrained by the obligation to find a particularized set of facts, yet he ended up adopting an additional or alternate basis preferred by Roberts and the mastiffs. The first case was *Butler v. United States*, a constitutional challenge to the AAA. Roberts's majority opinion ultimately turned on whether the tax levied on the processors of agricultural products to pay farmers who agreed to curtail production was permissible under the Spending Clause. But in conference,

Stone recalled, the chief justice "recommended that the statute be overturned for improper delegation." Only after "a painful elaboration" of his position did Hughes say that if the Court were to reach the merits, he would join in an opinion declaring the Agricultural Adjustment Act "an invasion of the reserved power of the states."[77]

According to Stone, Roberts and the mastiffs rejected Hughes's nondelegation argument and insisted on holding that the regulation of agriculture was beyond the reach of the federal government. The dissenters then had their say, and Hughes closed by stating that "he was willing to put the case on the ground of unconstitutional regulation" and calling for a vote. He would join the majority opinion, announced in January 1936, which did not mention the nondelegation issue, but only after persuading Roberts to include language that permitted a more expansive interpretation of the Spending Clause in the future.[78]

Two months later, when the *Carter* case came on for oral argument, the Court had another opportunity to strike down an agency on nondelegation grounds. The Guffey Act was vulnerable for leaving too much discretion to the boards and private bodies that administered the statute, for exceeding Congress's power under the Commerce Clause, for setting prices in an industry not affected with a public interest, and for forcing coal operators to offer miners the same wages and hours their competitors did. Further, if the justices decided that either the price-fixing or the labor-standard provision was unconstitutional, they had to decide whether the infirm section was severable or whether the whole statute fell.

Months after the decision, Stone's clerk, Thomas Harris, revealed that the Court had been "hopelessly divided" in conference. The mastiffs wanted to invalidate the statute's price-fixing provisions and overrule *Nebbia*, but Roberts, *Nebbia*'s author, refused.[79] Sutherland was forced to declare the labor provisions unconstitutional because they regulated production, "a purely local activity," rather than interstate commerce, and because they impermissibly delegated the power to set wages and hours to a dominant faction of coal operators and miners. "This is delegation in its most obnoxious form," Sutherland wrote, "for it is not even delegation to an official or an official body, presumptively disinterested, but to private persons whose interests may be and often are adverse to the interests of others in the same business." Finally, he held that because the labor provisions were bad, the entire statute fell, notwithstanding its severability provision.[80]

Hughes, writing alone, concurred in the result. He addressed the price-setting provisions and found them valid under the Commerce and Due

Process Clauses as well as a constitutional delegation of legislative power. The Guffey Act, he wrote, created "elaborate machinery for the fixing of prices of bituminous coal in interstate commerce" and subjected the commission's orders to judicial review. He decided that the labor provisions were bad under the Commerce and Due Process Clauses and an invalid delegation of legislative power, but, unlike the majority, he thought them severable from the rest of the statute and so wrote separately to indicate that he would join with the dissenters in voting to uphold its price-setting mechanism.[81]

Hughes's discussion of the shortcomings of the labor provisions under one strand of the Court's Commerce Clause jurisprudence, devoted to conduct that burdened or obstructed or tended to burden or obstruct interstate commerce, was especially revealing. He argued that the Guffey Act exceeded Congress's reach not because labor disputes were intrinsically local but because the statute authorized coal operators and unions to set wages and hours "according to their own views of expediency." Congress could create an agency to settle labor disputes that actually threatened the flow of interstate commerce, but it could not use its "protective authority as a pretext" to "assume control of virtually all the activities of the people." Hughes thus hinted that he would vote to uphold a statute directing an independent commission to regulate labor disputes or conditions once it found that the regulated conduct injured or threatened the free flow of interstate commerce.[82]

Hughes's dissent in *Morehead v. New York ex rel. Tipaldo*, announced on the final day of the term, also showed his attentiveness to the structure and procedures of the agency that implemented a policy. The case was the latest stage in a long campaign to regulate the hours and wages of working women. After the Supreme Court struck down Washington, DC's minimum wage law in 1923, Frankfurter asked Benjamin Cohen to draft a distinguishable statute for New York. Cohen ably complied, but, in *Tipaldo*, the mastiffs, joined by Roberts, rejected his handiwork.[83] Hughes commenced his dissent with a lengthy description of the "careful and deliberate procedure" set out in the statute. Under such a law, he wrote, one need not fear "arbitrary procedural action."[84]

Had *Butler, Carter* and *Tipaldo* come in a different term, the continuity of Hughes's votes with his long-held views on the administrative state might have been more apparent. In the 1935 term, however, he was often counted among the "six old men who constitute the majority" and sought "a true judicial despotism."[85] Observers also missed the moderate nature of the term's leading rate case, *St. Joseph Stock Yards*. The dispute arose under the Packers and Stockyards Act of 1921, which empowered the secretary of agriculture to set the fees charged by stockyards and associated businesses. St. Joseph Stock Yards charged that the rate the secretary had set for its services was confiscatory under the *Smyth* doctrine and asked a three-judge trial court to weigh the evidence itself. The judges, hoping to avoid that burdensome task, claimed that the Supreme Court had not yet followed the *Smyth* doctrine in a case arising under the Packers and Stockyards Act. They applied the substantial evidence standard and upheld the rate order.[86]

Hughes, famously reluctant to overturn a precedent, was not yet ready to abandon the *Smyth* doctrine. Indeed, he welcomed the opportunity to affirm it, even as he upheld the secretary's order.[87] Ratemaking, he observed, was "a field peculiarly exposed to political demands." To treat findings of fact as conclusive when constitutional rights were involved was "to place those rights at the mercy of administrative officials."[88]

Brandeis fumed that Hughes was "crazy about 'confiscation.' He has a mania on the subject—driven by fear and that blinds his judgment, so that his very considerable brains are not at work."[89] Yet the chief justice's gloss on the *Smyth* doctrine in *St. Joseph Stock Yards* ought to have reassured regulators. First, Hughes announced that in determining constitutional facts, judges should take the regulators' "reasoning and findings" into account. Second, judges were normally not to accept evidence not already presented to the Secretary.[90] Third, complainants bore a heavy burden of proof. As Tushnet has noted, Hughes's deferential approach was not the same as the substantial evidence standard, but the difference between the two was not great.[91]

That Hughes, in the midst of the Supreme Court's battle with the New Deal, declined to abandon a judicial check on "unscrupulous" administrators is not surprising; what perhaps is surprising, at least to those who overlook Hughes's earlier decisions, is that he instructed the lower courts to overturn rate orders only in extreme cases. Hughes was still not ready to remove the judiciary from the field of economic regulation, but he did call an orderly retreat that left most of the ground to the expert mediation of conflicting political interests.

The Constitutional Reconciliation of 1937

What Stone called "one of the most disastrous" terms in the history of the Supreme Court ended on June 1, 1936. A year later, Hughes was back in command of his Court. In the 1936 term, he and Roberts joined with Brandeis, Cardozo, and Stone to uphold a state minimum wage law for women in *West Coast Hotel Company v. Parrish* and the NLRA in *NLRB v. Jones &*

Laughlin Steel Corporation. The same majority upheld the unemployment insurance provisions of the Social Security Act, whose fate had been uncertain after *Butler*.[92] Van Devanter announced his retirement in May 1937, and the remaining mastiffs were unlikely ever again to run away with the Court. To be sure, the battle over Roosevelt's plan to pack the Supreme Court by appointing one justice for every sitting member over seventy-and-one-half years of age still raged, but Hughes had mortally wounded it with an open letter demonstrating that the Court was not, as FDR had claimed, behind in its work. "Hughes has played a bad hand perfectly while we have played a good hand badly," lamented Corcoran. By the end of July, the plan was dead.[93]

A full account of why Roberts and sometimes Hughes voted with the conservative justices in 1936 but with the liberals in 1937 is beyond the scope of this book. For our purposes it suffices to note that the structure and procedures of agencies powerfully influenced Hughes's votes. When, as in New York's minimum wage law and the price provisions of the Guffey Act, statutes required agencies to operate within limited delegations, hold adequate hearings, and adopt appropriate findings of fact, Hughes interpreted the relevant constitutional doctrines to uphold an agency's actions. When *Panama Refining*, *Schechter*, *Butler*, and *Carter* presented him with agencies lacking in these respects, he applied those doctrines aggressively. Contemporaries saw this pattern, too. One NRA lawyer, for example, read *Schechter* as the Court's signal that the "Commission form of regulation" was the only way to avoid "irresponsible and chaotic bureaucratic action."[94]

In the spring of 1937, Hughes privately complained, "We've had to be not only the Court, but we've had to do the work that should have been done by the Attorney General."[95] The work he had in mind was not simply stating the government's side of a case but also teaching the New Dealers the first principles of administrative law and procedure. By the 1936 term, however, the improved quality of New Deal lawyering should have reassured Hughes that the legislative mistakes of the Hundred Days would not be repeated. (The labor provisions of the Guffey Act were the exception that proved the rule.) Although Hughes may never have said as much, Roberts later did. "The real change that came about was the lawmaking itself," the justice told Hughes's biographer in 1947. "After a few jolts, Cong[ress] and [the] ad[ministration] learned how to frame constitutional laws."[96]

Certainly, the NLRA better respected the principles of the liberal state than did NIRA or the Guffey Act. Although most observers thought the statute doomed after *Carter*, some realized that the NLRB, which protected an individual's right to organize and bargain collectively, was a different creature than the NRA or the NBCC, which enabled groups to set wages, hours, and working conditions for entire industries.[97] Further, the NLRA required the board to find facts in accordance with the Court's decisions under the Commerce Clause.[98] Its category of "unfair labor practices" mimicked the FTC Act, the constitutionality of which was well-established.[99] The NLRB had given the Jones & Laughlin Corporation ample opportunity to present evidence, and the board's lawyers had carefully compiled a record showing how the company's behavior burdened or threatened to burden the free flow of commerce. "The facts found by the Board support its order," Hughes wrote, "and the evidence supports the findings."

The NLRB's procedures ensured that those findings were made after a vigorous, adversarial exchange between lawyers for employers and the board. The NLRA required "complaint, notice and hearing," Hughes noted. "The Board must receive evidence and make findings. The findings as to the facts are to be conclusive, but only if supported by the evidence." Finally, the board knew that "all questions of the jurisdiction of the Board and the regularity of its proceedings, all questions of constitutional right or statutory authority" were subject to judicial review in enforcement proceedings. Presumably, the NLRB would behave itself rather than risk a public rebuke.[100]

In 1937, then, the Supreme Court and the New Deal reconciled, on terms set by the chief justice rather than the president. Henceforth administrators would follow procedures, including findings of fact on a record, that allowed private parties to contest an agency's actions and to permit courts to make sure that it had acted within statutory and constitutional limits. Having ensured that the American administrative state would proceed on liberal rather than fascist or corporatist lines, Hughes could return to the task of fine-tuning the courts' after-the-fact scrutiny of administrative decisions and the expert-mediated interest-group bargains they represented.

Dicey at Bay

Through June 1937, Hughes could count on the four mastiffs to join in any assertion of judicial power to review facts aggressively, but, starting that summer, the Court's composition changed. The appointments of Hugo Black in August 1937, Stanley Reed in January 1938, and Frank Murphy in January 1940 substituted New Dealers for the conservatives Van Devanter, Sutherland, and Butler. Although Frankfurter and Douglas (appointed in January and March of 1939, respectively) replaced the liberals Cardozo and Brandeis, the new justices had strongly condemned judicial review of agencies' fact finding and were eager to back their words with deeds.[101] After 1937, Hughes's challenge became how to keep justices who would travel further and faster in the direction of deference to administrators from winning a majority that unambiguously renounced the jurisdictional and constitutional fact doctrines.

Recall *Crowell*'s admonition that courts should accept agencies' determinations of most facts, even if doubtful, so long as administrators had substantial evidence for finding them as they did. After *Jones & Laughlin*, some lower courts, suspecting the NLRB of playing favorites, overturned its factual determinations after paying only lip service to the substantial evidence standard. When they did, the Hughes Court reprimanded them. In December 1938, Hughes reminded the lower courts that the NLRB had only to show that it had acted on "such relevant evidence as a reasonable mind might accept as adequate to support a conclusion." Later, Stone, writing for himself, Hughes, Roberts, Butler, and McReynolds, did affirm the Seventh Circuit when it ruled that an order of the board lacked substantial evidence, but when the same court applied the standard aggressively in 1940, the Supreme Court reversed per curiam. When the Seventh Circuit tried again, Douglas, writing for all the justices save McReynolds, told them to stop substituting their "judgment on disputed facts for the Board's judgment."[102]

The Supreme Court reinforced such warnings by keeping a tight rein on the two doctrines that permitted de novo review of fact finding. In 1938, a study of the jurisdictional fact doctrine found that the "great majority" of judges who cited *Crowell* did so while *upholding* an agency's order. Hughes himself distinguished the decision in a challenge to a finding by the ICC that an electric interurban railway was within the purview of the Railway Labor Act. His Court never again used the jurisdictional fact doctrine to overturn an agency's order.[103]

The *Smyth* doctrine entered a similarly moribund state. *Railroad Commission v. Pacific Gas & Electric Company* continued Hughes's quarrel with Butler over valuing the rate base. The case turned on procedural issues: did the commission consider reproduction cost when valuing a utility's property and, if not, did its failure to do so violate the Due Process Clause? Hughes, writing for the majority, decided that the commission had considered evidence of reproduction costs and volunteered, with a citation to the *Minnesota Rate Cases*, that the Constitution did not require rate makers to base their decisions "upon conjectural and unsatisfactory estimates."[104]

But two Roosevelt appointees wanted the Court to renounce *Smyth v. Ames* altogether. In a startling dissent from a per curiam decision, Hugo Black, in January 1938, traveled far from the issue at hand to attack the doctrine.[105] A year later, Black joined Felix Frankfurter's attack on the *Smyth* doctrine in *Driscoll v. Edison Light & Power Company*. Frankfurter, who privately dismissed the Court's opinions in rate cases as "miserable obfuscation," argued that in setting rates, commissions struck a balance of conflicting social interests. That process did not present "questions of an essentially legal nature in the sense that legal education and lawyers' learning afford peculiar competence for their adjustment." Courts should limit themselves to ensuring that commissions observed "those procedural safeguards in the exercise of legislative powers which are the historic foundations of due process."[106] Despite Black's and Frankfurter's efforts, *Smyth* survived Hughes's chief justiceship, but only briefly and without the Court overturning a ratemaker's order.[107]

By 1939, the triumph of the substantial evidence standard was apparent. The New Deal lawyer Milton Katz thought it had prevailed because judges realized that "a conscientious commission, on the average, does a more competent and intelligent job of finding facts within its own field than a conscientious court." Now, Katz maintained, "the primary role of the courts is to see to it that the commissions remain conscientious" by correcting "unfairness, abuse of discretion, laziness, sloppiness," and the like.[108]

To illustrate the courts' new role, Katz might have cited a sensational exchange between the chief justice and a member of Roosevelt's Cabinet in May 1938. The controversy demonstrated that under Hughes the Supreme Court did not abandon the rule of law but merely swapped Dicey's version of it for a procedural variant that looked to lawyers to keep administrators in check. The variant required administrators to observe, in the historian Laura Kalman's acute phrase, "due process, the lawyer's means of control."[109] Hughes did not insist that administrative hearings follow the ordinary legal manner of the ordinary courts of the land in every respect. He disliked trying cases; the pleadings and motions beloved by litigators were to him "a maze of legal technicalities."[110] Still, he firmly believed that agencies had to respect the fundamentals of due process as developed in the courts if the rule of law was to survive after the close judicial review of agency fact-finding had ended.

Fair Play

The Packers and Stockyards Act entrusted the job of setting "just and reasonable" rates for the meatpacking industry to the Bureau of Animal Industry of the US Department of Agriculture (USDA). Under its long-serving chief, the veterinarian John R. Mohler, the bureau followed "a live-and-let-live policy" with the industry, including the agents who accepted livestock at stockyards and marketed them to meatpacking companies. The bureau set rates at the larger stockyards high enough to support dozens of these "commission men."[111]

In 1930, the bureau started the process of setting new rates for commission men in the Kansas City yards. It held hearings from December 1930 through February 1931 and again from October to November 1932. In keeping with the bureau's usual practice, the trial examiner merely presided over the hearings and did not, as happened at other agencies, write an intermediate report setting out his findings and recommending a disposition. The Kansas City commission men could consult a transcript of the hearings, but, as the date of their argument before the secretary of agriculture approached, they had no way of knowing how the USDA proposed to dispose of their case.

The argument did not take place until March 1933, the frenetic first month of the New Deal. The presiding official was not Secretary Henry A. Wallace but his assistant, Rexford Tugwell, a member of FDR's original Brain Trust. J. S. Bohannan, a lawyer in the office of the department's solicitor, filed no brief, made only a few general comments, and remarked, "I think I can fairly say to you that I do not believe that any of the members of these commission firms are receiving too much money." With little to argue against, the lawyer for the commission men, John B. Gage, replied just as generally. After the hearing concluded, Gage was sent a transcript of the oral argument, and he submitted a brief for Wallace's consideration. He heard nothing until the secretary announced his decision in June.[112]

In the interim, a committee consisting of the Bureau of Animal Industry's lawyer, the bureau's economists, and Bohannan of the solicitor's office pored over more than 11,000 pages of testimony and exhibits, and drafted tentative findings of fact and a tentative order. All freely discussed the case with the department's solicitor, Seth Thomas. At last, Wallace received the proposed order and findings, as well as the record and briefs, at a meeting with Mohler, his lawyer, Solicitor Thomas, and his subordinate Bohannan. The secretary told the gathering that he saw no need to support dozens of commission men at the expense of the nation's hard-pressed farmers and that he intended to lower rates and force marginal firms out of business. Wallace's order, supported by 180 findings of fact, set rates far lower than the commission men could have anticipated and signaled for the first time the USDA's new policy of "forcing consolidations" in the trade.[113]

It happened that Wallace was scheduled to speak in Salina, Kansas, soon after he announced his order. After his address, he was beset by irate Kansas City commission men. As they told the story, the embattled Wallace "admitted

FIGURE 3.1 "Fuehrer Wallace." On February 16, 1938, shortly before *Morgan v. United States* arrived at the US Supreme Court for the second time, Clifford K. Berryman, cartoonist for the *Washington Star*, depicted Secretary of Agriculture Henry A. Wallace as Hitler, saluting goose-stepping farmers passing in review.

Source: Courtesy of the Library of Congress, LC-USZ62-50894.

that he had not personally read the record or considered the case." In July, fifty commission men sued in federal district court to block the enforcement of the new rates because they had not received the "full hearing" due them under the Packers and Stockyards Act. When their case reached the Supreme Court in 1936, the justices, in an opinion by Hughes, unanimously sent it back to the trial court to give the commission men the chance to prove that Wallace had not really considered the evidence before issuing his order.[114]

When the case returned to the Marble Palace in March 1938, the justices were satisfied that Wallace had adequately considered the record, but they spotted a different procedural mistake. Bohannan, the lawyer representing the department in the hearing, had also prepared the findings of fact and the order Wallace issued, and he had done so without giving the commission men a chance to contest his version of the dispute. Stone, Brandeis, Hughes, Roberts, and McReynolds all asked questions going to this mingling of quasi-prosecutorial and quasi-judicial functions and suggesting that the commission men ought to have had a chance to counter the government lawyer's statements to Wallace. In conference, Hughes allowed that what constituted a "full hearing" in an administrative matter was "relative" but asserted that a proceeding in which an administrator "took what his bureau disclosed to him" without revealing it to the other side "emphatically" was not a full hearing.[115]

The Court announced its decision on April 25, 1938. "Congress, in requiring a 'full hearing,'" Hughes wrote, "had regard to judicial standards—not in any technical sense but with respect to those fundamental requirements of fairness which are of the essence of due process in a proceeding of a judicial nature." He could now see that Wallace had sufficiently considered the evidence; but the hearing he afforded the commission men was unfair in other respects. Wallace had adopted findings "prepared by the active prosecutors for the Government, after an ex parte discussion with them and without according any reasonable opportunity to the respondents in the proceeding to know the claims thus presented and to contest them." In this, he failed to act "in accordance with the cherished judicial tradition embodying the basic concepts of fair play."[116]

While the New Deal's lawyers pondered the decision, Wallace attacked it. On a nationally broadcast radio program and in a private letter to Hughes, he merely protested that he had inherited the procedures he had followed in the Kansas City case from his Republican predecessors and that he had reformed them soon after the Court's first decision in the case.[117] Then, in a letter to the editor of the *New York Times*, he argued that the justices' real complaint was not with the Department of Agriculture but certain "newer quasi-judicial agencies," by which he presumably meant at least the NLRB. Wallace restated this charge the next day in a letter delivered to the desk of every member of the US Senate.[118]

Hughes was not long in responding. "The multiplication of administrative agencies is the outstanding characteristic of our time," he told the American Law Institute. Many, such as the ICC, had demonstrated a "capacity for dealing expertly with intricate problems." But lately, Hughes had detected a tendency to celebrate the "flexibility" of agencies and "to deprecate the work of the courts." This was shortsighted and would ultimately hurt agencies' standing with the public, he warned. "Whatever the shortcomings of the courts, and whatever the need of administrative bodies, it is still the courts which stand out as the exemplars of the tradition of independence and impartiality." The wise administrator would act in "the spirit of the just judge."[119]

The journalist David Lawrence praised Hughes for insisting upon "the standards of fairness that have prevailed for centuries wherever English jurisprudence has been accepted as the legal exponent of human liberty." Wallace received rougher treatment. Correspondents called his letter to the *Times* "a mendacious piece of bureaucratic impertinence" and "one of the most inane utterances of the most cockeyed administration this country has ever known." Another counseled, "You only reveal yourself as small, vindictive and ridiculous when you attempt to lecture the court on its duty."[120]

Following the decision, a journalist reported that "virtually all of the quasi-judicial commissions of the Federal Government are beginning this week to reexamine their procedure in the light of the chief justice's ruling to see whether they are giving the citizens a full and fair hearing in accordance with the time honored judicial processes of fairness and equity." The SEC's general counsel circulated *Morgan* to the commissioners the day it was decided. He later recommended that issuers of securities receive better notice of the flaws in their registrations and that the lawyers who prepared the SEC's findings of fact have their own section within the Legal Division. At the USDA, the solicitor's staff worked out the implications for the many statutes the department administered. Ultimately, the lawyers concluded that Secretary Wallace "should not, in the absence of the adverse party or his representative, discuss the merits of the case with any employee of the Department who acted as an investigator, witness or attorney in the proceeding, or who supervised the development or presentation of the particular case for the Department."[121]

Days after *Morgan* was announced, the NLRB withdrew several cases from the federal courts and instructed the attorneys who prepared its findings not to discuss cases with trial attorneys or trial examiners. In the few cases in which the board did not require an intermediate report, it employed an alternative Hughes had sanctioned in his decision: it proposed findings on its own, permitted parties to except to them, and then heard arguments on the exceptions themselves. In fall 1938, the FCC adopted this procedure as its usual practice in issuing radio licenses and claimed that under it "the proprieties as set forth in the second *Morgan* case are completely satisfied." When the Bituminous Coal Division was organized the following year, *Morgan* haunted its legal staff. Lawyers for the coal operators invoked it so frequently that the division's general counsel instructed his staff to "err on the side of giving due process."[122]

As the agencies altered their procedures, the Department of Justice decided on an administration-wide response. In September 1938, Charles

Wyzanski, who had left the Solicitor General's Office for private practice, told Attorney General Cummings that agencies' procedural missteps had given ammunition to the New Deal's critics and troubled even "serious and disinterested students of public affairs." He proposed that administrative procedure be studied across the federal government.[123] In January 1939, Cummings's successor took up Wyzanski's suggestion and created the Attorney General's Committee on Administrative Procedure. One of the topics proposed for consideration was *Morgan*'s implication that "the ideal of even-handed justice would seem to require a pretty thoroughgoing separation of the prosecuting and the judicial staff." The committee's report, issued during Hughes's last term on the Court, followed the chief justice in urging that trial examiners have a more independent role in agencies' adjudication of individual disputes.[124]

A Lawyer's Administrative State

When Hughes left the Supreme Court in June 1941, he had completed a life's work. As a progressive reformer and governor, he had created the nation's leading example of the expert-staffed regulatory commission, "an answer with legs," the historian Daniel T. Rodgers writes, "that was, from the early progressive years through the New Deal and beyond, capable of application to many different circumstances."[125] He championed commission government over socialism in the progressive era and corporatism during the New Deal, but he also saw that the same independence that promised to put commissions beyond party politics might also make them irresponsible. When he looked to the courts for an answer, he realized that the traditional Anglo-American notion of the rule of law was too restrictive. With other Supreme Court justices, he translated it into legal doctrines that gave greater freedom to administrative discretion. Although he remained convinced of the need for after-the-fact judicial review long after others were prepared to abandon it, as early as 1920 he saw that the better solution was to design agencies' structure and procedures so that the affected concerns and their counsel could channel administrative discretion along reasonable lines. Courts would intervene to structure agencies' proceedings in their own image so that the affected parties could bring egregious decisions to their attention. Otherwise, the judges were to give administrators their lead.

Two groups threatened this entente between the courts and the agencies. First, members of a legal profession that closely identified with courts would have to be convinced that administrative discretion would not threaten their own interests and ideals. Second, the professional politicians who still dominated the nation's legislatures had to be persuaded that the new agencies would not provide governors and presidents with an independent source of political power.

Between 1938 and 1941, it seemed as if the lawyers and politicians had joined forces and were marching on Washington. Ultimately, however, both groups saw that requiring agencies to follow court-like procedures met their concerns as neatly as it solved the judges' puzzle of reconciling administrative discretion and the rule of law.

4

New York, 1938

IN APRIL 1938, New York's first constitutional convention since 1915 convened in Albany. When it adjourned in late August, one of the amendments slated for a referendum that fall was an "anti-bureaucracy clause," a provision that would greatly increase New York courts' oversight of the state's agencies. A few weeks later, the state parties held their conventions. Democrats nominated Robert F. Wagner to another term in the US Senate; to face him, Republicans unexpectedly chose John Lord O'Brian, a Buffalo lawyer who had served in the US Department of Justice in both Republican and Democratic administrations. O'Brian did not unseat Wagner, but his attacks on the senator's legislative offspring, the NLRB, won O'Brian the support of New York City's civic elite and an endorsement from the *New York Times*, which had previously backed Democratic senatorial candidates. Even President Franklin D. Roosevelt grew alarmed. In the last days of the campaign, he summoned NLRB members to the White House to ask them to change their procedures and "help Bob Wagner get re-elected."[1]

The battle over the antibureaucracy clause and the O'Brian-Wagner senatorial contest showed that the new administrative agencies had opened fault lines within the major political parties and the legal profession. "Old Guard" or "regular" politicians, who played by longstanding rules of patronage politics, and trial lawyers sought to control the new agencies by requiring courts to review their finding of facts under the weight-of-the-evidence standard. But a newer breed of "liberal" politicians, oriented toward issues that mattered to urban professionals, and corporation lawyers did not insist on an appeal from agencies to the courts on factual matters as long as administrators observed the "basic concepts of fair play" that Charles Evans Hughes had championed in *Morgan*. By rejecting the antibureaucracy clause, New York voters showed that they were unwilling to sacrifice administrative agencies to the principle of judicial supremacy, but the surprisingly large turnout for O'Brian suggested that they wanted those administrators to observe the fundamentals of due process as developed in those "exemplars of independence and impartiality," the courts.[2]

Dividing over the Administrative State

By 1938, the statebuilding of the New Deal had presented New York's traditional politicians with an unhappy prospect. Urban professionals and others who wore their partisan affiliations lightly threatened to use administrative agencies as the basis for new, executive-directed parties that could circumvent party bosses' control of legislatures and distribution of patronage. In the twenties, Old Guard Republicans had contained an earlier burst of administrative state building with patronage appointments and strict judicial review. When the Democrats regained the White House in 1933, Franklin D. Roosevelt's campaign manager turned postmaster general also ensured that "the grand old boys of the Party" got their due.[3] In Roosevelt's second term, however, issue-oriented professionals in the administration, for whom the term "New Dealers" came to be reserved, plotted to remake the Democratic Party by centering it on the presidency, mobilizing voters with administratively disbursed benefits, and realigning Republicans and Democrats into conservative and liberal parties. Every favorable NLRB ruling, federal loan, radio license, or social security payment was a link between the state and a potential member of a liberal political party. Thus, as the political scientist Martin Shefter has written, the new bureaucracies promised to "perform for the administration precisely those functions served by party organizations in cities and states governed by centralized political machines."[4]

A series of dramatic events convinced many observers that Roosevelt had signed onto the New Dealers' project. Roosevelt's executive reorganization and Court-packing plan of 1937 seemed calculated to strengthen his hand against rival branches of government. His attempted "purge" of anti-administration Democrats in the primaries of 1938 looked like a bid to become the master of the Democratic Party. NLRB rulings favoring affiliates of the Congress of Industrial Organizations (CIO) seemed the quid pro quo for the labor group's $470,000 contribution to the president's reelection campaign in 1936. A newspaper exposé and congressional investigation of the partisan use of Works Progress Administration funds unfolded over the summer of 1938. Although Roosevelt's actual intentions remain obscure, such developments were enough to drive conservative Democrats in Congress into a coalition with Republicans to block further New Deal legislation and to investigate the NLRB.[5]

With a former governor in the White House, New York's political affairs were thoroughly enmeshed in national politics. Five factions operated under the banners of three different political parties. One group of Democrats coalesced around the state's "little New Deal," presided over by Governor Herbert Lehman. It included financial regulation of public utilities, municipal power plants, unemployment insurance, an improved worker's compensation law, a minimum wage for women, an ambitious program of public housing, and a state labor relations board.[6] The state's regular Democrats, led by Alfred E. Smith, resisted the New Dealers, who denied them patronage and plotted to weaken them through reapportionment.[7] The leader of the Smith faction in Albany was Robert Whalen, a lawyer who looked upon the New Deal as a species of mob rule.[8]

The Republicans were also divided. The Old Guard, a conservative alliance of upstate farming and business interests, had strenuously opposed New York's little New Deal and wanted to "stand pat" until the Roosevelt recession of 1937–38 returned them to power. Their leader in the state senate was George Fearon, a hard-boiled lawyer from Syracuse.[9] Since early 1938, they had lost ground within the party to a growing contingent of urban liberals, who accepted the basic policies of the New Deal. In New York City, this group drew heavily from the civic elite, including great corporation lawyers like Arthur Ballantine, Herbert Hoover's treasury undersecretary, and Hoover's two solicitors general, Charles Evans Hughes, Jr. and Thomas Thacher. In the state legislature, they joined with Democrats to pass many of Lehman's measures; they worked to elect Fiorello La Guardia mayor of New York; they blocked Fearon's nomination for governor in 1936; and they outraged the Old Guard by joining in a fusion ticket with the American Labor Party (ALP) in 1937.[10]

The ALP was the fifth political faction afoot in 1938. It had been organized in 1936 to give trade unionists, socialists, Republican fusionists, and independents a chance to support Roosevelt without having to back Tammany Democrats. The leaders of CIO affiliates, such as Sidney Hillman of the Amalgamated Clothing Workers of America and David Dubinsky of the International Ladies' Garment Workers Union, dominated the ALP at its founding, but room was also made for George Meany, president of the New York State Federation of Labor, and for several affiliates of the American Federation of Labor (AFL). The ALP turned out almost 275,000 votes for Roosevelt in 1936 and helped elect politicians from the liberal wing of the Republican party under the fusion agreement of 1937, but it suffered grievously when Meany led AFL affiliates out of the party in the spring of 1938. The ALP would give Lehman and Wagner their margins of victory later that year but more as the tail of a Democratic kite than as an independent labor party.[11]

In this political context, the wrangling over the antibureaucracy clause reinforced the tendency of New York's political groups to divide into anti- and pro-New Deal camps. Both regular Democrats and Old Guard Republicans saw the controversy as a chance to savage the New Dealers for their alien, oppressive bureaucracies. New Deal Democrats, liberal Republicans, and Laborites countered that the clause would paralyze the administrative measures that all modern societies needed. But if liberal Republicans like Congressman Bruce Barton accepted collective bargaining and social security as "part of our American scheme of things," they refused to merge with the Democrats to form a New Deal party. "The next national campaign will not be fought by a liberal party and a reactionary party," Barton declared in 1938. "The next campaign will be between a Republican liberal party and a Democratic radical party."[12]

New York's lawyers also had a stake in the controversies of 1938. Most of the state's lawyers were sole practitioners or members of small partnerships and represented private individuals in local courts.[13] They regarded administrative hearings as, at best, second-rate imitations of judicial trials and, at worst, travesties in which lay officials ignored the law of evidence and freely engaged in ex parte contacts. Further, as Charles E. Wyzanski, Jr., observed, most trial lawyers were "not professionally equipped to handle controversies in an unfamiliar forum and with an unfamiliar technique." Many were active in their local political parties; they dominated the New York State Bar Association (NYSBA); and they must have accounted for most of the 120 lawyers among the 168 delegates at the constitutional convention in 1938.[14]

A very different bar had emerged in New York City after the Civil War, when a cohort of lawyers discovered that incorporations, securities, mergers, and reorganizations were far more lucrative than courtroom advocacy. Around 1900, these "corporation lawyers" organized multidepartment firms in which associates, recruited from the top of their classes at case-method law schools, competed for partnerships. "As a rule they are not conspicuous in public life," a journalist said of these Wall Streeters. "They are the silent, shrewd, polished, keen, erudite men who are the brains behind the vast organizations of capital they have helped create." Their fees were fabulous: $500,000 to Francis Lynde Stetson for organizing US Steel; $1,000 a day to Elihu Root on another matter; $1 million to James Dill for settling a quarrel between two steel barons; and another $1 million to William Guthrie for breaking a railroad magnate's will. Although some, like Charles Evans Hughes and Root, passed up retainers that would mire them in lucrative but routine work, others, like Paul Cravath, happily accepted the bargain.[15] Corporation lawyers might serve on ad hoc commissions or take appointive offices at the request of Republican presidents; Hughes was among the few who subjected themselves to popular elections. Their exclusive preserve was the Association of the Bar of the City of New York, known colloquially as "the City Bar."[16]

New York's public utility commission persuaded many corporation lawyers of the merits of the administrative state. Wall Streeters had lined up against Hughes's bill in 1907; four years later, they frankly conceded their error. "It is hard to believe that such opinions were entertained by intelligent men of affairs," Cravath marveled. "Many of us now think the corporations would be better off if the commission were endowed with wider powers. One reason for this feeling is that we are relieved of our annual struggle with the Legislature, which was a perfect nightmare."[17] When New York's utility companies attempted to write strict judicial review into the state constitution at the constitutional convention in 1915, Root, the convention's president, blocked the effort. Administrative agencies were "inevitable," he explained the following year, because they furnished "protection to rights and obstacles to wrongdoing which under our new social and industrial conditions cannot be practically accomplished by the old and simple procedures of legislatures and courts as in the last generation." Further, commissioners were more reliable than legislators, who too often brandished "strike bills" to extort payoffs from utility companies, or judges who tried to comprehend the needs of modern industry with antiquated common-law doctrines.[18]

Thus the courtroom lawyers of the NYSBA and the corporation lawyers of the City Bar tended to divide on the question of judicial review of administrative orders. The trial lawyers tended to subscribe to Dicey's rule of law and to insist on weight-of-the-evidence review of facts in the ordinary courts of the land. In contrast, the corporation lawyers were far more accepting of administration, so long as administrators adopted something like the adversarial process of the courts when disposing of individual disputes. Their differences would become apparent at the New York State Constitutional Convention in the spring and summer of 1938.

Forming Ranks

The New York constitution of 1894 provided that the question of whether to convene a constitutional convention be put to voters every twenty years. Neither party displayed much interest as the referendum approached in fall 1936, but, after their sweeping victory in the general election, the state's Democrats believed they could use the convention to entrench the little New Deal through reapportionment and other measures.[19] George Fearon understood the stakes. "If the New Dealers control the coming convention," he warned, "you are going to have the same contempt for American institutions, the same disregard for our courts, the same centralization of authority, the same greed for power, the same disregard for individual and minority rights that we have had in Washington." But Fearon's fears proved unnecessary: when the convention delegates were chosen in the fall of 1937, Republicans won a clear majority, thanks to La Guardia's landslide reelection as New York City's mayor and the ALP's refusal to endorse the full Democratic slate.[20]

Among the elected delegates were two Republican lawyers from western New York, Ernest Leet and Arthur Eugene Sutherland, Jr. Both were alumni of the Harvard Law School. Leet graduated in 1926, returned to Jamestown, New York, and joined Robert H. Jackson's law firm. Sutherland graduated a year earlier and served as Justice Oliver Wendell Holmes's legal secretary before settling down to a substantial practice in Rochester. Sutherland was best known for his defense of a local grocer convicted of violating the state's milk control law, which produced the constitutional landmark *Nebbia v. New York* (1934).[21]

Leet's galvanizing encounter with the *droit administratif* was the denial by the state Motor Vehicle Bureau of his request that a stenographic record be made of his client's hearing in 1929. On that occasion he mobilized the Jamestown bar and forced the "dictatorial, vicious and undemocratic" bureau to back down, but he remained convinced that administrators oppressed New Yorkers in ways that were beyond the power of lawyers to correct. All they could do, Leet complained, was advise would-be clients to see "the right person" or to work through "political channels."[22]

In late 1937, in anticipation of the constitutional convention, Leet tried and failed to rally the bar associations of western New York and the state Republican Party behind an amendment to increase judicial scrutiny of agency fact-finding.[23] His failure left the initiative to a committee appointed by Governor Lehman, which, in turn, asked Louis Jaffe, a New Dealer on the University of Buffalo Law School faculty, for a report on the issue. In a draft of "Judicial Review of State Administrative Decisions," Jaffe denounced *Ben Avon* and *Crowell* as "excesses of judicial review" and opposed any change in New York law. Although these passages were purged from the final report, they helped Leet persuade the NYSBA to take a stand.[24] In March, it created a committee on administrative law with a New York City lawyer, Edward Gluck, as its chair and Leet and Sutherland among its members.

At the committee's invitation, scores of trial lawyers mailed in complaints about the state's administrators. Some lawyers reported that they had been forbidden to read or object to trial examiners' reports; others, that they had not been allowed to file a brief or argue before the official who actually decided their disputes. Some complained that referees in worker's compensation disputes would "decide cases only one way"; others, that the Alcoholic Beverage Control Board did not give their arguments "a fair determination"; still others, that sales tax officials did not produce "proper records of hearings."[25]

Above all, the NYSBA lawyers objected to the substantial evidence standard. At the constitutional convention, the conservative Democrat Robert Whalen recalled an occasion when an employer sought his advice on whether to challenge a worker's compensation award in the courts. The worker had jammed his thumb and was laid off for a month, Whalen explained. The employer paid his wages in full and his doctor's bill and hired him back after his recuperation. Yet when the State Industrial Board learned of the accident, it set the matter down for a hearing on its own motion. The workman swore that he had suffered no permanent injury. "I can grasp a hammer just as well as I ever could," he testified. Three doctors, appearing on behalf of the employer, agreed, but the commission's own doctor testified that the worker had lost 40 percent of the use of his hand. The commission followed its doctor's testimony. Although the weight of the evidence argued for no award, the testimony of the commission's doctor was "substantial evidence in the case to support the finding," Whalen explained. "There was nothing to do but advise the employer that an appeal to the Appellate Division would be utterly futile."[26]

Whalen declared the case an egregious example of a common phenomenon. Time and again, he had seen his appeals of administrative orders dismissed with a shrug. "Well, there is evidence in the case to support the findings," the judges had said. "What can we do?" Whalen thought it a great "anomaly" that the factual findings of a commission, "composed perhaps of a former barkeeper or street cleaner," were "absolutely conclusive and beyond the power of courts to review," when those of "a trained judge" were not.[27]

Although the NYSBA's trial lawyers would have nodded sympathetically, the corporation lawyers of the City Bar saw more advantages than disadvantages in the administrative process. The ABA had in 1933 created the Special Committee on Administrative Law, but it had yet to propose legislation that the organization could support. In October 1937, the ABA chieftains tried to energize the committee by appointing a new chairman, the former Harvard law dean Roscoe Pound. To counter this move, the City Bar, under the patrician Henry Stimson, created its own committee, with Felix Frankfurter as a member and John Foster Dulles as chair.[28]

Dulles took the job "with some reluctance and hesitation" and did not "feel particularly qualified to deal with this important subject," yet he quickly became a prominent and effective critic of heightened judicial review. He did find it "disheartening to be trying to defend the administrative procedure of a body like the S.E.C. when it goes on in ways which, justifiably or not, make litigants before it feel that they have not been accorded a treatment which meets the elemental requirements of justice." But the solution was for the agencies themselves to reform their procedures, not to "throw upon the courts the burden of curing" their deficiencies.[29] As Dulles would later explain, "What people want is quick, efficient action. You go to a skilled surgeon and he finds a diseased spot. He takes a knife and cuts it out with expertness, sureness of touch and a minimum of suffering. The body, relieved, goes on living. That is the kind of treatment which business and financial people, with whom I come in contact, expect of administration." Dulles would willingly exchange "a certain amount of classic legal protection" for the "valuable quid pro quo" of a quick and decisive conference with an expert official.[30]

Dulles's committee would not meet until May 11, and it followed developments in Albany from a distance. In contrast, at the convention Leet and Sutherland actively pursued the interests of the NYSBA trial lawyers—in Sutherland's case, as a member of the convention's Judiciary Committee. Their most effective opposition came not from the corporation lawyers of New York City but the liberal Republicans and New Dealers of Buffalo's bench and bar.

Anti-Bureaucracy Politics

When the constitutional convention convened on April 5, 1938, liberal Republicans seemed to have the upper hand. One of their number, Charles Sears, presiding judge of the Appellate Division in Buffalo, was chosen to chair the Judiciary Committee. As the convention proceeded, however, the prospect that Liberal Republicans might join with New Dealers to pass major reforms drove Old Guard Republicans into opposition. Sears kept his chairmanship, but increasingly, regular Republicans and Tammany Democrats combined to seize the initiative.[31]

Previews of the convention made no mention of judicial review of administrative agencies.[32] The New Dealers were satisfied with the deferential state of the law, and the Republicans, Leet complained, lacked "any coordinated and intellectual approach to these problems." Nor did the NYSBA at first provide any guidance, as its administrative law committee could not unite on a single proposal. Over thirty amendments treating the judicial review of agency decision-making or the reform of administrative procedure were introduced in the first weeks of the convention. Gluck convened a meeting of the various sponsors in an attempt to settle on a single measure, but Philip Halpern (a liberal Republican on the University of Buffalo's law faculty) and the counsel for the Department of Education opposed any attempt to heighten judicial review.[33]

Rebuffed, Gluck tried for a narrower consensus in a joint meeting of the NYSBA committees on administrative law and on the constitutional convention. When it ended, Gluck thought all had agreed on language borrowed from a bill just approved by the ABA's Board of Governors. It directed reviewing courts to set aside findings that were "clearly erroneous or not supported by substantial evidence." Upon further consideration, however, several participants objected that the words "clearly erroneous" had no generally accepted meaning among the bench and bar and might not be read to require weight-of-the-evidence review. At last, in mid-July, the NYSBA's lawyers arrived at a solution. Borrowing from New York's Civil Practice Act, they proposed that state judges should overturn an agency's finding of fact whenever there was "such a preponderance of proof against" it that a jury verdict to like effect would be set aside by a trial court "as against the weight of the evidence." The Democrat Whalen and the Republican Sutherland introduced a resolution embodying the proposal, and it was referred to the Judiciary Committee.[34]

The City Bar committee followed the NYSBA's attempts to constitutionalize weight-of-the-evidence review with growing dismay. "Administrative law is in an evolutionary stage and inevitably subject to defects inherent in the early development of the process," Dulles wrote to Frankfurter. Constitutionalizing it now would lead to "undesirable rigidities and excessive detail." To Sears, Dulles acknowledged that administrators unfamiliar with the "judicial approach" to fact-finding sometimes abused their quasi-judicial powers. The remedy was not to let courts second-guess administrative fact-finding but to persuade administrators to act in "the judicial spirit of fairness and impartiality." Weight-of-the-evidence review would produce needless cost and delay, destroy administrators' "sense of responsibility," and prevent administrative tribunals from evolving into "useful aids to society."[35] Frankfurter, after huddling with Sears in Buffalo, telegrammed Dulles that the judge was "most anxious to have you appear personally before his committee because of [the] great weight which you will carry in averting real danger of adoption of mischievous provisions." That proved impossible, however: Dulles was "leaving at the end of this week to sail on the Eastern Yacht Club Cruise."[36]

Meanwhile, at Leet's behest, Roscoe Pound treated the Judiciary Committee to a preview of his report for the ABA's Special Committee on Administrative Law. Sears countered with two New Dealers, Francis Shea, dean of the University of Buffalo Law School, and the Columbia law professor Walter Gellhorn.[37] For days the committee remained deadlocked. At last, on July 19, it narrowly adopted the NYSBA measure, which had been amended to apply only to newly created agencies, a compromise insisted upon by representatives of the Education Department and the worker's compensation commission. Sears dissented because he opposed weight-of-the evidence review of most fact-finding; Whalen, because existing agencies were excluded.[38]

Before the convention could take up the Judiciary Committee's recommendations, however, news of the report of a second ABA committee studying administrative law in 1938 reached the convention. This committee had conducted a state-by-state survey of judicial review of administrative decisions, and it came to the stunning conclusion that New York courts had been engaging in "practically no inquiry...into questions of fact." Particularly alarming was its observation that New York courts had interpreted the phrase "weight of the evidence" to require only the existence of substantial evidence in the record. The NYSBA had assured politicians that its proposal would require courts to engage in an independent review of the record. The clear implication of the second ABA report was that the proposal would work no change in the law.[39]

From the opening of the convention, the NYSBA lawyers had tried to keep the debate on administrative law from becoming openly partisan. Once judicial review became a question of "New Deal against Old Deal," Gluck realized, "emotion and politics" would be in the saddle. After the second ABA report became public, emotion and politics took the reins from the lawyers. On the evening of August 3, the Democrat Whalen, identified in the press as "one of the most outspoken anti–New Dealers in the convention on either side of the house," moved the adoption of a substitute for the Judiciary Committee's report to provide for "judicial review...upon both the law and the facts" of any quasi-judicial order of the state's administrative agencies.[40] Whalen would exempt only three groups of administrators: tax assessors, worker's compensation commissioners, and "the educational system of the State." Nothing suggested that these officials were exceptionally faithful to the norms of judicial procedure; indeed, Whalen had illustrated the dangers of the substantial evidence standard with a worker's compensation case. His real aim, a delegate charged, was partisan, to take "a whack... at the New Deal."[41]

The delegates debated Whalen's substitute, which newspaper reporters had dubbed "the anti-bureaucracy clause," well past midnight.[42] Smith marshaled the anti–New Deal Democrats in support of the proposal, which he praised as a breakwater against "this wave that is going all over the country, of just taking hold of everybody and telling them what street they get off at." Old Guard Republicans closed ranks with Smith's Democrats. George Fearon promised that Whalen's amendment would ensure that "some old lady, or some old man" wrongly denied a social security payment would get "a fair review by an impartial system." W. L. Burke rose to defend "the common man, the working man, the poor devil who would have to take it unless given some right of review of the actions of these boards."[43]

On the other side of the question, Sears and Halpern spoke for the liberal Republicans. Sears invoked Charles Evans Hughes; Dulles; Stimson; and Cuthbert Pound, chief judge of the state's highest court, as opponents of weight-of-the-evidence review.[44] For the New Deal Democrats, Robert F. Wagner predicted that New Yorkers would "overwhelmingly" reject a measure that would cripple unemployment insurance and other social welfare programs. Maldwin Fertig, a member of New York City's transportation board, warned that the clause would paralyze his agency but then blundered by invoking the authority of a recent symposium in the *Yale Law Journal.* Sutherland interrupted to ask Fertig to list its contributors; Felix Frankfurter's name drew jeers and laughter. Another delegate's question—did Fertig know "anything about the functional approach, as used in the Yale Law School in the teaching of law?"—produced more guffaws.[45]

The conservative coalition of Old Guard Republicans and Tammany Democrats easily prevailed, and Whalen's amendment was cleared for final approval by a vote of 84 to 33. Liberal Republicans accounted for "at least half" of the negative votes; New Deal Democrats made up the balance.[46]

From August 4 until the final vote two weeks later, the antibureaucracy clause was the subject of wide and overwhelmingly negative comment. "Courts have enough to do already without taking on the review of boards and commissions at the request or behest of any aggrieved individual or corporation," protested the patrician New York City lawyer Charles Culp Burlingham. "Shall the justices of New York's Supreme Court be required to count the number of bacilli in contaminated milk?" demanded the *Rochester Times-Union*. "Are they to be asked to grade examination papers for civil service jobs, and to pass on the eligibility of applicants for relief?" Even the Gannett chain of newspapers, not known for its liberal bent, came out against the clause. The New York State Federation of Labor denounced its likely effect on unemployment insurance and the state's labor board (which was more evenhanded in disputes between AFL and CIO unions than its national counterpart).[47] The liberal Republican Edward Corsi scoffed at the notion that the clause would "give the little fellow relief against the encroaching power of bureaucracy." Instead, it would help "utility companies, railroads, oil companies and other large interests, who can hand down the cost of litigation to the consumer." Governor Lehman called the clause "extremely dangerous and unwise"; Mayor La Guardia thought it a brazen bid to establish "government by the courts."[48]

When the antibureaucracy clause came before the convention for final passage on August 18, the NYSBA's lawyers tried to keep the debate on the proper plane. Leet called it "the most constructive step that we have taken here to restore our State government to a government of laws and not of men." Sutherland was still more lofty. "Now and then behind the particular and the specific there can be seen some great trend in the course of modern government," he declaimed. The "sudden and disproportionate growth in the executive branch" and the tendency to "exclude courts from sitting in judgment on all questions where their decision may come in conflict with executive desires" were not confined to New York or even the United States; they were part of "a world-wide process" that had "lately seen its greatest extension in some of the European states." Some delegates, Sutherland believed, were "impatient of the more deliberate processes of the Legislature and of the courts," but he hoped "that this body, with a solemn feeling of responsibility that rests upon every member here," would vote to preserve "something in our government which has today been thrown away in governments in other countries."[49]

Then the politicians took over. A member of the Smith bloc declared a vote for the Whalen amendment a vote against the "so-called sociological thought of the day, which builds up these bureaucracies." Another delegate, who confessed to being neither a "brain truster" nor "a brilliant jurist," likened the clause to a switch cut from a tree "out behind the barn" and hung over the front door to warn a child to stop misbehaving. "Now we are putting a switch in the Constitution," he explained. "We are going to make these administrative bureaus toe the line." Fearon successfully proposed an amendment that would permit courts to remand orders to the agencies that issued them and added the state social security board to the list of exempted agencies. (Evidently, word that federal administrators would cut off the state's funds if the clause were adopted overwhelmed Fearon's earlier solicitude for old ladies and old men.) A last bid by Sears to substitute a more agency-friendly measure failed, and the antibureaucracy clause was approved for submission to the voters in November.[50]

Wagner fretted in a memorandum to Roosevelt that "the vice of the proposal is obscured by its technical nature and attractive 'anti-bureaucracy' label." He need not have worried. In the weeks between the convention and the general election, opponents of the clause all but drowned out its supporters. La Guardia called it "outrageous, disgraceful," and "a vicious threat to orderly administrative government." "In Germany they do it with a brown shirt," he declared, "but here they do it with a black robe."[51] Every New York City newspaper save the *Sun* came out against the clause; so did the Democratic, American Labor, Socialist, and Communist parties. The Republicans endorsed the measure, but the party's gubernatorial candidate, Thomas Dewey, joined other liberal Republicans in opposing it. So did the Chambers of Commerce of Brooklyn and New York State, the Merchants Association of New York, AFL and CIO affiliates, the Citizen's Union, and the City Bar.[52] Gluck and Leet campaigned vigorously for the clause but were answered by other lawyers. Frank Shea, for example, neatly invoked the rise of totalitarianism in Europe as an argument *against* intrusive judicial review. "The lesson of the consequences of a people's losing faith in a democratic government's capacity to respond to their essential needs is too current and too appalling," he observed. Under the antibureaucracy clause, he predicted, generalist judges would frequently overturn expert administrators. Administrators, in turn, would soon stop caring about their decisions and succumb to "the irresponsibility of negligent, half-hearted action."[53]

In the end, the antibureaucracy clause was defeated by a more than two-to-one margin. The result was "a striking indication that the voting public were conscious of the movement toward a more inclusive executive branch, and favored it as the most effective means of carrying out the multitude of new and complex duties they expected government to perform," Sutherland reluctantly concluded. Evidently, the popular support for the US Supreme Court that pollsters had discovered during the battle over the Court-packing plan did not translate into an endorsement of strict review of agency fact-finding. In that context, at least, La Guardia's dismissive reference to "gown-government" may have come closer to capturing the popular mood.[54]

The defeat of the antibureaucracy clause showed that New York voters rejected Dicey's rule of law when it would deny them the benefits of administration. As it happened, a second issue on the ballot that November became something like a referendum on whether administrators should observe court-like procedures and thus be subject to the rule of law in different guise. John Lord O'Brian had played no role in the constitutional convention of 1938. For most of the summer he had been in Chattanooga, closeted with the general counsel for the Tennessee Valley Authority (TVA), as the two planned their second defense of the agency before the Supreme Court. On September 29, after a late evening at the TVA offices, O'Brian returned to his hotel to find a sheaf of messages from Thomas Dewey, calling from the New York State Republican Convention. O'Brian phoned Dewey, who had just been named the party's gubernatorial candidate, and learned that Dewey wanted him to run for the US Senate against Robert F. Wagner. O'Brian told Dewey he did not want the job and went off to bed. The next morning he saw in the newspapers that he had been chosen after all.[55]

The Legal Progressive and "The G– D—Labor Board"

O'Brian was sixty-four years old in the fall of 1938. The nomination "comes at a late time in my career," he told a reporter soon after his selection. "I had no ambition for public office."[56] Even so, O'Brian still believed, with his hero Elihu Root, that the law was a "public profession," and he was still willing to put a remunerative law practice on hold to act on that belief. His mother, a devout Episcopalian, had instilled in him a sense of Christian stewardship at an early age, and it survived an undergraduate education at Harvard, thought to be a godless place during the presidency of Charles Eliot. O'Brian did study with William James and George Santayana, but he also helped run a boys club at a Boston settlement house. The most galvanizing event of his college days was a talk given to Episcopalian students by an alumnus then serving as the police commissioner of New York. O'Brian would never forget Theodore Roosevelt's admonition that college men should not let "their own ideals and high standards" keep them from entering the political ring.[57]

After Harvard, O'Brian returned to Buffalo, studied law, and gained some prominence as a speaker at literary events, a lawyer, and a lay minister to Episcopalians in the city's hinterlands. In 1906, he was elected to the state assembly, where he consistently supported Governor Charles Evans Hughes in the battle to reform state government. The two had met when the young assemblyman spotted a legislative loophole Hughes had missed. They saw each other regularly over the remainder of the session, and the governor asked O'Brian to join his reelection campaign.[58]

Hughes proved to be O'Brian's entrée to the patrician corporation lawyers of New York City. In 1909, Theodore Roosevelt appointed him US Attorney for the Western District of New York; his duties brought him into contact with his counterpart in the Southern District, Henry Stimson. In 1913, O'Brian was a good-government candidate for mayor of Buffalo and was much celebrated by the civic elite despite his defeat. When New York's corporation lawyers, under Root's leadership, convened a committee to plan for the Constitutional Convention of 1915, they invited O'Brian, a delegate, to participate. During the convention, he, Stimson, George Wickersham (William Howard Taft's attorney general), and Charles Sears shared living quarters, which the state's politicos dubbed the "House of Lords." As chairman of the Rules Committee, O'Brian became Root's lieutenant and confidante. He cherished his memory of their frank discussions and considered Root "the greatest man I have ever known."[59]

Other political and official assignments followed. Roosevelt asked O'Brian to second Stimson's nomination for governor in 1910, when the aloof New York City lawyer was engendering little enthusiasm among upstate Republicans. O'Brian was a member of the state's delegation to the Republican National Conventions in 1916 and 1920 and a contender for the Republican gubernatorial nomination in 1920 before giving way to a party stalwart. He was mentioned as a possible gubernatorial nominee in 1928, 1934, and 1936.[60] He also made time for stints as a government lawyer. Woodrow Wilson's attorney general kept O'Brian on as a US Attorney until 1914, then appointed him special counsel in the prosecution of a German provocateur, then made him chief of the Department of Justice's War Emergency Division. In that capacity he defended the Espionage Act of 1917 and personally ordered the prosecution of Eugene Debs, but he also instructed US attorneys not to "suppress honest, legitimate criticism of the administration or discussion of government policies," demanded solid evidence before interning enemy aliens, and disbanded his unit before a new attorney general, Mitchell Palmer, could get hold of it. Later stints of government lawyering included a turn as Assistant Attorney General for the Antitrust Division, the defense of TVA in the *Ashwander* and *Nineteen Companies* cases, and the general counselship of the War Production Board.[61]

In 1938, O'Brian did not expect to defeat the New Deal's great tribune in Congress, who enjoyed broad support among New York's workers and immigrants. At least two major legislative landmarks —the National Labor Relations Act of 1935 and the Housing Act of 1937—were informally known as "Wagner Acts," and the senator had helped pass many others. Although Wagner was in poor health, he still had the energy to campaign, over the protests of his advisors, "at every dinky club-house, rally, and gathering" in New York City.[62] O'Brian's defense of TVA gave him a measure of bipartisan appeal, as Attorney General Robert Jackson backhandedly acknowledged in announcing the postponement of the argument of the *Nineteen Companies* case until after the election. "We are not unappreciative of the compliment implied," Jackson deadpanned, "when the Republican convention finds its best man for this high office on the legal staff of this Administration."[63] But most New Yorkers knew so little about the Buffalo lawyer that he was obliged to issue a press release titled, "Who Is John Lord O'Brian?"[64] One friend spoke of "the tremendous odds" O'Brian faced; another, who thought the task hopeless, told him, "I could hardly escape wondering why you could bring yourself to undertake it."[65]

As low as expectations for his candidacy were, O'Brian went out of his way to lower them further. "The people need not expect pyrotechnics," he told reporters. "It is vitally important that the truth be told concerning certain vital policies of the administration with which my opponent has identified himself; and on this basis I intend to wage my modest campaign." Yet, from his first speech on October 15, 1938, O'Brian discovered that the issue he cared most about as a lawyer—ensuring due process within a growing administrative state—directly addressed a major political controversy of the day, the NLRB's seeming favoritism for the industrial unions of the CIO over employers and the craft unions of the AFL. By attacking the procedures of the NLRB, he could defend a cause he believed in and gain ground on his opponent, who was too closely identified with the board to shrug off its shortcomings. In early November even Wagner's lieutenants thought O'Brian might win.[66]

O'Brian had long held something like Charles Evans Hughes's view of the administrative state. The charge that administration interfered with individual freedom left him unmoved: "social forces" had already "inevitably narrow[ed] the scope of the individual's activity"; administration promised to widen it again. But the expansion of the federal government during World War I and its aftermath made him fear that "the old American idea of government by laws" might succumb to "a continental conception of administrative law foreign to the spirit of the American Constitution." Not only the Bureau of Internal Revenue and the FTC but also the postmaster general's suppression of radical literature and the deportation of leftists illustrated how "the edicts of subordinate officials ... whose powers lie outside the control and review of the courts" menaced liberty, he warned in 1920.[67]

For O'Brian, as well as for Hughes and the City Bar leaders, the solution was not heightened judicial review but procedural reform. "It is impossible for the Appellate Courts on a cold record to deal with questions on the weight of the evidence," he told the American Law Institute in May 1939. The "crucial question," O'Brian maintained, was how "findings of fact are to be arrived at" within an agency and whether its procedures were consistent with our "tradition of fair play."[68]

Before his senatorial campaign, O'Brian had on two notable occasions insisted that federal agencies observe court-like procedures. The first, in 1936, occurred after the SEC charged the brokerage firm White, Weld & Company with manipulating the price of a company's stock. The SEC commissioners recruited Yale law professor Thurman Arnold to preside over the administrative hearing. O'Brian moved for a bill of particulars to limit the SEC's case, and he objected so frequently and presented his own case so methodically that a despairing Arnold declared the hearing "perfectly interminable." Finally, Arnold took over the examination of O'Brian's witnesses himself. "I irritated John Lord Bryan [*sic*], who is a very nice person," Arnold reported to his wife. "After protesting vigorously, he asked for an adjournment and said he would shorten his case. I hated to do it, but if I let them run they will be going all winter."[69]

O'Brian entered a second suit, brought by the US Department of Agriculture's Bureau of Animal Industry against the meatpacker Swift & Company under the Packers and Stockyards Act, in November 1936. Many New York City wholesalers had reported to the bureau that Swift gave small retailers discounts and easier credit than they received and that the company shipped its goods only on railroads and steamships that bought its products for their dining cars and commissaries. But when the bureau's lawyer arrived in New York to prepare for the hearing, he found that the wholesalers and purchasing agents were too afraid of Swift to tell him even the names of their own salesmen. The leading wholesaler proved to be wholly untrustworthy; other jobbers had made statements that "were not in accord with the facts, or facts to which they could testify." Under the circumstances, the lawyer had to elicit testimony that he knew would not "stand up in any court action" in the hope that, when "confronted by these statements under oath," witnesses might be induced to "come much nearer to telling the truth." "It is a case of digging for evidence," the lawyer confessed to his superior. "Hearsay testimony is being put in merely to develop leads whereby real evidence may be obtained later on. These people will not come in and tell their story without being subpoenaed and put on in the open hearing. All the meat industry up here seems to be afraid of the big packers."[70]

O'Brian saw what the government was up to and protested that Swift was being "persecuted under the guise of a government hearing."[71] As he had before Arnold, the Buffalo lawyer moved for a bill of particulars to limit testimony. He also insisted that every invoice be shown to date from a relevant time period and repeatedly objected to testimony as "incompetent, irrelevant, and immaterial." "No criminal case was ever conducted with more technicality than Mr. O'Brian is attempting to inject in the record," the bureau's lawyer complained. He understood that the bureau might lack the funds to conduct "a long drawn-out hearing"; still, he was "prepared to go the limit." The hearing proceeded, and the trial examiner upheld some (but not all) of the complaint's counts. O'Brian persisted as well. He restated his evidentiary objections before Secretary Henry A. Wallace and objected to having to proceed without a brief from the government. When Wallace ruled against him, O'Brian appealed to the federal judiciary, which fully exonerated his client.[72]

O'Brian had no similar experiences with the NLRB, but only, it seems, because he never appeared before it.[73] Still, as chair of the ABA's Standing Committee on Labor, Employment and Social Security, in 1936 he produced a report that criticized the NLRA on structural and procedural grounds. The board's lawyers acted "virtually as prosecutors" and argued before the NLRB's own trial examiners, who were predisposed to rule against employers, the report charged. Facts found by the NLRB were practically binding upon a reviewing court, thanks to the substantial evidence standard. In sum, the board was violating "the traditional requirements of fair play" and had therefore lost "the confidence of the public at large."[74]

Businessmen had their own, more heated verdict on the NLRB, captured in the title of a widely noted article in *Fortune* magazine: "The G– D---- Labor Board." A well-funded litigation campaign had kept the board in limbo for almost two years after its creation in 1935.[75] After the Supreme Court upheld the constitutionality of the NLRB in the *Jones & Laughlin* decision, however, the agency received thousands of requests to hold elections for collective bargaining agents and thousands of complaints against employers. As the board's activity picked up, the economy slowed down. The "Roosevelt recession" gave employers and their congressional allies a new line of attack. Senator Edward Burke, for example, told an appreciative US Chamber of Commerce that the board's orders would "snuff out the fires of industry and send millions of workers into the line of the unemployed."[76]

Congressional conservatives like Burke, a Nebraska Democrat outraged by Roosevelt's channeling of the state's patronage through the Progressive Republican George Norris, viewed the NLRB as part of a New Deal plot to remake the Democratic Party. Their fears grew during the 1938 primary season, when the president campaigned against Democrats who had opposed the Court-packing plan. The purge failed almost everywhere, but it convinced party stalwarts that their combat with the New Dealers was mortal. After the November elections, congressional leaders made their opposition public. Their votes for the ABA's bill to reform administrative procedure, a ban on political activity by federal employees, and a law to remake the labor board were intended to block the New Dealers' schemes.[77]

The NLRB had another dangerous enemy in the AFL, which objected to the board's recognition of CIO affiliates as workers' representatives. When the board certified the CIO's longshoremen's union instead of the AFL affiliate in June 1938, the older federation mounted, in the historian Christopher Tomlins's words, an "all-out war against the NLRB." In August, AFL president William Green asked Roosevelt and Wagner to amend the act and denounced the labor board as "a travesty on justice." Meanwhile Green's general counsel met secretly with employers' lawyers in search of common ground. The AFL's lawyer favored a new administrative tribunal to hear appeals from the NLRB; employers' lawyers countered with weight-of-the-evidence review in the federal courts. At its annual convention in October, the AFL directed its Executive Council to study both proposals. In the interim, it endorsed a more modest set of reforms.[78]

More generally, public opinion was running against the NLRB in fall 1938. Although the Supreme Court consistently upheld the board, newspaper and magazine editors and columnists consistently condemned it. *Collier's*, for instance, declared the NLRB "the most glaring example" of the "rank partisanship of some of our federal boards." A Gallup poll conducted that summer found that more than two-thirds of those with an opinion of the board thought it biased in favor of unions.[79] Another poll, published just after the congressional elections, found that 70 percent of respondents believed the NLRA should be revised or repealed, up from 62 percent in May. So widespread was dissatisfaction with the NLRB that a sarcastic reference to the Wagner Act was sure to get a laugh at the New York constitutional convention. Once, when Wagner declared some proposal unfair, George Fearon leapt to his feet. "This is just too much, Mr. Chairman, when the author of the

National Labor Act gets up and talks about fairness," the Republican stalwart cried. "God forbid that he should be any judge of the meaning of the word."[80]

In short, once O'Brian got over the shock of being nominated, he must have warmed to the idea of campaigning against Wagner and the NLRB, because it gave him the opportunity to argue for the reform of the administrative state in an unusually receptive political environment. Just the presence of the antibureaucracy clause on the ballot was advantageous, because it would make O'Brian's procedural reforms seem more moderate and reasonable. A clue to his thinking can be found in one of his conversations with Root during the constitutional convention of 1915. "I expressed the view that it was foolish for us to try to dogmatize too much about the future operation of any of these measures that we were talking about; that after all the thing to do was to get a fundamental principle firmly established and then trust to public opinion and let it grow, let it evolve." O'Brian remembered his unsuccessful campaign for mayor of Buffalo in just these terms. Although he had never had much chance of winning, he considered the campaign a success because it demonstrated the power of the city's "good government" crowd and ultimately brought in much needed reforms and an entirely new group of local officials. "My campaign," he believed, "had in reality accomplished its objectives in spite of my defeat."[81] If O'Brian could do for due process in 1938 what he had done for good government in 1913, he would not have to defeat Wagner to win.

"Fair Play" Politics

Within a week of O'Brian's nomination, the *New York Times*' Arthur Krock declared the race "one of the most interesting contests in the current campaign." If O'Brian mounted "a frontal attack on Senator Wagner," Krock wrote, his campaign would become a referendum on "the extremes of the New Deal." In particular, "Mr. O'Brian has everything to gain and nothing to lose by making an issue of the Wagner act." The CIO had already endorsed the incumbent, but the AFL could still be divided, "unless Mr. Wagner goes so far in proposing amendments as to vex his CIO followers." In addition, a vigorous attack on the NLRB would give the businessmen who might otherwise stay home a reason to turn out. "Mr. Wagner will be a hard man to beat this year," Krock acknowledged, but if O'Brian was bold "it might be done."[82]

O'Brian opened his campaign in Buffalo on October 15, less than a month before the election on November 8. In an address to a group of young Republicans, he criticized Wagner for "bungling" the administration of public relief, for backing NIRA, and for his silence on Roosevelt's Court-packing plan. O'Brian's main target, however, was the NLRB. The Roosevelt recession, O'Brian observed, had returned business and labor to "just about where we were in 1933." It was the product of "the general sense of insecurity and uncertainty... resulting from the operations of the National Labor Act," which had "split the ranks of labor and... brought confusion and demoralization into business and industry" throughout the nation.[83]

O'Brian, who had once defended Buffalo's clothing workers during a strike, declared himself in full accord with the Wagner Act's basic principles.[84] He wanted to see collective bargaining firmly established, workers free to present their complaints "informally and inexpensively," and labor disputes "quickly disposed of by a fair hearing." But the NLRB's hearings could not be fair, he argued, as long as the board combined within itself the functions of prosecutor and judge. The NLRB "files a complaint with itself," O'Brian explained. "To hear and try out the complaint the Board appoints a Trial Examiner whose salary is paid by it." Next, "the Trial Examiner holds a hearing or trial and later reports his recommendations to the Board. The Board itself then reviews the record and makes the final decision upon the complaint originally filed by it, prosecuted by it, and heard by its Trial Examiner." If the record thus produced contained "any substantial evidence which will support its decision on the facts, the findings of the Board as to these facts are binding upon the courts."[85]

O'Brian knew that the ancient maxim "no one should be a judge in his own cause" had often been leveled against administrative agencies without success.[86] As James Landis, dean of the Harvard Law School, argued, "a succession of practical legislative judgments" suggested that the dangers the combining of prosecutorial and judicial functions posed for the administrative process were worth braving because courts were unable to handle certain classes of disputes. These dangers could be kept at bay if administrators developed "a spirit of professionalism," consistently followed their own precedents and procedures, and justified their orders with "detailed and informative" findings of fact.[87] Had O'Brian known of the actual practice of fact-finding at the NLRB, where, as Louis Jaffe later acknowledged, lawyers sometimes found "facts as we wanted to have them be," he might have shown that the board was not living up to liberal lawyers' own standards.[88] Under the circumstances, the best O'Brian could do was to distinguish the NLRB from, say, the ICC, on the rather unconvincing ground that the labor board dealt with "fundamental questions of human right and even of human liberty," whereas other agencies handled "minor administrative questions"—hardly an apt description of the regulation of the nation's railroads and trucking industry![89]

O'Brian promised to reform national labor policy in four ways. First, he endorsed most of the changes called for by the AFL at its convention, including notice of hearings to all interested parties, a ban on "secret reports and files," and the hiring of better trial examiners. Second, in a dispute between rival unions, O'Brian would let employers ask the board to hold an election to determine which one should represent their workers. The NLRB only allowed employees to request an election. Third, he would separate the functions of prosecutor and judge. The existing NLRB would continue to investigate disputes and prosecute complaints, but "a different and impartial board" would be created to rule on them. Finally, O'Brian promised to end "the partiality and open partisanship" of the current members of the board, presumably by blocking their reappointment. He closed with an appeal to New York's workers: "Whatever may be said by partisans or professional leaders I feel confident that the suggestions which I have made will, on reflection, commend themselves to the great mass of the rank and file of wage earners themselves, and I rest my plea for reasonableness on that confidence."[90]

In appealing to labor, O'Brian probably remembered the friendly reception Buffalo's workers had given him during his mayoral campaign.[91] Yet, his repeated endorsements of the principle of collective bargaining and the AFL reforms brought him no show of support from workers or unions. Instead, middle-class and elite voters came out for him with unexpected enthusiasm. A cadre of young adults, known as the First Voters League, organized a "John Lord O'Brian Minute Men Division" to canvass New York City. League members showed up at rallies holding banners proclaiming "Youth Wants O'Brian" and "John Lord O'Brian for Senate," with the capital letters *J, O, B*, and *S* in boldface.[92] More weighty was the financial support of New York City's legal elite. A citizen's committee, including such legal titans as Arthur Ballantine, Charles Evans Hughes, Jr., Stimson, and Paul Windels, was formed under the chairmanship of a member of the City Bar and funded six statewide radio addresses. On October 21, Stimson weighed in, with a lengthy letter to the *New York Times* that attacked Wagner for failing to oppose the Court-packing plan and for the NLRB's one-sidedness. O'Brian, in contrast, had displayed "the courage, the fair-mindedness, and the ability of a great citizen and public officer" and "the kindliness and uprightness of a loyal friend."[93]

As late as October 23, the *New York Daily News* thought the Wagner-O'Brian race "so one-sided" that the average voter refused to "get steamed up over it." On that date, however, O'Brian challenged Wagner to debate "in what respect, if any, should the national labor relations act be amended?"[94] The gambit presented Wagner with a dilemma. In all likelihood he knew of procedural irregularities at the NLRB from his meeting with AFL leaders and talks with the board's regional director in New York. As Krock had reasoned, with the AFL in open revolt, Wagner could scarcely pretend that the administration of what he liked to call "my labor relations act" was beyond reproach. But were he to explain how his statute and the board should be reformed, he risked alienating the CIO and opening the door to drastic changes by congressional conservatives.[95]

Until O'Brian's challenge, Wagner's preferred course was to concede that the act was not perfect, to promise to consider "any proposal to strengthen and improve the basic purposes of the law," and to deride his critics. He urged audiences not to be fooled by the "synthetic coating of liberalism" recently applied to the "reactionary Republican elephant." Republicans were still plotting "to press the thorns of industrial slavery and yellow dog contracts upon the sweated brow of labor." So-called liberals in the GOP's ranks were "indulging in camouflage"; they were "last minute hitchhikers seeking a free ride on the progressive bandwagon." Republicans revealed their true colors when their party endorsed the constitutional convention's antibureaucracy clause, which would "hamstring the Public Service Commission and clog the courts."[96]

Because so many newspapers had excoriated the NLRB—even the *Daily News*, solidly in the senator's camp, attacked it—Wagner knew that the press would applaud O'Brian's challenge, and he took several days to formulate a response.[97] At last, on October 25, he replied that although he would have happily debated his opponent a week earlier, the intervening publication of O'Brian's answers to questions submitted to the candidates by the *New York Times* showed that his opponent was committed to the same views as "Mr. Hoover, Mr. Landon and their spokesmen in the United States Senate." His own views, Wagner continued, were "in square opposition" and had already been reported "times without number." He then released his responses to the *New York Times*' questions. In combining investigatory and quasi-judicial functions, he argued, his statute had followed the example of the ICC, the FTC, and "innumerable other Federal and State regulatory agencies." The Supreme Court had upheld the NLRB's procedures in *Jones & Laughlin*, a decision, he suggested, that "Mr. Henry L. Stimson" might want to read. The statute was not one-sided; it simply addressed a specific evil, violent resistance to workers' rights to organize and to bargain collectively. Wagner closed by observing that he had never maintained that the NLRA was perfect; but he neglected to say how it might be improved.[98]

"How lame and cheap his excuse!" exclaimed the *Herald Tribune*. "How disappointing!" Wagner had passed up the chance to debate "a subject of vital moment to the country with an opponent at once thoroughly respectful and worthy of his steel." "Every voter on Election Day should cast for him not a ballot but a white feather." Other newspapers piled on. The *New York World Telegram* called Wagner's refusal "a big campaign surprise—and disappointment"; the *Syracuse Post-Standard* thought the senator was running scared; the *New York Daily Mirror* demanded, "Is Senator Wagner a statesman or a stooge?" and depicted him hiding under his bed from the lightning bolt of O'Brian's "debate challenge." O'Brian called Wagner "a standpatter and not a liberal." "The public can judge which of us is the more sincere," he told a gathering of Republican women. "Senator Wagner has not only refused to meet me in debate"; he had entirely ignored the main issue of the campaign, "how jobs can be restored to the people who want work."[99]

Over the next days Wagner defended his refusal to rebut O'Brian's "calculated sophistry" face-to-face. Proposals to reform the act were best hammered out around a conference table, he told a newspaper editor. They were not "firebrands to be tossed aloft in a political scramble in the hope of luring a few stray votes." Republicans pressed their advantage. Although Wagner already had the endorsements of the CIO-led American Labor Party and the AFL's state federation, O'Brian renewed his bid to win the support of rank-and-file workers with promises to support the AFL's reforms and to oppose the reappointment of board member Donald Wakefield Smith, thought to be biased in favor of the CIO.[100]

Stimson replied to Wagner with another lengthy letter in the *New York Times*, in which he observed that *Jones & Laughlin* had merely settled the constitutionality of the Wagner Act's procedures, not whether they were a sensible way to handle a matter "full of class feeling, bias, and counter-bias." The ICC and FTC were inapt comparisons: they protected "all classes of persons" involved in transport or trade. The NLRB was the champion of a single class. Stimson claimed that resentment over "the unfair treatment of litigants under the system now in effect in the Labor Law" had been "one of the main impelling motives" behind the constitutional convention's adoption of the antibureaucracy clause. He promised to continue to oppose that ill-conceived measure, but Wagner's intransigence hindered "those of us who are pleading for a fair chance for the development of a proper system among our regulatory commissions."[101]

Wagner, of course, did not need Stimson's vote. He could weather some defections by independents; even the *New York Times*' endorsement of O'Brian on November 1 was surmountable. What alarmed the Wagner camp in the last week of the campaign were reports that "some factions of Labor are not supporting the Senator."[102] A fortnight earlier staffers had joked that O'Brian was "The Man Nobody Knows"; now they endured sleepless nights over the "almost inconceivable" prospect that Wagner might lose.[103]

The defeat in November 1938 of any of several prominent Democrats, including Michigan governor Frank Murphy, who had refused to intervene in the sitdown strikes in the auto industry, would be a blow to the New Deal's prestige, but the loss of as stalwart a congressional champion as Wagner would be a calamity.[104] Moreover, a victory by O'Brian or by District Attorney Thomas Dewey in his challenge to Governor Lehman would reveal the weakness of the New Deal in Roosevelt's home state, which Democrats would have to carry to retain the presidency in 1940. "For the first time since Franklin D. Roosevelt crushed Herbert Hoover and shattered the Republican organization with the power of his New Deal appeal," the *New York Daily News* reported, "the political dominance of the President is in peril."[105]

On the day Wagner refused to debate O'Brian, Roosevelt announced that he would deliver a radio address on behalf of state Democrats on the Friday before the election. Asked at a press conference about his party's chances, Roosevelt affected nonchalance. In fact, he was very concerned. Although he usually kept his distance from the NLRB, Roosevelt had already summoned its members to the White House.[106]

Two recollections of the meeting, both by Chairman Warren Madden and recorded years later, survive. According to Madden, Roosevelt said that Wagner was "somewhat frightened" about his chances and that the senator considered the labor board "his principal handicap for reelection." Roosevelt then asked the board to amend its rules to permit employers as well as employees to petition for an election. "He did not expand at all on this notion," Madden explained. "Apparently, it was purely political." (It was, in fact, one of the reforms O'Brian had proposed in his first campaign speech as well as the practice of New York's labor relations board.) Roosevelt seemed to think letting employers call elections "wouldn't hurt," the NLRB chairman recalled, and that "Wagner could use [the change] to give the impression that the board was, after all, reasonable."[107]

Madden balked. Employers "really didn't have any rightful interest" in the board's elections, he protested, because they selected representatives for workers, not their bosses. Besides, employers were sure to petition for an election before unions were ready. "It would be like holding a political election before the campaign," the chairman protested. The "election would be held, the union would be defeated, and that would be the end of the union."[108]

Roosevelt "purported to see the rightness of that" and asked Madden to draft a paragraph for his radio address. Madden did, but when the president spoke from Hyde Park, he barely mentioned the labor board. Instead, after confiding that he was glad he had passed up a run for governor in 1918, when he was Dewey's age, Roosevelt turned to the Wagner-O'Brian race. "Just as a Governor is required to be much more than a good prosecutor, so a United States Senator must be much more than a good lawyer." New York's senators had to be leaders in Congress, and no one had worked more effectively "for the benefit of those who need the help and support of government against oppression and intolerable conditions of living" than Robert F. Wagner.[109]

Roosevelt continued his efforts in the remaining days of the campaign. "The President is fighting harder for Wagner than for any other individual facing the electorate," reported the *Daily News* on the Sunday before Election Day. "He is making personal phone calls and putting all the great weight of the White House... into the fight." Both candidates fought to the finish as well.

FIGURE 4.1 John Lord O'Brian leaving New York City for Buffalo to vote in the general election of November 8, 1938.

Source: Courtesy of the Library of Congress, LC-USZ62-111157.

O'Brian explained that his campaign was "based not on political doctrines" but "solely on the power of ideas." He called his public philosophy "reasoned liberalism" and claimed it could reconcile the "increased degree of governmental activity" in Washington with "the maintenance of the individual's freedom and sense of responsibility." Wagner complained that a group "of clever lawyers, including my opponent and also a former member of the Hoover Cabinet"—that is, Stimson—were tempting voters with the plea, "Of course the Labor Act is constitutional, but it is un-American, and we want a chance to fix it." He warned his supporters not to "trust your fortunes or your future to the wolves in sheep's clothing who are seeking to trick you into their camp."[110]

On Election Day, O'Brian carried every county above the Bronx save Albany, but a large majority in New York City gave Wagner the victory, by some 440,000 votes out of over 4.5 million cast. Dewey, who lost by only 64,000 votes, later told O'Brian that he had been sure the Buffalo lawyer would win, because of the eminence of his backers. Although O'Brian cut Wagner's margin of victory by over 40 percent from 1932, he could not persuade enough workers to vote for him. "I couldn't come back into New York politics and in four weeks recover what reputation I'd had years before and at the same time sell myself to a brand new generation," he explained. "It just wasn't in the cards."[111]

But did O'Brian succeed in his larger aim, to show the need for reform of federal administrative procedure? O'Brian thought he had. "I feel confident that those views and recommendations we have made will ultimately prevail at Washington," he said after the election. The *New York Times* praised O'Brian for arguing that "the social program of the Roosevelt Administration can best be achieved if it is undertaken... with a greater sense of fair play than has marked some recent legislation." Even in defeat, the newspaper opined, his arguments "ought to affect the conduct of affairs at Washington." An old friend assured O'Brian that his message had "not been lost on the nation," thanks to the "Greek perfection" of "your dignity, your moderation, your clearness."[112]

Probably more important than O'Brian's display of classical virtue in forcing a reassessment of national labor policy was Roosevelt's expenditure of so much capital on what ought to have been the easiest of senatorial campaigns, together with the defeats of other New Dealers. A week after the election, with Frank Murphy turned out of his Michigan governorship and job-hunting in Washington, journalists reported that "a careful stock-taking has gone on in these last few days" among "the New Dealers whose great object is the transformation of the Democratic party into a New Deal or 'progressive' party." The New Dealers recognized "the validity of certain attacks on the

W.P.A. and the Labor Relations Board" and agreed that the NLRB's decisions "must cease to have a partisan flavor." Plans had "been laid to increase the assets and write off the liabilities," a journalist confided. Indeed, some moves were "already under way."[113]

Donald Wakefield Smith's renomination to the NLRB, pending in the Senate on Election Day, was put on hold. In April 1939 Roosevelt withdrew it and named William Leiserson, a labor economist, to straighten out the "mess" at the board.[114] "I get too many stories," Leiserson recalled Roosevelt telling him. "If you find what I'm told you're going to find, then I want you to clear those guys out of there."[115] Notwithstanding growing pressure from a congressional investigation, Madden resisted Leiserson's efforts to fire the "left wingers." By the summer of 1940, "many earnest New Dealers" considered the chairman a political liability and called for his sacking. Roosevelt did nothing until after his election to a third term; then he nominated the labor economist Harry Millis to the chairmanship and gave Madden a face-saving appointment to the US Court of Claims. The lawyers who led the NLRB's left wing promptly departed.[116]

Millis and his successor instituted a series of reforms that separated prosecutorial and judicial functions within the NLRB. Meanwhile, the Roosevelt administration blocked legislation to split the labor board into two independent bodies, an "Administrator" to investigate and prosecute complaints and a three-member board to hear and pass judgment on them. After the war, however, Congress intervened. First, the Administrative Procedure Act of 1946 (APA) strengthened the independence of trial examiners and instituted other procedural reforms for most federal agencies, including the NLRB. Then, in 1947, the Taft-Hartley Act separated the general counsel from the rest of the board. Nominated by the president and confirmed by the Senate, the general counsel was charged with investigating and prosecuting unfair labor practices. The board retained its power to oversee representation elections, but it could act only on cases the general counsel brought before it.[117] The formal separation of the "functions of prosecutor and judge and jury" for which O'Brian had campaigned finally became law.[118]

The Politics of Administrative Law

The events in New York in 1938 revealed the durability of America's peculiarly legalistic administrative state despite a strong political challenge. Many of the state's trial lawyers still believed that close judicial review—Dicey's rule of law—was the best way to prevent administrators from abusing their discretion. After the litigators called for weight-of-the-evidence review, professional politicians took it up to keep administration from becoming an independent source of political power. Yet New York's corporate bar, including some of the nation's most eminent lawyers, preferred administrative agencies to generalist courts and party-dominated legislatures. They joined liberal politicians in a campaign to persuade New Yorkers that they had far more to gain than to lose from administration. The election returns showed that, by an overwhelming margin, New Yorkers agreed.

But a vote against weight-of-the-evidence review was by no means a vote to free administrators from all legal constraint. As the delegates to the constitutional convention deliberated over judicial review, Chief Justice Charles Evans Hughes instructed the nation's administrators to "accredit themselves by acting in accordance with the cherished judicial tradition embodying the basic concepts of fair play."[119] In *Morgan*, Hughes suggested that agencies could retain their quasi-judicial duties if they isolated their adjudicators as the ICC did its trial examiners. Yet as early as 1920, Hughes noted that adjudicators could also be organized into their own administrative "court," such as the board that heard appeals from customs officials. In 1938, the NLRB's real or suspected sins against due process led employers and AFL unionists to argue that the board should be divided into quasi-prosecutorial and quasi-judicial bodies.

Had O'Brian been associated with employers or craft unionists, Wagner could have argued that the lawyer was simply pursuing his clients' interests by electoral means. That O'Brian arrived at this conclusion independently, after his own encounters with federal agencies, notwithstanding his defense of TVA in the courts, lent credibility to his arguments. Political observers interpreted his surprisingly strong showing as a sign that attacks on the procedures of the New Deal's agencies might succeed when calls for their abolition or subjection to judicial tutelage would fail. Thus, the legalism of the American administrative state was not simply a neat reconciliation of official discretion and the rule of law; it had considerable political appeal and lent political legitimacy to the nation's bureaucrats.

As the controversy over the administrative determination of individual rights quieted in New York, a committee of the ABA readied a bill that would soon roil Congress quite as much as the antibureaucracy clause had vexed the constitutional convention in Albany. Although the campaign to reform administrative law in the Empire State was soon forgotten, the battle in Washington has figured in many histories of the twentieth-century American state. Its most interesting feature is the often noticed and as often misunderstood role of a great legal intellectual.

5

Pound and Frank

IN SEPTEMBER 1938, Charles E. Wyzanski, Jr., late of the Solicitor General's Office, warned Attorney General Homer Cummings that New York's antibureaucracy clause "was plainly the advance signal of an approaching partisan attack on a national scale." Wyzanski was right: in early 1939 Representative Francis Walter and Senator Marvel Mills Logan introduced in Congress a bill proposed by the ABA to reform the procedures of federal agencies. Although Department of Justice officials thought the measure "strange," "fantastic," and "extremely unfortunate," they also expected it to attract considerable support.[1] And, in fact, a version of the "Walter-Logan bill" passed Congress in December 1940.

In Washington in 1939, as in New York in 1938, lawyers proposed a measure to defend their own professional ideals and interests that professional politicians took up to keep administrative agencies from becoming a source of political power for the executive. But the Walter-Logan bill had a longer gestation than did the antibureaucracy clause, and lawyers specializing in the work of administrative agencies played a greater part in shaping its terms. Unlike trial lawyers, who continued to regard the ordinary courts of the land as an indispensable check on administrators, agency-centered lawyers believed that conscientious commissions found facts better than did conscientious courts. Their main goals were to reform the structure and procedures of agencies and to create specialized, "administrative courts"; the bill's ambiguous provision on judicial review apparently was a concession to the ABA's true believers in Dicey's rule of law. In addition, the congressional leaders who made the Walter-Logan bill their own had more definite targets that did New York's politicos: (1) a corps of "janizaries" who had loyally served Franklin D. Roosevelt during the Court fight in 1937 and attempted purge of anti-administration Democrats in 1938; and (2) agencies, such as the SEC, that were engaged in fierce struggles with powerful economic interests.[2] Whether the bill would actually bring the rule of law to the new administrative state mattered less to the party chieftains than the prospect of plaguing the president's partisans with enervating litigation.

The battle over administrative reform in Washington acquired an intellectual component not evident in New York when Roscoe Pound took up arms against the advocates of administrative discretion. As dean of the Harvard Law School from 1916 to 1936, Pound had celebrated the legal profession and the judiciary as repositories of a vital form of social intelligence, the capacity to mediate between reason and experience. Administrators acted on expediency, not reason, he believed; they were the propagators of "justice without law." As long as he thought that American lawyers shared his understanding of their and the courts' place in the legal order, Pound could regard the growth of administration calmly, confident that the next turn of the historical wheel would restore "justice according to law." Yet as Pound stood his ground, "legal realists" to his jurisprudential left spoke of law in terms of social function in ways that elided Pound's fundamental distinction between courts and commissions. When legal realists took top posts in the New Deal and one, James Landis, succeeded him as dean, Pound believed his ideal of law as reason was under attack. After President Franklin D. Roosevelt proposed his Court-packing plan, he decided to act lest administrators acquire absolute power and lawyers succumb to the legal realist heresy.[3]

For all that, Pound was no disciple of Dicey. He rejected weight-of-the-evidence review in favor of structural and procedural reforms that enabled lawyers to call administrators to account. For his rivals, led by the corporation lawyer, New Deal administrator, and federal judge Jerome Frank, this shared premise was less significant than Pound's obvious intent to savage the legal realists and the agencies they led. In the end, the legal realists prevailed, and administrative law became just another specialty for the American lawyer. Although Pound survived until 1965, increasingly he did so as a ghostly presence haunting the basement of Langdell Hall, appearing in public only occasionally to confer upon the China Lobby, personal injury lawyers, and other embattled groups the waning prestige of his once-great name.[4]

Justice According to Law

Law was not Roscoe Pound's first love, but it was his longest and deepest attachment. Pound was born in 1870 in Lincoln, Nebraska, the son of a judge and a former schoolteacher who were as intensely interested in their children's education as Charles Evans Hughes's parents were in his. The result was another prodigy. Roscoe read at age three; at fourteen he entered the University of Nebraska, where the study of botany fascinated him. Upon graduation, he and his father tussled over his career. Judge Pound wanted his son to read law in his office; but he also permitted him to take graduate classes in botany. When his father offered to send Roscoe to the Harvard Law School, the son accepted, apparently because of the opportunity it provided to study with Harvard botanists on the side. The case method captivated him, however, and although he completed a doctoral dissertation in botany after returning to Nebraska, the law ultimately prevailed. As a young lawyer, he threw himself into organizing and defending the state's legal institutions. He was among the founders of the Nebraska State Bar Association, helped draft its constitution, and served for six years as its secretary. He was an officer of the state's bar examining commission. He called for Nebraska's judges to don the robe and deplored the persistence of lay judges. In 1901 he had the chance to experience the dignity and authority of the judiciary firsthand when he was appointed to a commission charged with reducing a backlog in the state supreme court. He was all of thirty years old.[5]

Above all, Pound devoted himself to raising the scholarly standards of the state's law school, the University of Nebraska College of Law, He started teaching jurisprudence and Roman law as an instructor there in 1895, joined the faculty in 1899, and became dean in 1903. He restructured the curriculum and introduced the case method. All the while he was working out a legal philosophy that he called "sociological jurisprudence," which combined recent German legal scholarship and the notion of "social control" developed by his university colleague, the sociologist E. A. Ross.[6]

Pound's big break came in 1906 when he addressed the annual meeting of the ABA in St. Paul, Minnesota. His speech, "The Causes of Popular Dissatisfaction with the Administration of Justice," was a sensational attack on the lawyer-run trial, in which masters of common-law pleading shaped lawsuits to their liking and reduced the judge to "a mere umpire" who was "to decide the contest, as counsel present it, according to the rules of the game, not to search independently for truth and justice."[7] So offended were ABA's trial lawyers that they voted down a motion to print the speech as a pamphlet and missed Pound's purpose, which was to reform the courts so that they could continue to dominate the American polity.[8] The law professors in attendance, however, realized that modern times required "socialized" courts and knew they had found a champion. Northwestern's law school dean

John Henry Wigmore declared Pound's St. Paul address "the spark that kindled the white flame of progress" and an assault on the "stout defenders of Things-As-They-Are."[9]

In 1907, Wigmore offered Pound a job and a reduced teaching load, and the Nebraskan never looked back. Soon he published brilliant attacks on what he termed the "mechanical jurisprudence" of *Lochner*-era judges.[10] When the University of Chicago made him a better offer, Northwestern countered with a raise that would have made Pound the highest-paid law professor in the country. Wigmore lost out, but Pound did not stay in Chicago for long. In 1910, he accepted a chair at the Harvard Law School, and in 1916, he became its dean. "His rise," writes the legal historian G. Edward White, "was one of the most meteoric in the history of academic law."[11]

Scholars have assumed that because Pound criticized courts, he enthusiastically supported their rival, the independent regulatory commission. In fact, he considered the commission's rise part of a worrisome recrudescence of "justice without law" and "personal government." This "executive justice" was "an evil," that would persist until the courts brought their "adjustment of human relations... into thorough accord with the moral sense of the public at large." Only when lawyers improved "the output of judicial justice," Pound maintained, would "the onward march of executive justice" be checked.[12]

In a series of writings, Pound fit the rise of administration into a cyclical interpretation of legal history, which posited "a constant movement back and forth between wide judicial discretion on the one hand, and strict confinement of the magistrate by detailed rules upon the other hand." When "justice according to law" became too rigid, a reversion to "justice without law" was required to "bring the administration of justice into touch with new moral ideas or changed social or political condition."[13] The result of entrusting new discretionary powers to the executive branch "has always been and will always be as crude and as variable as the personalities of the officials" involved.[14] Fortunately, over time the new ideas became embodied in "a new body of fixed rules" that courts could adopt. Thus infused with "enough of current morality to preserve its life," justice according to law could then resume its proper, dominant place.[15]

The common lawyers' opposition to the *droit administratif* in Tudor and Stuart England figured in Pound's historical imagination, much as it had in Dicey's, though without the triumphalism of the Oxford law don. Pound thought that Sir Edward Coke and his brethren bore some of the blame for the growth of equity jurisdiction and the creation of prerogative courts because of their blinkered defense of outmoded principles and procedures.

Although the common lawyers ultimately made chancellors more respectful of precedent and abolished the court of Star Chamber, they also belatedly saw the value of many equitable principles and incorporated them into English law. "The common law survived," Pound wrote, "and the sole permanent result of the reversion to justice without law was a liberalizing and modernizing of the law."[16]

Pound believed that history was repeating itself in his day. Boards and commissions had multiplied; judicial control over "arbitrary executive action" had loosened; "summary administrative powers" had been unleashed—all in reaction to an earlier period of judicial excess that had nearly paralyzed administration. "Almost every important measure of police or administration," Pound claimed, had "encountered an injunction." Courts of equity had even attempted to regulate grade crossings.[17] Because judges had been weighed down by "the old scholastic logic" and the "cumbrous, ineffective and unbusinesslike procedure" of their courts, the laity had turned to the executive for justice without law. In 1907, Pound counted scores of statutes that gave "wide powers of dealing with the liberty or property of citizens to executive boards, to be exercised summarily, or upon such hearing as comports with lay notions of fair play." Ten years later, Pound still saw "all manner of administrative tribunals, proceeding summarily upon principles yet to be defined," created at the expense of the courts. "We seem for a time to be willing to throw over a large part of our hard won justice according to law," Pound opined, "in the hope that summary adjustment of human relations and summary administrative regulation of human conduct may give wider recognition and more effective security to the claims of the socially dependent to a larger and fuller life."[18]

The growth of administrative justice was not the product of "maternalism or paternalism, or a decay of the ancient faith, or a loss of fiber in the American public, or anything of that sort," Pound explained. It was but a phase in a historical cycle, and it too would pass. "However much society may turn for a time to the unfettered common sense of the layman, we may be assured in the long run the paramount social interest in the general security will require administration of justice according to law."[19]

As Pound waited for lawyers and judges to formulate "the results of administrative experience" into legal principles, he complained about administrators and their ways.[20] He called *Local Government Board v. Arlidge* (1915), in which the House of Lords upheld a refusal to disclose a housing inspector's report declaring a building unfit for human habitation "a startling decision in the cradle of our common law" and "a reversion to a primitive justice without law."[21] He also faulted administrators who sought "the line of least resistance" rather than take a principled stand, as when New York's public utilities commission ratified a patently unlawful issuance of securities after ordering the company to reduce its capital stock by $100,000. "As a matter of fact," Pound fumed, "the capital stock had been watered something like two hundred and twenty-five thousand dollars and no possible rule of reason could be put behind authorizing one hundred and fifty-eight thousand dollars of improper securities conditioned upon a reduction of one hundred thousand of two hundred and twenty-five thousand inflated stock." He thought it obvious that the commission had made "a feeble compromise with no principle behind it."[22]

Pound's favorite illustration of unprincipled administration was *Carroll v. Knickerbocker Ice Company* (N.Y. 1916), the facts of which he exaggerated for humorous effect:

> Late in the afternoon of a hot day in the summer of 1914 an employee of an ice company in New York City came home in a very shaky condition, and responded to his wife's questions by explaining that a 300-pound block of ice had fallen upon him while at work putting ice in a cellar. A physician was called to whom he told the same story. He was removed to a hospital and died—of delirium tremens. The physicians testified that there were no bruises, discolorations or abrasions upon his body. Three witnesses who were present when the ice was put in the cellar testified that no such accident happened. In other words, it was evident that the death had no connection with activities either upon the ice wagon or the water wagon. But the statute provided that the workmen's compensation commission should not be governed by common-law rules of evidence or formal rules of procedure. Accordingly, the commission not only received the hearsay, which was entirely proper, but acted on it in the teeth of conclusive direct evidence, apparently conceiving, in its zeal to distribute the economic surplus, that any requirement that awards should be based on and sustained by evidence was technical and formal.

The case reminded Pound of a sixteenth-century sergeant-at-law's protest that the equity jurisprudence of his day was contrary to the Law of God. "God had given us a certain law in the scripture," the lawyer remarked, "but the chancellor gave us no law anywhere." The sergeant-at-law, Pound dryly observed, "would thoroughly understand a modern industrial commission."[23]

If Pound thus affirmed the lawyers' exasperation with lay administrators, he also counseled them to do more than "sound warning blasts and kick against the pricks." They should look to "the new economics and the social science of today" to understand the sources of popular dissatisfaction and to revise law accordingly. "We must have recourse to lawyers," Pound declared, if "our crude experiments with lawless justice" were to give way to "a legal fixation and systematization."[24] Just as the great antebellum judges John Marshall, James Kent, Joseph Story, Lemuel Shaw, John Bannister Gibson, and Thomas Ruffin had remade a feudal common law for the robust economy of the new nation, so should twentieth-century jurists engage in the "creative, constructive, legal thinking" needed to renovate the outdated jurisprudence of Victorian America.[25]

Dean Pound and Mr. Try-It

As long as he believed that lawyers and law professors joined him in thinking that the discretion of administrators ought to be recast as "justice according to law," Pound regarded the expansion of the administrative state without alarm. In well-received addresses to bar associations from Vermont to Utah, he presented the challenge calmly and with due regard for lessons to be learned by looking beyond the common-law world. He reminded Oklahoma's solons that "the epoch-making achievements of legal history have resulted from infusions into the law from without rather than from professional creative activity from within."[26] Further, Dicey had erred by equating the rule of law with the supremacy of common-law courts. "The administrative tribunals of France," he lectured Utah's lawyers in 1927, "are in spirit and in conduct... ordinary courts." Dicey's "confident distinctions" between England and the Continent had "at least [lost] their edge."[27] In 1928 he reminded ABA members that Magna Carta was not the last word in governance and claimed that "Continental Europe has shown signs of moving in our direction as we have in theirs."[28]

Pound did not have to rely solely on the applause of practitioners for affirmation, for it came in comforting quantities from other sources as well. All traced the origins of the campaign to reform the courts, culminating in the adoption of the Federal Rules of Civil Procedure, to his St. Paul address.[29] In 1925 the University of Wisconsin offered him its presidency and a princely salary, which Pound declined rather than abandon his "life's work," legal education and legal research. President Herbert Hoover appointed Pound to a commission to investigate criminal law enforcement and Prohibition, headed by the former Attorney General George Wickersham. Pound wrote its final report, published in 1931. As he completed it, he was widely mentioned for the seat on the World Court left vacant when Charles Evans Hughes became Chief Justice.[30]

Pound's equanimity survived into Franklin D. Roosevelt's first presidential term. The "constant swinging back and forth from reliance mainly on rules to reliance chiefly on personal judgment and discretion" was surely evident during the Hundred Days, he wrote in June 1933, but "a new process of crystallizing will presently supervene. The new institutions will presently fall into a legal mode," and "in the end we shall lose little that is significant in our inherited law."[31] He also took the Supreme Court's liberal decisions of 1934 in stride. Neither *Home Building and Loan Association v. Blaisdell*, which upheld a moratorium on mortgage foreclosures, nor *Nebbia v. New York* were "sudden and radical departures," he assured *New York Times* readers. Each was "in line with an established view of what is reasonable."[32]

Yet as Pound entered his sixties, he increasingly found himself embroiled in unsettling conflicts. One source of aggravation was the Harvard Law School faculty. Some of its members faulted Pound for not standing up to Harvard University president Abbott Lawrence Lowell when he vetoed appointments. Others objected to Pound's torpedoing of attempts to incorporate the "functional approach" of legal realists at Columbia and Yale into the Harvard Law School curriculum. Even jurisprudential traditionalists rankled at his micromangement of the law school, his refusal to reimburse professors for trivial unauthorized expenditures, his growing irascibility, and his lengthy absences while serving on the Wickersham Commission. Joseph Henry Beale complained that Pound was "growing nuttier and nuttier"; another professor wrote that Pound would not tolerate opposition.[33] By 1931, Frankfurter, once an ally, deplored the dean's "pathetic" vanity. "He must know all the law that anybody knows or can possibly exist," he complained to Learned Hand, "and he naively believes that all his former students... are merely echoes of him."[34]

In early 1934, Harvard's new president, James Bryant Conant, alarmed by the feuding, started attending meetings of the law faculty and found it to be "the most quarrelsome group of men I ever encountered." Yet Pound continued to behave badly. In July, Frankfurter fumed that "R.P. is a liar and a double-crosser." A worse provocation occurred in October 1934 when, on the steps of Langdell Hall, the German ambassador conferred upon Pound an honorary degree from a Nazified University of Berlin.[35] At last, in September 1935, Pound announced his retirement, effective a year hence. "My chief reason for giving up the Deanship," he privately explained, "is that I do not care to be responsible for teaching that law is simply a pious fraud to cover up decisions of cases according to personal inclinations or that there is nothing in the way of reason back of the legal order but it is simply a pulling and hauling of interests with a camouflage of authoritative precepts."[36]

As his explanation suggests, by 1935 Pound, once the nation's most eminent legal progressive, had been outflanked by intellectuals to his left. As Pound made no discernible progress on his great work on sociological jurisprudence, other scholars, especially at Columbia and Yale, reimagined law in light of advances in empirical social science. The impatience of these "legal realists" with Pound burst into view in 1930, in what the legal historian N. E. H. Hull has called "perhaps the most famous controversy in the history of American jurisprudence."[37] In *The Bramble Bush* (1930), Karl N. Llewellyn declared that the law was not Pound's lawyer-mediated encounters between experience and reason but simply what officials "do about disputes," regardless of whether "the people who have the doing in charge... be judges or sheriffs or clerks or jailers or lawyers." In a related article, Llewellyn accused the Harvard Law School dean of succumbing to outdated "precept-thinking." "At times [his] work purports clearly to travel on the level of considered and buttressed scholarly discussion," Llewellyn wrote, "at times on the level of bedtime stories for the tired bar; at times on an intermediate level, that of the thoughtful but unproved essay."[38]

Still more provoking to Pound was Jerome Frank. Frank had graduated from the University of Chicago Law School in 1912 with the highest grades ever recorded and had joined a leading corporate firm in the Windy City. During the 1920s, he plunged into various reform projects, such as municipal ownership of Chicago's street railways, and cultivated the city's literati. In 1928, he moved his family to New York City so that his daughter could undergo psychoanalysis, a process that so fascinated Frank that he underwent it himself. At one of the city's few corporate law firms that would hire even an assimilated Jew, Frank joined the reorganization branch of the Wall Street practice, in which teams of lawyers representing the various stakeholders of a bankrupt company negotiated the reduction of existing debt, attracted additional capital, and launched the concern as a new and viable enterprise. Some reorganizers, including the masterful Robert T. Swaine, a partner at the great corporate law firm of Cravath, Henderson and De Gersdoff, vigorously defended their enormous fees, but the avariciousness of the Wall Street bar dismayed Frank. Unhappy in his work, he looked to writing for satisfaction.[39]

The result was *Law and the Modern Mind* (1930), which Frank wrote on his daily commute. Working from Freudian principles, Frank developed the argument that jurists who insisted on certainty in the law were emotionally immature. Back of their lofty invocations of precedent and principle was a childish search for an infallible substitute for their own, all-too-fallible fathers. Frank illustrated his point by reviewing the work of particular judges and legal scholars. Pound came in for a skewering, to the delight of Llewellyn but the dismay of its subject, who accused Frank of misquoting him. "I cannot afford to discuss anything with one who uses such tactics," Pound wrote to Llewellyn, "and should like to suggest to you whether you can afford to identify yourself with him." Llewellyn defended the legal realist movement from Pound's attack in an article published under his own name but that warmly acknowledged Frank's assistance.[40]

Frank's relationship with another brilliant and iconoclastic lawyer, William O. Douglas, proved even more momentous for his career. After graduating second in his class at the Columbia Law School in 1925, Douglas went to work at the Cravath firm, where he put in long hours on one of the biggest corporate reorganizations of the twenties. In 1927, he escaped to the Columbia Law School faculty and the following year moved to the Yale Law School. At some point, Douglas sought out Frank for help on a technical aspect of the reorganization practice. After *Law and the Modern Mind* appeared, Douglas joined his colleague Thurman Arnold in getting its author appointed as a research associate at Yale, a post that came with few obligations beyond the smuggling of liquor to New Haven.[41] Even so, Frank wrote an attack on corporate reorganizations that brought a vigorous rejoinder from Swaine. Frank and Douglas collaborated on another article on the subject; and Douglas continued to consult Frank after Frank left New York to become General Counsel to the AAA. Thereafter, Yale law professors sent Frank some of their best graduates and lent their own services on a temporary basis.[42]

Pound discerned alarming implications in Llewellyn's and Frank's writings. If law was just what officials did or an artifact of the psyche, then "justice according to law" was a myth; and politics, an unchained monster. So closely did Llewellyn's and Frank's arguments stand in Pound's thinking that he conflated them under the rubric of "give-it-up" philosophies. Both men, it seemed to Pound, had abandoned the search for law as something more than the threat of force against those the politically powerful deemed obnoxious.[43] Thus, he privately described *Law and the Modern Mind* as "a highly sensational book chiefly important as revealing the frame of mind of a group of men who believe that law is whatever those who administer it choose to do."[44]

Pound tried to contain the jurisprudential left by subsuming their insights within a more comprehensive view of law. Llewellyn and Frank had hold of a part of the elephant, Pound implied, while he saw the creature whole. That this strategy might fail became evident when Pound appeared on a panel with Frank at the annual meeting of the AALS on December 30, 1933. Pound spoke first. He conceded that the new jurisprudence had "its eye on something significant." In some sense, "everything that enters into or affects the judicial process is 'law.'" But legal precepts and principles were a distinct and crucial source that existed apart from the factors the realists stressed. He concluded on a chivalric note: "So, Mr. President, as one who has borne the heat of the day in jurisprudence for a generation, I can only say to those who are coming forward to do battle: '*Venite fortior me post me.*'"[45]

Anyone expecting Frank to meet Pound in direct combat was disappointed. To be sure, Frank repeated his denial of the existence of a priori legal principles. "Principles are what principles do," he famously declared. Yet he was far more interested in giving the law professors a dispatch from the New Deal. Frank's most memorable conceit was a contrast of two fictional government lawyers, "Mr. Absolute" and "Mr. Try-it." Mr. Absolute believed that "the true, pertinent legal principles must prevail," whatever the consequences. In fact, because of an unconscious predisposition, Mr. Absolute was bound to

FIGURE 5.1 Roscoe Pound, dean of the Harvard Law School, standing behind his desk in Langdell Hall in 1934, photographed by Fabian Bachrach.

Source: Courtesy of Louis Fabian Bachrach and the Harvard Law School Library.

arrive at the functionally desirable result, yet because he had to "attitudinize to himself," he "wast[ed] time, proceed[ed] unnecessarily by indirection, and burn[t] up his energies needlessly." In contrast, Mr. Try-it commenced with the desirability of a given program. He forthrightly looked for ways to justify it and generally succeeded in finding "satisfactory premises" for his conclusions. "There are, so to speak, plenty of vacant premises," Frank punned, and others could "be sufficiently repaired or remodeled."[46]

Pound could have scarcely encountered more galling evidence that "give-it-up" theorists and their legion of Mr. Try-its were running the New Deal while he endured the slights of a squabbling faculty in Cambridge. A militant tone, previously reserved for private communications, crept into Pound's public statements and publications. In January 1936, he favorably contrasted equity courts' power of "visitation" over corporations with the free-wheeling authority of public service commissions and the SEC under the Public Utility Holding Company Act of 1935. "Much more danger of arbitrary action has arisen" under administrators, he warned, "than exercise of the visitatorial jurisdiction by the courts could possibly carry with it."[47] He warned an international collection of jurists gathered at Harvard that law—"the voluntary subjection of authority and power to reason"—was under attack around the world and "most aggressively and persistently in the United States."[48] Pound once wrote as if the containment of administration by the common law was inevitable. In August 1936 he thought it very much in doubt.

Pound stepped down from the deanship in September 1936; on February 5, 1937, he left San Francisco on a globe-circling trip. That same day, President Franklin D. Roosevelt announced his Court-packing plan. Pound's initial response, based on telegraphic descriptions of the plan, was dismissive. "It looks to me like just a big bluff," he announced upon landing in Honolulu. "This talk about forcing retirement of justices over 70 is stuff, just plain stuff." The seriousness of the affair ultimately dawned on him, however. Although the great battle for judicial supremacy was won before Pound returned to the United States, a reporter found him in a fighting mood when he finally debarked in New York City. The Court-packing plan "was one of the most outrageous things that ever occurred in American legal history," he fumed dockside on August 31, 1937.[49]

Before the Court-packing plan, Pound cautioned lawyers against mounting an "obstinate, rear-guard action" against reform.[50] In its aftermath, he was ready to stand with them in defense of the common law. As it happened, the ABA chieftains were about to give him the chance to do just that.

The ABA Discovers Administrative Law

In 1932, Louis Caldwell, the first Washington partner of the eminent Chicago law firm now known as Kirkland & Ellis, proposed that the ABA create a committee to reform the procedures of federal agencies. Caldwell, who had been the first general counsel of the Federal Radio Commission, was convinced that professional politicians had captured his old agency and turned radio licenses into "a form of patronage," secure in the knowledge that the substantial evidence standard immunized their awards from reversal in the courts. The commission's lawyers framed findings of fact "with an eye not so much to the evidence as to justify an *a priori* decision," he complained. As long as they got substantial evidence into the record, they knew that a reviewing court would uphold the award of a license.[51]

"To my surprise and dismay," Caldwell recalled, the ABA president made him chairman of the new Special Committee on Administrative Law and told him to report at the association's next meeting. The Hundred Days intervened, and Caldwell found that his modest project of law reform had pitched him into the vortex of New Deal politics.[52]

Had a more conventional lawyer headed the Special Committee, its reports might have called for the intrusive review of administrators by the US Courts of Appeals, in line with Dicey's equating the rule of law with de novo review by one of the "ordinary Courts of the land." But Caldwell was a learned and cosmopolitan figure, who had turned down Wigmore's offer to teach at Northwestern's law school. He believed that the administrative courts of France, Germany, Fascist Italy, and Stalinist Russia afforded "interesting tests of the adequacy of certain methods of administration." Some independent body should review administrators' orders on the facts as well as the law, he believed, but he preferred a specialized administrative court, such as the Board of Tax Appeals, to common-law judges unfamiliar with an agency's organic statute, regulations, and practices.[53]

George Norris, a progressive US senator from Nebraska, had introduced a bill for such a court in 1929. At the time Congress was puzzling out how to reroute appeals from customs officers, which went to a specialized administrative court, and those from the patent office, which overwhelmingly went to a heavily burdened US Court of Appeals for the District of Columbia. Ultimately, the legislators decided to create a new Court of Customs and Patent Appeals. Norris's bill, in contrast, would have created a more capacious "U.S. Court of Administrative Justice," with appellate jurisdiction over tax rulings, claims against the federal government, and mandamus actions against federal officials as well as customs and patent matters.[54]

The bill was the product of Ollie Roscoe McGuire, counsel to the Comptroller General of the United States, who was Norris's protégé. "Colonel" McGuire—the honorific was the residue of some long-forgotten service to a Kentucky governor—would later help James Montgomery Beck, a former solicitor general, write the anti-statist screed, *Our Wonderland of Bureaucracy* (1932) and churn out wildly bombastic articles and speeches under his own name. He wangled his way onto the Special Committee on Administrative Law in 1933 and replaced Caldwell as chair in 1936.[55]

McGuire persistently advocated the creation of "an administrative court" to hear appeals from across the federal bureaucracy. Just as persistently, he encountered opposition from two camps. The first consisted of customs, patent, and tax lawyers, who were satisfied with their existing arrangements with the Court of Customs and Patent Appeals and the Board of Tax Appeals.[56] The second was a member of McGuire's own committee, the Minnesota lawyer Monte Appel, who insisted on full review by the federal judiciary. Anything less, Appel protested, would transgress "the basic Anglo-American concept of the supremacy of law administered in one court, the same court, over public official and private citizen alike."[57]

In January 1937, McGuire abandoned the administrative court bill for a wholly new approach.[58] His new bill would establish a review board within each agency and department, give a broad class of aggrieved persons the right to challenge an agency's actions, and require administrators to decide individual cases on written records and to make findings of fact.[59] Appeals from an internal review board went first to the agency's chief administrator and then into the courts. The courts were to review the agency's interpretations of the law and verify that substantial evidence supported its order, but they were not to engage in weight-of-the-evidence review, because, McGuire explained, this would "substitute the discretion of the courts for the discretion of the administrative officers."[60] Finally, the new bill would require agencies to promulgate their rules and regulations for review by the US Court of Claims, which, unlike courts created under Article III of the Constitution, could issue advisory opinions.[61]

Since its founding, the Special Committee had deplored the combination of prosecutorial and judicial powers in the same agency, so its abandonment of an independent appellate court was, as Caldwell protested, "almost a complete volte face." It entrusted the finding of facts, "on which 99 out of 100 cases turn," to departmental employees who were certain, in Caldwell's opinion, to vote as their superiors wanted them to. Appel, who thought McGuire was angling for an appointment as Comptroller General, filed a minority report, and asked for permission to make his case to the ABA's Board of Governors before the House of Delegates convened in Kansas City in September 1937. The board declined but sent McGuire's and Appel's reports to the House without a recommendation. During the ensuing debate, a revered delegate from Georgia almost defeated the measure with an impassioned invocation of the rule of law. "I am opposed to bureaucratic government," he solemnly declared. "The only source of justice as I know it, is the courts." With defeat looming, the ABA leaders proposed that delegates approve the bill "as a declaration of principle" and that a final version be prepared, "subject to the approval of the Board of Governors," in time for the next session of Congress. The motion, which did not specify who was to revise the bill, carried by a vote of 55 to 51.[62]

The new ABA president, Arthur T. Vanderbilt, voiced the leadership's dismay after the meeting. "The Administrative Law Committee, now, as formerly, has been a one-man committee," Vanderbilt observed. Although "there have been brilliant men on the Committee, they have shown a flair for breaking out at the wrong time." Convinced that administrative law was "going to be our hottest spot during the present year, second only to the Supreme Court fight," Vanderbilt announced his intention to secure as chair "an outstanding man ... who will look at the thing in a very broad way, and who will be prepared to give a large amount of time" to the job.[63] On October 5, 1937, just over a month after returning to the United States, Roscoe Pound accepted the chairmanship of the Special Committee on Administrative Law.[64]

Chairman Pound

As Ernest Leet was trying to rally New York's lawyers to the cause of weight-of-the-evidence review, then, Vanderbilt looked to Pound not only to produce a "broad and deep" study of administrative law but also to "get the matter down out of the clouds so that the Committee can present concrete recommendations for action by the Congress or the State Legislature."[65] Pound saw his mission differently. He recalled his service, after his St. Paul address, on an ABA project to revise civil procedure. Although all around him had been demanding a new code of procedure, attempts to produce one had led only to "haggling over words and phrases." Instead, Pound wrote a report that set out some fundamental principles. With those articulated, lawyers found that they could work out the details on their own.[66] In fall 1937, Pound similarly believed that if he restated the meaning of "our common-law doctrine of supremacy of law" for an administrative age, someone else could come up with a statute.[67]

Through the winter of 1937–38 and into spring, Pound persevered despite many aggravations. One was Colonel McGuire, who continued on the Special Committee despite his dim view of the man who had replaced him as chair. "While a great lawyer, or rather law student," he complained to Vanderbilt, "I know of no particular accomplishments of his in the field of administrative law." McGuire repeatedly demanded that Pound convene the committee and plagued the chair with "a good many sarcastic remarks" about his failure to do so. Vanderbilt, who also endured "the fulminations of the disagreeable Colonel McGuire," still wanted more than the scholarly study Pound proposed. "I do not believe we can stop there at this time," he wrote in December 1937, "when the reorganization of the Executive Departments is pending in Washington, and when the report of the previous Committee, as voted on by the House of Delegates in Kansas City, must be regarded as a mandate to the Committee, even though the vote was a very close one."[68] In April 1938, Vanderbilt dispatched a member of the Board of Governors to Cambridge to ask Pound to produce a bill in time for its meeting a few weeks hence. When Vanderbilt's ambassador arrived, Pound was still reeling from the latest escapade of his alcoholic second wife, who had abruptly decamped to Manhattan a few days before.[69]

"Harassed," as he said, "beyond belief," Pound convened his five-member committee in Washington, DC, in late April. Only two other members, Colonel McGuire and the lawyer and political scientist Walter F. Dodd, attended, although Pound held the proxy of the former secretary of the interior James R. Garfield. McGuire and Dodd wanted the committee to report some version of the Kansas City bill; Pound and Garfield did not; the view of the fifth member, the Oregon lawyer Robert Maguire, was unknown.[70] Somehow, a compromise emerged. The committee would endorse no legislation, but Colonel McGuire would meet with the subcommittee of the Board of Governors and help it revise the Kansas City bill for the board's consideration. The bill would thus be that of the board's own subcommittee and not the Special Committee on Administrative Law.[71]

The Board of Governors adopted the subcommittee bill when it met in Washington in May 1938, when Secretary Wallace's quarrel with Chief Justice Hughes was the talk of the capital. The situation was awkward for all concerned. The ABA had its bill but not Pound's imprimatur. Pound had in the report a prominent vehicle for his views, but if he publicly objected to the bill, he might provoke Colonel McGuire, Dodd, and the Oregon lawyer (who, Pound learned in May, supported the Kansas City bill) into writing what would become the majority report.[72]

The ABA chieftains did as much as they could to create the impression that Pound's committee had endorsed the bill without forcing Pound to declare otherwise. Thus, when the galleys of the advance program for the House of Delegates meeting in Cleveland arrived, Pound discovered that the bill had been appended to his report, which now included references endorsing the legislation. With only an hour to edit the proofs, he struck out several passages and decided that the result finessed the matter of the bill's authorship.[73] In fact, the publication of Pound's report with the revised Kansas City bill in *ABA Reports* and ambiguous references to the bill's parentage when the House of Delegates met in July 1938 led contemporaries and historians alike to think that the Harvard law dean had drafted the Walter-Logan bill.[74]

In Pound's mind, at least, there had never been any confusion. In May, when Walter Dodd forwarded suggestions for revising the bill to Pound, he refused to consider them. "As the bill was given form by the Board of Governors, I do not know just what power our Committee has with reference to it," he replied. In June Pound urged Vanderbilt to recommit the measure. In September he assured the prominent tax lawyer Robert Miller that his committee "had nothing to do with that bill.... Our report made no reference to it, but it was appended to the report I suppose by action of the Board of Governors. I certainly should not have thought of recommending the bill in the form in which it was appended to the report." Pound also disavowed authorship of the bill to Jerome Frank, who then demanded that Pound and the ABA state whether the dean endorsed it. In an open letter to Colonel McGuire, who had been restored to the chairmanship of the Special Committee, Pound finally declared that although he was not the author of bill, that fact "did not mean, and in my judgment cannot be taken to mean, that I am out of accord with the Committee or the Association on the subject."[75]

The dean's logic was impeccable; still the statement left in doubt whether Pound *was* in "accord with the Committee or the Association" and, if not, how he differed with them. One might deduce from the New Dealers' later characterization of Pound as one of the ABA's "extreme conservatives" that he objected to the bill's departures from Dicey's rule of law.[76] But although other lawyers opposed the bill on these grounds, Pound did not.

Consider first the internal review boards, which were to replace trial examiners as agencies' principal adjudicators. An appeal of an individual administrator's decision was to a three-person board appointed by the head of the agency. This internal review board would hold a hearing, make findings of fact, and reach a decision. That decision, in turn, was appealable to the agency's head (or a designee). Only after that official approved, rejected, or modified the order of the internal review board could a disputant go to the courts.[77]

Robert Miller believed that if tax matters went to such a board, rather than to the existing, independent Board of Tax Appeals, its members would be "dominated by the views of the Secretary just as other parts of the Treasury are of necessity dominated." Within Pound's own committee, James Garfield objected that the members of a board would "be influenced by, if not controlled by, the opinion of the Executive heads of the Department or Commission appointing them." In contrast, Pound saw "something to be said on both sides" of the question. True, a board's members might be overly solicitous of the wishes of their agency head, "to whom they must look for promotion, if not for the very tenure of their positions." Yet their reports would also provide superiors with "a clear record of what is done and on what basis and by whom." Although "not immune from objection," internal review boards could, Pound concluded, correct "obvious abuses now existing perhaps as well as any plan which may be devised."[78]

Further, Pound rejected weight-of-the-evidence review. "There comes a time when we should stop reviewing facts," he told a Senate subcommittee in May 1938. "If we are really assured there is a determination of facts," we need not substitute "the judicial tribunal for the administrative tribunal."[79] Judges should uphold most findings of fact whenever they had "a reasonable support in substantial evidence." Their job was to ensure that an agency "kept within the limits prescribed by law with respect to power, and that its proceedings are in accordance with processes of law." Sir Edward Coke's view, that "there is to be no matter of misgovernment, but that it should be remedied by King's Bench," was no more valid than Karl Llewellyn's claim that law was whatever officials said it was. "One is as extreme as the other."[80]

The reform Pound most wholeheartedly endorsed was surprisingly modest. "What seems to me most important from a good many months' study of the matter," he wrote to the corporate lawyer Cornelius Wickersham, "is to provide a speedy and effective judicial review." Too often, he maintained, those who would challenge an administrator's ruling had to negotiate a bewildering maze of common law writs, injunction suits, and statutory appeals. "The technicality, confusion, delay and expense in review procedure," he told Wickersham, made administrators' pleas to be relieved of judicial review persuasive and discouraged lawyers from appealing their orders. With the chances of prevailing so uncertain, clients looked to "political influence" for relief.[81] But fix the appellate process, Pound reasoned, and lawyers could go to the courts. The courts would insist on due process within the agency. Due process within the agency would make further judicial review unnecessary.

Pound, then, converged on about the same position that the Supreme Court did during Hughes's chief justiceship and New York voters evidently did in the general election of 1938. The rule of law required "fair play" from administrators; if individuals had their "day in commission" they were not also owed a "day in court." Had Pound stated his views dispassionately, he would be seen today as what he in fact was: another sign of an emerging consensus that the structural and procedural reform of agencies would keep Tocqueville's nightmare at bay. Yet, as so often happens when Americans discuss their state, politics prevailed. Initially, the politics were academic: Pound wished to strike a blow against law professors who rejected his vision of legal education as the transmission of a taught legal tradition centered on the courts. That the person who replaced him as Harvard's dean was James M. Landis was particularly galling, for Landis had chaired the SEC, defended the Court-packing plan, and written *The Administrative Process* (1938), a powerful defense of the administrative state.[82] But Pound vied with "the jurists of the left" not merely for preeminence within the legal academe but also for the hearts and minds of American lawyers, whom he counted on to keep the state in check. Pound's academic opponents, including the fellow traveler Jerome Frank, understood the stakes in similar terms. They had come to enjoy unprecedented power as lawyers and administrators in the New Deal, and they would not surrender it without a fight.[83] Finally, as in New York, professional politicians saw their own interests in administrative reform and made it a rallying point for opposition to the New Deal.

Sound and Fury

Imminent peril is a boon to any polemicist. Pound's peril was the global spread of "administrative absolutism," which he defined as "a highly centralized administration set up under complete control of the executive for the time being, relieved of judicial review and making its own rules." The term "at once conjures up visions of Tudor and Stuart excess and calls into play prejudices born of emotion and tradition," a law professor observed. Pound chortled that it affected law professors and agency lawyers "very much as a red rag does a bull." The phrase also flattered the legal profession. In joining Pound's crusade to keep administration "under and a part of the legal order," lawyers were not simply protecting their lucrative expertise in the ways of the courts but also "safeguarding individual interests and preserving the checks and balances" that were "fundamental in our American polity."[84]

Pound's starting point was Llewellyn's claim that, in the dean's paraphrase, "law is whatever is done officially." Such a position, Pound maintained, implied that law, "in the usual and longest continued" sense of the term, "the body of authoritative grounds of and guides to decision," was illusory. Whether they knew it or not, Llewellyn and his followers were subscribing to the "Marxian" doctrine of the disappearance of law, "the proposition recently maintained by the jurists of Soviet Russia that in the socialist state there is no law but only one rule of law, that there are no laws—only administrative ordinances and orders."[85]

Pound set out the steps in his reasoning elsewhere. A fuller definition of law helped. It was, he wrote, "the body of authoritative precepts recognized or established as rules of conduct and of adjustment of relations among men, to be applied by the tribunals and administrative agencies of a politically organized society in determining controversies." This definition assumed that individuals had conflicting interests requiring adjustment, a condition that obtained under capitalism but would not obtain, Pound's authorities on Soviet law held, after private property was abolished. With no private property to differentiate and divide individuals, social classes would disappear, and the simple disputes that remained could be resolved administratively on an ad hoc basis. Law was "the typical agency of social control" in societies organized around the individual, the Soviet jurist Evgeny B. Pashukanis claimed (in Pound's paraphrase), but "administration was the characteristic form of regulation in a social organization marked by 'unity of purpose.' " Or, as Piotr Stuchka held, "Communism means, not the triumph of socialist law, but the triumph of socialism over law, for law will wholly disappear with the abolition of classes and their opposing interests."[86]

Even when stated more fully, Pound's argument was tendentious. He loosed Llewellyn's behaviorialist definition of law from its original context, derived from it a claim that administrators should be completely untrammeled by law, and projected that position onto an ill-defined cabal of "administrative absolutists" without ever showing that any of them actually endorsed so extreme a view. Further, he never demonstrated that the legal realists read the Soviet jurists or considered whether the two groups differed in any important respect. He thus engaged in a highbrow form of red-baiting.

The legal philosopher Morris Cohen pleaded with Pound to drop the slur. Cohen saw "nothing particularly Marxian" in the view that law was what officials do. One might as well call the legal realists Hobbesian, he observed. Besides, the immediate inspiration for Llewellyn and his associates was not

Marx but Eugen Ehrlich, an Austrian jurist whom Pound counted as an influence. "I am sure that Messrs. Frank, Llewellyn and [Underhill] Moore can in no way be charged with being Marxists," Cohen insisted. He added that "for many members of the American Bar Association the characterization of any view as Marxian is itself a judgment of condemnation."

Pound did not budge. "I have read Marx, Engels and their orthodox interpreters on this point thoroughly and repeatedly," he replied. To Cohen's caution against throwing around "vague labels like Marxian," Pound countered that "it did not occur to me that the characterization of any view today as Marxian necessarily involved condemnation."[87] So profound was Pound's immersion in a scholarly world of his own making that one cannot quite dismiss his protest out of hand. Still, with Stalin's show trials a very recent memory and the House Committee on Un-American Activities just starting its search for subversives, Pound's characterization of his jurisprudential rivals was recklessly inflammatory and intentionally provocative.[88]

Pound was just as tendentious in the most famous passage of his report, a list of "tendencies which may be noted in administrative action in the whole English-speaking world":[89]

1. A tendency to decide without a hearing, or without hearing one of the parties.
2. A tendency to decide on the basis of matters not before the tribunal or on evidence not produced.
3. A tendency to make decisions on the basis of preformed opinions and prejudices.
4. A tendency to consider the administrative determining function one of acting rather than of deciding.
5. A tendency to disregard jurisdictional limits and seek to extend the sphere of administrative action beyond the jurisdiction confided to the administrative board or commission.
6. A tendency to do what will get by; to yield to political pressure at the expense of the law.
7. A tendency to arbitrary rule making for administrative convenience at the expense of important interests.
8. A tendency at the other extreme to fall into a perfunctory routine.
9. A tendency to exercise of jurisdiction by deputies.
10. A tendency to mix rule making, investigation, prosecution, the advocate's function, the judge's function, and the function of enforcing a judgment, so that the whole proceeding from end to end is one to give effect to a complaint.

A social scientist would have felt obliged to study agencies to see how often these "tendencies" became manifest in actual practice. Although the Commonwealth Fund's monographs and term papers from Frankfurter's seminars were readily available, Pound ignored them. Aside from an occasional reference to the Wickersham Commission's studies of deportation and Prohibition, he usually contented himself with judicial opinions, gathered from around the common-law world. His sole authority for the "tendency to do what will get by; to yield to political pressure at the expense of the law" was a reference to the parable of Mr. Absolute and Mr Try-it from Jerome Frank's 1933 address to the AALS.[90]

To avoid the appearance of partisanship, Pound, a lifelong Republican, repeatedly illustrated his tendencies with incidents from the administration of Prohibition by Republican presidents. [91] Although he also referred to five New Deal agencies, only one of them seemed a particular target. The Petroleum Administrative Board appeared anonymously as the culprit in *Panama Refining*, "a case not so long ago in this country of administrative carrying on of a prosecution on the basis of a non-existent administrative rule."[92] The Federal Communications Commission indulged in various procedural irregularities; one of its lawyers deprecated judicial review of administrative agencies.[93] The National Bituminous Coal Commission tried to set coal prices without first holding a hearing.[94] The NLRB gave the lie to Landis's claim that the "interpretation of sociological and economic data flourishes less happily in the overheated atmosphere of litigation than in the calm of scientific inquiry."[95]

With these agencies, Pound only noted procedural shortcomings. With the SEC, where William O. Douglas was chairman and Jerome Frank a member, he weighed in on a fiercely contested regulatory initiative.[96] Pound wrote his report shortly before Congress passed the Chandler Act, which transformed the corporate reorganization practice that had been so lucrative for Swaine and other Wall Streeters. The statute required that disinterested trustees be appointed to develop reorganization plans; neither they nor their lawyers could be officers, directors, underwriters, or creditors of the bankrupt corporation. This provision ended the Wall Streeters' practice of working out a plan around a conference table and then presenting it to a federal judge for perfunctory review and ratification. The act also permitted the SEC to appear as a party in reorganization proceedings, and it required federal judges to submit plans for major reorganizations to the SEC for comment.[97]

Douglas had laid the foundation for the statute with a lengthy investigation of corporate reorganizations. In 1934 he mercilessly interrogated Swaine, his old boss at the Cravath law firm, about his part in drafting legislation concerning railroad reorganization. Afterward, Swaine complained to Douglas, "You stood me on my head and shook all the fillings out of my teeth."[98] Sometime later, the Cravath lawyer devoted the better part of an appearance at the Yale Law School to denying that he was an avaricious perjurer. "I wish I had been able to broadcast the speech to you," a professor told Douglas. "I am sure you would have enjoyed hearing Swaine out-Swaine Swaine."[99]

In his report, Pound twice sided with Swaine against Douglas and Frank, without ever acknowledging that Swaine was the great champion of the corporate reorganization practice and might still be smarting from his rough treatment by Douglas. First, to illustrate the tendency of administrative absolutists to "make decisions on the basis of preformed opinions and prejudices," Pound approvingly quoted what he thought was Swaine's characterization of Douglas's investigatory reports as "essentially briefs" for the SEC's legislative agenda.[100] Second, he endorsed Swaine's complaint, made while the Chandler Act was before Congress, that the measure would insert "a politically constituted administrative bureau" into private litigation. Unless "the bar takes it upon itself to act," Pound warned, "there is nothing to check the tendency of administrative bureaus to extend their operations indefinitely even to the extent of supplanting our traditional judicial regime by an administrative regime."[101]

Such thrusts demanded a response, and Jerome Frank immediately rose to the defense of the SEC, to which he had been appointed in December 1937. Already scheduled to defend the Chandler Act at the ABA meeting in July 1938, he revised his remarks to include a rebuttal to Pound.

"Your Committee's report defames Chairman William O. Douglas," he declared. "A more honest, fair-minded man never lived. Patient justice is a quiet passion with him." Frank accused Pound of the very tendency to act on "preformed opinions and prejudices" that the former law dean detected in Douglas. After all, had Pound followed the standard of objectivity he demanded of agencies, he would have had to read the 18,000 pages of testimony taken during Douglas's investigations. Pound was "a voracious reader, in almost every language," Frank allowed, but his report gave no indication that he had performed such a feat.[102]

In his prepared remarks, Frank claimed that he was not acting on "personal pique." After delivering them, however, he acknowledged that "an article of mine, without indicating my name, is summarized in the report." Later correspondence revealed that Pound's use of the parable of Mr. Absolute and Mr. Try-it had wounded him deeply. Pound had implied that he was "the kind

FIGURE 5.2 Jerome N. Frank takes the oath of office as a member of the Securities and Exchange Commission on December 27, 1937, as Chairman William O. Douglas looks on. *Source*: Courtesy of the Library of Congress, LC-DIG-hec-23817.

of a lawyer who 'yields to political pressure at the expense of law,' " Frank protested, when, as the AAA general counsel, he had "continuously been in hot water" for opposing on legal grounds the demands of agribusinessmen and administrators.[103]

Pound shrugged off Frank's protests. The legal realist's thesis in *Law and the Modern Mind* that "objectivity in decision is impossible," Pound scoffed to Colonel McGuire, made Frank's objections a "case of Satan rebuking sin." To Frank himself he wrote, disingenuously, that he had not had "your Commission or any other commission particularly in mind, but rather the whole question of what I have been calling administrative absolutism."[104] Yet just before writing to Frank, Pound had held the members of the Investment Bankers of America spellbound as he explained how, under the influence of European ideas, "young lawyers newly appointed to give counsel to administrative bureaus" were discarding the doctrine of the supremacy of the law in favor of "the supremacy of the bureau." He described Frank as "a leading exponent of administrative absolutism, who now holds a high administrative office, with *jus vitae necisque* over private enterprise," and claimed that

Frank believed "that every item of the judicial process is shaped wholly and inexorably by the psychological determinants of the individual judge." The danger of such a theory in the hands of "an official empowered to apply law of his own making in his own way speaks for itself," Pound declared. In a corporate reorganization, he would be "like the man who intervenes in a brawl, not to stop the fight but to go in and take part in it on the side of one of the combatants."[105]

Frank defended the SEC against Pound's "intemperate, reckless charges" in an address to the Georgetown Law Alumni Club. His colleagues were "men mindful at all times of the legal limitations on their powers; scrupulous in respecting those limitations; untiring in their efforts to preserve the rights of citizens to full, fair hearings; and above all, entirely aware of the inestimable value of our judicial system and the importance of the legal profession." They had never sought immunity from judicial review. In fact, they sought not administrative absolutism but to be "the patient servants of the judiciary."[106] Frank closed by carrying the fight to his opponent. A dissenting member of the Wickersham Commission had complained that its final report was based on "secret evidence," one of the evils Pound deplored in his ABA report. Here was "the clue to Dean Pound's distemper," Frank announced. "Having in mind the operations of the Wickersham Commission in which he participated in 1930–1931, he perhaps believes that all Commissions now operate in the same undemocratic fashion."[107]

"I am no admirer of Dean Pound," announced Chester Lane, the SEC general counsel, but "some of this seems to be hitting below the belt."[108] But Frank was not finished. Before the Chicago Bar Association, he acknowledged that the decision to issue a "stop order," halting the sale of a security pending an investigation, was wholly committed to the SEC's discretion; but Frank countered that the commission had adopted detailed regulations to limit the staff's discretion. Anyone looking to curb official absolutism, he argued, should start not with the SEC but the police, who worked under the aegis of the courts. "Has the SEC ever used the rubber hose?" Frank demanded. "Has it ever deprived a citizen, suspected of wrongdoing, of food for many hours; kept him from obtaining counsel while subjecting him to protracted questioning; kept him sleepless in a rat or mosquito infested room; called witnesses to testify against him by the use of fake subpoenas—or done any one of the outrageous, indecent, inhuman and unfair acts all too frequently practiced or condoned by state prosecuting attorneys?"[109]

The quarrel between Pound and his academic opponents continued well into the 1940s. Pound restated his case before bar associations, expressly criticized Landis, and deprecated the research monographs of the Attorney General's Committee on Administrative Procedure.[110] Frank replied at book length in *If Men Were Angels* (1942) that the former dean was aiding renegades in investment banking, the stock exchanges, and the utility industry.[111] Other New Dealers accused the dean of indulging in an emotional "spree," committing "the Aristotelean fallacy of all or none," relying upon "ludicrously inadequate" evidence, and reaching conclusions that were "false and, in the view of many, even absurd." Privately, they spoke of him as "a great man with a terrible weakness—vanity—which is now eating him up in his old age."[112]

Doing Something about "Those Fellows Downtown"

Back of this scholarly quarrel was a controversy that was anything but academic. In January 1939, the ABA's House of Delegates finally approved a modestly revised version of the Kansas City bill. Soon thereafter, two Democrats, Senator Mills Logan of Kentucky and Representative Francis Walter of Pennsylvania, introduced variants in their respective houses of Congress. In each, the New Deal's critics quickly appreciated its serviceability for their own partisan ends.

By 1939, a conservative coalition of Republicans and anti-administration Democrats had concluded that Roosevelt was attempting to use administratively distributed largesse and policies to create an independent political base and keep a New Dealer in the White House after 1940.[113] The judiciary could no longer be counted on to prevent the president's advisors from putting administration to partisan use, because, as a journalist had it, his appointees had made the Supreme Court so "pro-government" that it upheld "ANYTHING done by administrative agencies." Congress would have to create its own check on "overzealous regulatory agencies" and "downtown braintrusters" who considered legislators "so dumb as not to be entrusted with plans BEFORE they are hatched." The Walter-Logan bill came with the ostensibly nonpartisan imprimatur of the ABA and the apparent endorsement of a former dean of the Harvard Law School. If, as even its proponents privately conceded, it was poorly drafted, its passage would disrupt the targeted agencies while the courts worked out sensible interpretations of its provisions. In the interim, the New Deal's critics could "make hay" with the bill and "talk of dictatorship" in the general election of 1940.[114]

After only a perfunctory hearing in April, the House Judiciary Committee voted Walter's version of the bill out on July 13, 1939. The Senate Judiciary

Committee unanimously approved it on May 17, 1939, without holding hearings. In July, William King, an anti-administration Democrat from Utah, won Senate approval of the bill on a surprise voice vote, but majority leader Alben Barkley, who owed his position to FDR, quickly forced a reconsideration and scheduled a debate for 1940. Although Roosevelt had already signaled his opposition to the bill, the House passed it in April 1940 by a vote of 279 to 97. (Only 93 of 221 Democrats—"including most of the New Dealers"—voted against it.) In the Senate, Barkley held off consideration until after the election. At last, on November 19, the Senators took up the House bill. Weakened by amendments, it passed by a vote of 27 to 25. Eleven Democrats joined all the Republican senators still in Washington in the two-vote majority.[115]

Congressional backers often praised the Walter-Logan bill in general terms, without distinguishing among administrative agencies. For example, Mills Logan declared that it would prevent "the entire subordination of both the legislative and judicial branches of the Federal Government to the executive branch." One congressman believed it would control the administrative "Frankenstein" Congress had created before it could "rise up and smite the very functions of the House and of the United States Senate." Another thought it promised to "recapture a part of the power of Congress which it should never have delegated to the bureaucrats." Yet, as Congress exempted more and more "old-line" agencies, such as the ICC, from its provisions, the true purpose of the bill, to punish agencies that had become a source of power for the New Dealers, became apparent. At last, its proponents gave up the charade. When a pro-administration congressman charged that the bill "was framed to cripple" the NLRB and the Wage and Hour Division of the Department of Labor, his interlocutor replied that those agencies deserved such a fate.[116]

Of all the New Deal agencies the Walter-Logan bill menaced, none was more alarmed than the SEC, then known as "the greatest New Dealers' nest in Washington."[117] If the bill were to become law, its lawyers warned, "unscrupulous and powerful" interests would exploit its technicalities, and the commission would be reduced to the status of a "second or third rate agency, with about the authority of a notary public to take depositions."[118] Nor were they alone in their animosity toward the bill. The Sullivan & Cromwell lawyer Alfred Jaretzki, Jr., declared it "unsound and unworkable" and faulted its drafters for taking an "*a priori* approach to a problem that can be dealt with adequately only after a careful study of the actual working of the many administrative agencies" it would govern. His partner, John Foster Dulles, agreed that it displayed "a complete lack of comprehension of the nature of the administrative process."[119]

The SEC's lawyers objected to three provisions in particular.[120] First, the bill threatened to disrupt the agency's making of rules and regulation, when even the corporate bar was satisfied with its exercise of rule-making power.[121] The bill gave agencies one year to hold public hearings and issue rules and regulations to implement a new statutory mandate. Anyone "substantially interested in the effects" of a rule could seek an advisory opinion on its legality from the US Court of Appeals for the District of Columbia.[122] If the D.C. Circuit upheld the rule, parties could also challenge it in the course of a normal lawsuit in any federal circuit court. Chester Lane, the SEC general counsel, warned that the passage of the bill would be "the opening gun for a crack-pot's field day" and predicted that "resourceful obstructionists" would fully exploit this "opportunity for harassment."[123]

The Walter-Logan bill also promised to expand the range of actions subject to review in a formal hearing within an agency and an appeal into the federal courts. Statutes and case law usually provided for review only of an administrator's final order. Interlocutory actions, such as decisions to investigate, could not be challenged until administrators finally disposed of a dispute. In contrast, the Walter-Logan bill allowed anyone aggrieved by "a decision of any officer or employee" of an agency to initiate proceedings, and it defined "decision" as "any affirmative or negative decision, order, or act in specific controversies which determines the issue therein resolved."[124] SEC officials feared that the language reached the issuance of a stop order or a trial examiner's ruling on the admissibility of evidence.[125] Writing from the Solicitor General's Office, Paul Freund agreed. The provision was so "vague and all-inclusive," he complained, that it was hard "to imagine any determination, however trivial or however inappropriate for reexamination in a formal hearing" that it excluded. Lane scoffed that under the bill a lawyer "kept out of the building by the janitor because it is after four-thirty" was owed a hearing before the full commission and an appeal into the courts.[126]

Finally, SEC officials opposed the bill's standard for reviewing agencies' findings of fact. Had it simply directed courts to set aside findings "not supported by substantial evidence," few would have objected to that deferential standard of review. But the bill also told judges to set aside findings of fact that were "clearly erroneous." Under the well-established canon of statutory interpretation that "redundancy is not to be imputed to the legislator," the drafters must have contemplated some circumstances in which a finding supported by substantial evidence was nonetheless clearly erroneous.[127] SEC commissioner Robert E. Healy could think of none and guessed that the courts would ignore the language and continue to defer to agencies.[128] Others thought that the bill authorized judges to throw out evidence as incredible or to find facts themselves, even though that would make agencies little more than "technical advisor[s] to the courts."[129]

To these objections, congressmen had what was, for their purposes, a sufficient response: Roscoe Pound, "one of the greatest legal authorities of our time," approved of the bill.[130] In May 1939, Pound wrote to Francis Walter that the measure was "in the direct line of progress." When Walter Gellhorn went to Capitol Hill to offer Walter the research services of the Attorney General's Committee on Administrative Procedure, the congressman declined. "I want you to know that we are definitely and unalterably opposed to administrative absolutism and that we have got to do something about those fellows downtown who think they can run the government any old way that pleases them," he told Gellhorn. "I have a letter here from Dean Pound—a beautiful letter—saying that this bill would be the best possible thing that could happen to the country and would go further than any other piece of legislation to preserve our form of government." In November 1939, an Ohio Republican also invoked Pound. No legal scholar "stands out more indisputably above the clamors and passions of the day," he declaimed. "When he speaks in terms of our national future, all of us, Republican, Democrat, or dissenter, must pay heed."[131]

Pound unambiguously endorsed the Walter-Logan bill after Landis attacked it in the May 1940 issue of the *Harvard Law Review*.[132] Enactment of the bill would be "a great step forward in administrative law," he wrote to Edward R. Burke, a leading anti-administration Democrat from the dean's home state of Nebraska. It would provide "a simple, expeditious, nontechnical mode" of administrative and judicial review without replacing "the discretion reposed by law in administrative agencies by the discretion of a court." Objections were mere phantoms conjured up by those who believed "that administration should be a fourth branch of government."[133] The letter permitted William King to invoke that "outstanding figure in the legal firmament," Dean Roscoe Pound, when the Senate finally took up the bill in November. "Administrative absolutism stalks triumphantly through the land," King warned. "The efforts to defend and protect the government which the founders of the Republic transmitted to us meet with strong and, too often, bitter opposition."[134]

"Government by Bureaucracy" (and Lawyers)

By lending "a great name" to the critics of the New Deal, Roscoe Pound won the enmity of a postwar generation of administrative law scholars, but he could not save the Walter-Logan bill.

Although the Senate removed some of the bill's most objectionable features, including the "clearly erroneous" standard of review, Roosevelt promptly vetoed it, and in a message drafted by Attorney General Robert H. Jackson blamed the bill on the same interests that had championed New York's antibureaucracy clause: "lawyers who desire to have all processes of government conducted through lawsuits and... interests which desire to escape regulation."[135]

Although the Senate would hold more hearings in 1941, an era in the history of the administrative state ended with Roosevelt's veto. It had commenced with the discovery by Charles Evans Hughes of the independent regulatory commission as a device for escaping patronage politics and applying expertise

SNEAKED OVER WITH 44 SENATORS ABSENT.

WEDNESDAY, NOVEMBER 27, 1940.

FIGURE 5.3 "Sneaked over with 44 Senators Absent." Daniel R. Fitzpatrick, cartoonist for the *St. Louis Post Dispatch*, published this critical view of the Walter-Logan bill on November 27, 1938.

Source: Courtesy of the State Historical Society of Missouri.

to any number of economic and social problems. Whether a public utility commission fixing the rates railroads could charge for carrying freight or a worker's compensation commission deciding when one person was in another's employ, these bodies proceeded on a case-by-case basis, mimicking the courts, whose jurisdiction over the problem they had partially ousted. Lawyers trained in the common-law tradition reflexively looked to the courts to keep administrators in check. Even in 1940, many still did. Yet by then the courts had long since concluded that close after-the-fact review of administrative fact-finding would swamp their dockets and keep agencies from doing the jobs they were created to do. The judges shifted their efforts to prescribing procedures that allowed lawyers to press their clients' cases and contest administrators' jurisdiction, as they had long done in "the ordinary courts of the land." And the agencies responded. After *Morgan*, many "judicialized" their procedures by making trial examiners more independent and their decisions more authoritative. The research monographs and the report of the Attorney General's Committee on Administrative Procedure prompted additional procedural reforms. When Congress adopted the Administrative Procedure Act in 1946, it was less a landmark "bill of rights" for the administrative state than a codification of the agencies' own best practices for formal adjudication.[136]

Performed against this backdrop, the attempt to reform federal administrative procedure in 1939–40 was a strange political drama, in which characters spouted hyperbolic dialogue that accorded poorly with the reforms they proposed. Roscoe Pound denounced "administrative absolutism" but opposed entrusting fact-finding to the ordinary courts of the land under the weight-of-the-evidence standard; with his ally on the ABA committee James Garfield, Pound wanted to see agencies adopt procedures that followed "the recognized rules that should govern Courts of first instance."[137] Congressmen warned of "bureaucrats gone mad with power," spied a rapidly approaching "totalitarian state," and likened the SEC's investigatory powers to "the tyrannies of the Gestapo of Germany, or the Russian Ogpu." Yet the final version of the bill abandoned heightened judicial review, left procedures at many agencies unchanged, and targeted the agencies that most aggressively battled big business. That sufficed for Southern Democrats and Republicans, who acted less from devotion to the rule of law than from hatred of the circle of New Dealers plotting to win Roosevelt a third term.[138]

In vetoing the Walter-Logan bill, the president complained that it would subject civilian agencies mobilizing for national defense to "endless and innumerable controversies at a moment when we can least afford to spend either governmental or private effort in the luxury of litigation."[139] Pearl Harbor opened a new chapter in the history of the administrative state, with regulation that was far more extensive and intrusive than that of the New Deal, including an "avalanche" of rule making and informal decision-making about war contracts and other public benefits. "Lawyers who had barely heard of administrative law," Arthur Vanderbilt wrote in 1942, "now met it in their offices—and in their homes."[140] Litigators did not suddenly abandon their preference for judicial over administrative tribunals, but they became far less susceptible to attempts to demonize something so familiar. Bar leaders still blustered that "government by bureaucracy is arbitrary, and actually there is no place for lawyers in it," but the practitioners themselves, who were busily helping clients negotiate a maze of wartime regulations and procedures, knew better.[141] No longer simply "officers of the court," they accepted a new role of holding America's "centralized administration" to the social rationality that they knew of as law.[142]

Conclusion

GOOD ADMINISTRATION

NOT MANY TOURISTS, I believe, list Elihu Vedder's murals in the Library of Congress among their sights to see when they visit Washington, DC. Even those who find their way to the Bibles Gallery, located on the first floor of the Thomas Jefferson Building, leave after taking in the Gutenberg Bible and the Giant Bible of Mainz. Only if they stray into the vestibule of an unused entrance to the Main Reading Room would they encounter Vedder's murals, painted just before the turn of the twentieth century. *Corrupt Legislation* has as its central figure "a woman with a beautiful but depraved face, sitting in an abandoned attitude" (as an art critic described her). The path to her throne is overgrown with weeds, "showing that under such a corrupt government the people have abandoned a direct approach to Justice." In her left hand she holds a set of scales, onto which a man is placing a sack of coins, "secure of her favors in return for his bribe." At his feet, amid more gold, lies "an overturned voting-urn, filled with ballots, signifying his corrupt control of the very sources of power." The "book of Law, which he is skilled to pervert to his own ends," sits open in his lap. Behind him is his factory, smoke billowing from its stacks, but the factory to the woman's right is still and in disrepair. Standing before it, "a poorly clad girl, representing Labor," appeals to the woman for employment but is waved away. At Elmira, Charles Evans Hughes decried official favoritism that "makes one man rich and drives another man into bankruptcy." *Corrupt Legislation* was Vedder's sexualized portrayal of the same phenomenon. Wrote the art critic: "The sleek respectability of the pious-faced briber, the slatternly wantonness of the woman he prostitutes, the mute protest of the chimney stack, the piteous appeal of the destitute haggard child—at a glance is revealed the hideous loathsomeness of the whole dirty business."[1]

FIGURE C.1 *Corrupt Legislation* (1896), by Elhu Vedder.
Source: Courtesy of the Architect of the Capitol and the Library of Congress, LC-DIG-ppmsca-07353.

Good Administration is a striking contrast. Now the central female figure is chastely robed and serene. The scales she holds in her right hand are in equipoise; her left hand rests on a shield "quartered to represent the even balance of parties and classes which should obtain in a well organized democracy." On the shield appear "emblems of a just government, the weight, scales, and rule." To her left, a handsome young man drops a ballot into a voting urn. Under his arm he carries a book, signifying that "education should be the basis of suffrage." To her right, a lovely girl winnows wheat over another voting urn, "so that the good grains fall into its mouth and the chaff is scattered." Behind them is a thriving wheatfield, "a last touch of intelligence and virtue, and in itself, symbolic of prosperous and careful toil."[2]

Taken together, the two murals suggest a response to those who, like FreedomWorks' Dick Armey and Matt Kibbe, argue that bureaucracy necessarily violates a constitution "based on private property and the rule of law" and the people's right "to simply be left alone."[3] At the dawn of the twentieth century, the alternative to commission government was not a lost realm of

FIGURE C.2 *Good Administration* (1896), by Elihu Vedder.
Source: Courtesy of the Architect of the Capitol and the Library of Congress, LC-DIG-ppmsca-07352.

individual freedom but a different political regime, in which industrialists and party bosses combined to promote their own interests. Reformers were not the only people who believed that administration would deliver them from a corrupt polity. Even the eminent corporation lawyer Elihu Root, counsel to Andrew Carnegie, considered the public utility commission as great a reform as had ever "been wrought in the public life of our country," because it ended an "old and vicious system" of legislative control.[4] Being left alone meant being left to the will of those who had already amassed economic and political power. It still does. Solicitor General Stanley Reed's warning in 1935 is still apt: "Claims of individual liberty may in reality be claims to domination over others."[5]

For all that, no one thought that Good Administration would stay good on her own. As Hughes said in 1920, "The pressing problem is how we are to adapt government to imperative needs and remain free."[6] America's poorly staffed and partisan legislatures made the *Rechtsstaat* a nonstarter, so Americans opted for what Ernst Freund called the "trial-and-error method of evolving standards."[7] At first, judges tried to review individual administrative decisions, but they soon discovered that they could not keep up with agencies' burgeoning dockets or match administrators' expertise. Judicial review had turned out to be "a pretty weak staff to lean on," Robert H. Jackson concluded in 1939. Walter Gellhorn agreed: "Judicial review of bad administrative decisions is a poor substitute for good administrative decisions in the first place."[8] Due process—Hughes's "fair play"—had intrinsic value for individuals, but it also enabled lawyers to keep administrators from self-aggrandizing, playing favorites, and resolving disputes perfunctorily. Judicializing administrative procedure also addressed the interests of two vitally interested groups. Lawyers found that expertise acquired in courts remained valuable in the new administrative state. Professional politicians realized that due process kept executives from using administrative decisions as their own form of individually targeted patronage.

Although much about how Americans govern themselves has changed since 1940, the history recounted here remains relevant in at least two ways. First, the notions of the rule of law that emerged in the early twentieth century are part of a repertoire of methods of holding administrators accountable that remains with us today.[9] For example, American liberals at last warmed to the *Rechtsstaat* in the 1960s and 1970s when Congress acquired the staff to formulate technical standards for environmental, health, and safety statutes in collaboration with public interest advocacy groups.[10] The public interest groups wanted to goad administrators into action, after regulators had become "almost the guardian angels of those they were to police."[11] Then libertarian foundations and political action committees deployed the concept against regulation. FreedomWorks, for example, challenged the Emergency Economic Stabilization Act of 2008 in court as an impermissible delegation of legislative power. The *Rechtsstaat* remains the favorite version of the rule of law of the ideological spokesmen for the Tea Party, if not the Tea Partiers themselves.[12]

With its deep roots in the common-law tradition, A. V. Dicey's rule of law has also had its enthusiasts. In the late 1960s and 1970s, for example, federal judges decided that "the Rule of Law" required them to review agencies' rulemaking more aggressively. "A court does not depart from its proper function when it undertakes a study of the record, hopefully perceptive, even as to the evidence on technical and specialized matters," Judge Harold Leventhal announced, "for this enables the court to penetrate to the underlying decisions of the agency, to satisfy itself that the agency has exercised a reasoned discretion, with reasons that do not deviate from or ignore the ascertainable legislative intent."[13] Of course, Dicey looked to judges to keep administrators from violating private rights; Leventhal, a former New Dealer, reviewed their actions to see whether they were vindicating public rights. Still, since 1970 the ordinary courts of the land have employed the "hard look" doctrine to engage in what has been, in practice, after-the-fact judicial review of the substance of administrative decisions.[14]

Dicey's rule of law has also reappeared beyond the regulatory context. After the attacks of 9/11, the United States launched a War on Terror that included the arrest and detention of suspected terrorists (some of them, US citizens) and the confinement at the American naval base in Guantánamo Bay of suspected unlawful enemy combatants captured overseas. In two decisions, issued on the same day in June 2004, the Supreme Court asserted the right of the federal judiciary to review military detentions. In *Hamdi v. Rumsfeld*, a challenge to the detention of a US citizen captured in Afghanistan but held in a naval brig in Charleston, SC, a plurality of the Court ruled that a citizen-detainee "must receive notice of the factual basis for his classification [as an enemy combatant], and a fair opportunity to rebut the Government's factual assertions before a neutral decisionmaker." In *Rasul v. Bush*, the Court also claimed for the judiciary the right to review the detention of enemy aliens captured outside the United States and detained at Guantánamo. "Even during the war on terror," the *New York Times* editorialized, "the government must adhere to the rule of law."[15] More recently, complaints that departures from normal judicial practice have kept the US Foreign Intelligence Surveillance Court from effectively policing the national security state shows that Dicey's ideal still speaks to Americans.[16]

More pervasive than either the *Rechtsstaat* or Dicey's rule of law has been a third approach to policing administrative discretion, namely, to look to the legal profession—a rule of lawyers—to keep administrators accountable. Lawyers could rely on due process to assert their authority in judicialized hearings, but because administrators so often acted informally, in proceedings that never came to a formal hearing, they also had to draw upon their long-standing role as mediators between state and society. How they conceived of that role has varied over time. In 1931, Hughes reminded government lawyers that they were not "wards of politicians" but "servants of the laws." If "true to the standards of your profession," he intoned, "you may well turn out to be the protectors of society from bureaucratic excesses." New Dealers also thought of lawyers as "professional watcher[s] of the system of power," but they were inclined to attribute their authority less to the mastery of legal principles than to their ability to fashion socially responsible resolutions of "snarled or complicated situations."[17] After New Dealers left government and founded Washington law firms to represent the businesses they used to regulate, they were inclined to see their role as ensuring that their clients' interests were taken into account in a pluralist process of policy making. In the 1960s and 1970s, "public interest" lawyers emerged to represent broader social interests that captured regulators had overlooked. Although they challenged the pluralist assumptions of their legal elders, they shared their belief that lawyers were uniquely qualified to represent social interests before the state.[18]

For a time, it seemed that economists might supplant lawyers as the dominant profession of the American state. Since the dawn of the twentieth century, Americans had used administration to address the shortcomings of unregulated markets. After the recession of 1973–74, however, business advocates argued that regulation was hurting the competitiveness of American industry and Americans rediscovered markets and market thinking.[19] The deregulation of several industries was the most dramatic result; less obvious but ultimately more pervasive was the spread of "cost-benefit analysis," the notion that regulation ought to pass a market-like test of costs and benefits. The Office of Information and Regulatory Affairs (OIRA) established during the final days of Jimmy Carter's presidency, reviewed agencies' regulations and returned those that failed for further study. One might have expected economists to have had the last word on such matters. Instead, lawyers contained the challenge to their hegemony by adding cost-benefit analysis and other forms of economic reasoning to their intellectual toolkits. Seven of OIRA's eleven administrators have had law degrees, and academic lawyers have attacked cost-benefit analysis as savagely as ever Robert Lee Hale did the *Smyth* doctrine.[20]

The history recounted here also remains relevant because it shows that the builders of the new administrative state did not succumb to alien ideologies; rather, they sought to preserve, not renounce, fundamental principles of American government. Hughes prevented commission government from evolving into socialism and corporatism; he and other judges had insisted on findings of fact on a formal record and judicialized hearings to force administrators to make their own, reasoned applications of legislative policy in ways that the affected parties could fairly contest. Of course, those threatened by the new regulatory agencies still objected that they transgressed principles that made the United States a beacon of liberty in a benighted world. Upon close inspection, however, these critics usually made their "exceptionalist" objections selectively, to defend a particular political, professional, or scholarly interest.

For example, during World War II, the Office of Price Administration (OPA), which regulated prices and rationed goods, carefully designed its hearings to comply with *Morgan*; still the ABA's president complained that, under the influence of "continental ideas," New Dealers there habitually violated "rights guaranteed to the people."[21] Popular support for the war effort carried the day while the nation was under arms, but business-financed campaigns against OPA's "bureaucratic control" prevailed in 1946.[22]

The Administrative Procedure Act of 1946 required most agencies to conduct formal hearings in line with the best practices of agencies before the war. One of the act's sponsors boasted that its safeguarding of the authority and autonomy of trial examiners was "a strongly marked, long sought, and widely heralded advance in democratic government." Yet Congress imposed a stricter separation of prosecutorial and judicial functions upon the NLRB in 1947. The board's general counsel became a presidential appointee who filed complaints without the board's approval; the NLRB itself was reduced to a mere "labor relations court." Less powerful interests had to make due with less in the way of "fair play." When the US Supreme Court directed immigration officials to extend the protections of the APA to deportation hearings, Congress promptly overturned the decision. Similarly, civil servants were hailed before loyalty-security boards drawn from the staff of their own agencies without the opportunity to learn the identity of their accusers—a practice that one lawyer likened to the procedures of the Gestapo.[23]

The pattern held for political actors and issues long after the New Deal. For example, by the start of the 1970s, the welfare rights movement persuaded courts to classify welfare benefits not as "gratuities" but "property" that could not be denied without a hearing that observed at least the fundamentals of due process.[24] The US Supreme Court's more recent assertion of judicial supremacy over Guantánamo's military commissions had its political constituencies as well. Military lawyers rallied to defend courts-martial from the challenge of a procedurally flawed rival. Diplomats who had long demanded that other nations observe human rights argued that denying detainees access to the federal courts would undermine "one of our country's most important diplomatic assets—our perceived commitment to the rule of law."[25]

The Tea Party's response to the legislative landmarks of President Barack Obama's first term brings the selective resort to exceptionalist arguments down to the present. The billionaire-funded advocacy groups FreedomWorks and Americans for Prosperity have attacked the American Recovery and Reinvestment Act, the Patient Protection and Affordable Care Act, and the Dodd-Frank Wall Street Reform and Consumer Protection Act for bringing "European-size government," "European-size taxes and a corresponding loss of liberty" to the United States.[26] The same could be said of Social Security and Medicare, and in fact, as the sociologists Theda Skocpol and Vanessa

Williamson write, the two national groups would privatize both programs and reduce "taxes on business and the wealthy." Yet few grassroots members of the Tea Party have foresworn their rights under those programs. As one confessed, "I guess I want smaller government and my Social Security."[27] Of course, many have accused President Obama of being a socialist, a Kenyan anticolonialist, or the devotee of some other foreign ideology; but, even after reading Friedrich Hayek's *Road to Serfdom*, with its forceful statement of the *Rechtsstaat* ideal, few seem ready to join the billionaires' war on discretionary federal programs that do not happen to benefit the wealthy.[28] When local Tea Parties speak of the rule of law, they do so to distinguish liberty from license, as in their pledge to uphold "the personal liberty of the individual, within the rule of law," or to add rhetorical firepower to a complaint about some exercise of discretion that they oppose on independent grounds.[29] Thus, Tea Partiers have invoked the rule of law in arguing that illegal immigrants should be deported, that President Obama ought to have sought congressional authorization before intervening in Libya in 2011, that the Department of Justice should not sell guns to Mexican drug cartels, and that the Internal Revenue Service should not target Tea Party groups when they apply for tax-exempt status.[30]

Such polemics obscure a vital fact: the American administrative state has been neither Tocqueville's nightmare nor Vedder's *Good Administration*. Its twentieth-century creators did not let the risk of misgovernment keep them from expanding the state to make life better, and they were not fooled by a vision of apolitical expertise into thinking that government would control itself. Instead, working under the particular political and professional conditions of their day, they imaginatively reworked the law they had to create the government they needed. We would do well to follow their example.

Acknowledgments

ONE MIGHT THINK, given how much time historians spend by themselves, with only their sources and their prose for company, that the writing of history is a solitary task. Historians know that it is a collective one. I owe a special debt to four scholars. As my senior colleague at the Georgetown University Law Center, Mark V. Tushnet long ago suggested that I study the legal history of the New Deal. He has since shared many insights acquired from his own study of the Chief Justiceship of Charles Evans Hughes, and his support of my work has been a continuing source of encouragement. John Mikhail assured me at a crucial moment that what I proposed to propose to publishers was in fact a book. I have turned to James Goodman for advice on writing, publishing, and life since our graduate student days; the friendship between our families has been a constant amid considerable change. Laura Kalman commented in detail on draft chapters; her scholarship has long modeled for me how to combine legal and political history; and our many exchanges at conferences and via e-mail have made being a legal historian fun. The autographed photograph of Roscoe Pound, which Pound gave her father Newton many years ago, hangs to my left as I write this. It constantly reminds me of my regard for Laura and of the collegiality of American legal historians.

I am also quite grateful for the comments of other scholars on drafts, in faculty workshops, and in the hallways of academic gatherings, including David Barron, Tomiko Brown-Nagin, Michael Ermarth, Daniel J. Gifford, Lewis Grossman, Kenneth Ledford, Renée Lettow Lerner, Victoria Nourse, William Novak, Aziz Rana, Reuel E. Schiller, John Henry Schlegel, Louis Michael Seidman, Brad Snyder, and Melvyn I. Urofsky. In addition, I benefitted greatly from careful readings of the manuscript by Barry Cushman, Alfred S. Konefsky, and an anonymous reviewer for the press. Ginny Faber improved the final draft with her expert and perceptive copyediting.

I am also indebted to Richard D. Friedman for sending me the relevant chapter of "Charles Evans Hughes as Chief Justice, 1930-1941" (PhD diss., Oxford University, 1979). Chapter 4 was inspired by Stanley N. Katz's "The Politics of Law in Colonial America: Controversies over Chancery Courts and Equity Law in the Eighteenth Century," *Perspectives in American History* 5 (1971): 485–518, and was first presented at a conference in Professor Katz's honor.

Chapter 1 first appeared as "Ernst Freund, Felix Frankfurter and the American *Rechtsstaat*: A Transatlantic Shipwreck, 1894-1932," *Studies in American Political Development* 23 (2009): 171–88. It appears here, in revised form, with permission. Chapter 4 was first published as "The Politics of Administrative Law: New York's Anti-Bureaucracy Clause and the Wagner-O'Brian Campaign of 1938," *Law and History Review* 27 (2009): 331–71. I especially thank David Tanenhaus for his editing of the article.

William E. Nelson kindly invited me to present a prototype of this book to the Golieb Research Colloquium at the New York University School of Law. I am especially grateful for the comments of Norma Basch, Richard B. Bernstein, Richard A. Epstein, Roderick Hills Jr., Daniel Hulsebosch, Deborah Malamud, Richard Pildes, and John Phillip Reid on that occasion. I am grateful for invitations to present drafts of chapters to the Cornell Law School Faculty Workshop, the Georgetown University Law Center Faculty Workshop, the George Washington University Legal History Roundtable, the Harvard Legal History Workshop, the Minnesota Legal History Workshop, the Minnesota Public Law Workshop, the NYU Legal History Workshop, the University of Pennsylvania Legal History Workshop, and the Yale Legal History Forum.

I am grateful to the following for their research assistance while students at the Georgetown University Law Center: Megan Buckley, Meghan Carr, Sterling Darling, Tucker Ewing, Owen A. McGillivray, Rita Mutyaba, Alexis Paddock, and Scott Turcotte. In addition, Carolyn L. Garner-Reagan tracked down documents for me in the Max Farrand Papers at the Huntington Library, Ross Brondfield verified John Lord O'Brian's defense of Buffalo striking clothing workers in sources at the Martin P. Catherwood Library at Cornell University, Jillian Cueller consulted records in the Registrar's Office at Columbia University, and Mary Rich of the Georgetown University Law Library tallied OIRA Administrators with legal training.

I am grateful to the following libraries, archives, and other repositories and their staff for responding to inquiries, assisting my consultation of their documents, and granting permission to refer to them here: the American Heritage

Center at the University of Wyoming (Shannon Bowen); Center for Oral History, Columbia University (Katherine Floess); Columbia Law School Library (Whitney Bagnall); Covington & Burling; the Kheel Center for Labor and Management Documentation and Archives, School of Labor Relations, Cornell University (Patrizia Sione); the Special Collections Research Center, Georgetown University Library (John Buchtel); the Harvard Law Library (Edwin Moloy, Margaret Peachy, and David Warrington), the Manuscript Division of the Library of Congress (Jeffrey Flannery, Bruce Kirby, and many others); the Massachusetts Historical Society (Sabina Beauchard and Anna J. Cook); Northwestern University Library (Kevin B. Leonard and Jim McMasters); the Rockefeller Archive Center (Erwin Levold); the Charles B. Sears Law Library, State University of New York at Buffalo (Christine Anne George and Karen L. Spencer); the Office of the Curator at the Supreme Court of the United States (Matthew Hofstedt); the Harry S. Truman Library and Museum (Sam Rushay); Special Collections Research Center, University of Chicago Library (Daniel Meyer); University of Virginia Law Library (Taylor Fitchett and M. Alison White); Special Collections and Archives, Olin Memorial Library, Wesleyan University (Jennifer Hadley); and Manuscripts and Archives, Yale University Library. For assistance in acquiring illustrations or permission to reproduce them, I thank Louis Fabian Bachrach; Jennifer Blancato, Museum Curator, Office of the Architect of the Capitol; Christine Colburn and Daniel Meyer, Special Collections Research Center, University of Chicago Library; Lesley Schoenfeld, Historical and Special Collections, Harvard Law School Library; Anne E. Cox, State Historical Society of Missouri; and the Prints and Photographs Division, Library of Congress. I am also grateful to the estate of Ida Klaus for permission to cite her oral history at Cornell's Kheel Center.

A fellowship from the John Simon Guggenheim Memorial Foundation has helped finance the research and writing of this work and a related book-in-progress. The Georgetown University Law Center, helmed by deans Judith Areen, T. Alexander Aleinikoff, and William M. Treanor, has also contributed summer writers' grants, a sabbatical leave, and a disbursement from the Reynolds Family Grant Fund. I thank both institutions for their support.

Finally, I am mindful of how little I could do without the love of my parents, Daniel P. and Ann R. Ernst; my sisters, Ellen Ernst Kossek and Ruth A. Ernst; and my children, Anna and Daniel. For the numberless, sustaining intimacies of our thirty years of marriage, I dedicate this book to Joy.

Abbreviations for Sources Consulted

MANUSCRIPT COLLECTIONS

AAA Records: Agricultural Stabilization and Conservation Service, Record Group 145, National Archives

ABA MSS: American Bar Association Microfiche Archive Collection, William S. Hein and Co., Buffalo, NY

Acheson MSS: Dean Acheson Papers, Harry S. Truman Library and Museum, Independence, MO

Arnold MSS: Thurman Wesley Arnold Papers, American Heritage Center, Laramie, WY

Baker MSS: Newton D. Baker Papers, Manuscript Division, Library of Congress

BCD Records: Bituminous Coal Division, U.S. Department of the Interior, Record Group 222, National Archives

Beck MSS: James M. Beck Papers, Department of Rare Books and Special Collections, Princeton University Library, Princeton, NJ

Brandeis MSS: Louis D. Brandeis Papers, Historical and Special Collections, Harvard Law School Library, Cambridge, MA

Butler Docket Books: Pierce Butler, Docket Books, Office of the Curator, U.S. Supreme Court

Cohen MSS: Benjamin V. Cohen Papers, Manuscript Division, Library of Congress

Commonwealth Fund MSS: Series 23, Legal Research Program, Commonwealth Fund, Rockefeller Archive Center, Sleepy Hollow, NY

Corcoran MSS: Thomas G. Corcoran Papers, Manuscript Division, Library of Congress

Cummings MSS: Homer Stille Cummings Papers, Alderman Memorial Library, University of Virginia, Charlottesville, VA

Cuneo MSS: Ernest Cuneo Papers, Franklin D. Roosevelt Library, Hyde Park, NY

Dimock MSS: Marshall E. Dimock Papers, Franklin D. Roosevelt Library, Hyde Park, NY

DOJ Records: U.S. Department of Justice, Record Group 60, National Archives

Douglas MSS: William O. Douglas Papers, Manuscript Division, Library of Congress
Dulles MSS: John Foster Dulles Papers, Princeton University Library, Princeton, NJ
Farrand MSS: Max Farrand Papers, Huntington Library, San Marino, CA
FF-HLS MSS: Felix Frankfurter Papers, Historical and Special Collections, Harvard Law School Library, Cambridge, MA
FF-LC MSS: Felix Frankfurter Papers, Manuscript Division, Library of Congress
Fisher MSS: Walter L. Fisher Papers, Manuscript Division, Library of Congress
Frank MSS: Jerome New Frank Papers, MS 222, Manuscripts and Archives, Yale University Library, New Haven, CT
Freund-E MSS: Ernst Freund Papers, Special Collections Research Center, University of Chicago Library, Chicago, IL
Freund-P MSS: Paul A. Freund Papers, Historical and Special Collections, Harvard Law School Library, Cambridge, MA
Gardner MSS: Warner W. Gardner Papers, Harry S. Truman Library and Museum, Independence, MO
Goodnow MSS: Frank Johnson Goodnow Papers, MS 3, Department of Special Collections, Sheridan Libraries, Johns Hopkins University, Baltimore, MD
Hale MSS: Robert L. Hale Papers, Columbia University Library, New York, NY
Hand MSS: Learned Hand Papers, Historical and Special Collections, Harvard Law School Library, Cambridge, MA
Hughes-Columbia MSS: Charles Evans Hughes Papers, Columbia University Library, New York, NY
Hughes-LC MSS: Charles Evans Hughes Papers, Manuscript Division, Library of Congress
Jackson MSS: Robert H. Jackson Papers, Manuscript Division, Library of Congress
Katz MSS: Milton Katz Papers, Harry S. Truman Library and Museum, Independence, MO
Keyserling MSS: Leon Keyserling Papers, Special Collections Research Center, Georgetown University Library, Washington, DC
Landis-HLS MSS: James M. Landis Papers, Historical and Special Collections, Harvard Law School Library, Cambridge, MA
Landis-LC MSS: James M. Landis Papers, Manuscript Division, Library of Congress
Levy MSS: Philip Levy Papers, Special Collections and Archives, Olin Memorial Library, Wesleyan University, Middletown, CT
Louchheim MSS: Katie S. Louchheim Papers, Manuscript Division, Library of Congress
McFarland MSS: Carl McFarland Papers, Mss 85-3, Special Collections, University of Virginia Law Library, Charlottesville, VA
Norris MSS: George W. Norris, Manuscript Division, Library of Congress
NRA Records: National Recovery Administration, Record Group 9, National Archives
NYSCC Records: New York State Constitutional Convention of 1938, New York State Archives, Albany, NY

O'Brian-B MSS: John Lord O'Brian Papers, MS 5, Special Collections, Charles B. Sears Law Library, State University of New York at Buffalo, Buffalo, NY

O'Brian-C&B MSS: John Lord O'Brian Papers, Covington & Burling, Washington, DC

Olney MSS: Richard Olney Papers, Library of Congress

Pound MSS: Roscoe Pound Papers, Historical and Special Collections, Harvard Law School Library, Cambridge, MA

PPF FDR: President's Personnel File, Franklin D. Roosevelt Library, Hyde Park, NY

Rowe MSS: James H. Rowe, Jr., Papers, Franklin D. Roosevelt Library, Hyde Park, NY

SEC Records: Securities and Exchange Commission, Record Group 266, National Archives

Stephens MSS: Harold M. Stephens Papers, Manuscript Division, Library of Congress

Stone MSS: Harlan Fiske Stone Papers, Manuscript Division, Library of Congress

USDA Records: U.S. Department of Agriculture, Record Group 19, National Archives

Vanderbilt MSS: Arthur T. Vanderbilt Papers, Olin Memorial Library, Wesleyan University, Middletown, CT

Wagner MSS: Robert F. Wagner Papers, Special Collections Research Center, Georgetown University Library, Washington, DC

Wigmore MSS: John Henry Wigmore Papers, Northwestern University Library, Evanston, IL

Wisconsin MSS: Law School General Correspondence, University Archives, Memorial Library, University of Wisconsin-Madison, Madison, WI

Wyzanski-MHS MSS: Charles E. Wyzanski, Jr., Papers, Massachusetts Historical Society, Boston, MA

ORAL HISTORIES

AJC OH: William E. Wiener Oral History Library, American Jewish Congress, Dorot Jewish Division, New York Public Library, New York, NY

COHC: Columbia University Oral History Collection, Columbia University, New York, NY

HST OH: Harry S. Truman Library and Museum, Oral History Collection, Independence, MO

NLRB OH: National Labor Relations Board Oral History Interviews, Kheel Center for Labor-Management Documentation and Archives, School of Industrial and Labor Relations, Cornell University, Ithaca, NY

NEWSPAPERS, PERIODICALS, AND OTHER PUBLICATIONS

ABAJ: *American Bar Association Journal*
ABAR: *American Bar Association Reports*
AdLR: *Administrative Law Review*
AHR: *American Historical Review*
AJCL: *American Journal of Comparative Law*
AL: *American Lawyer*

ALL:	*American Law and Lawyers*
ALR:	*American Law Review*
ALSR:	*American Law School Review*
ALReg:	*American Law Register*
AnLJ:	*Antitrust Law Journal*
APSR:	*American Political Science Review*
ARLR:	*Arkansas Law Review*
BDLJ:	*Buffalo Daily Law Journal*
BJIL:	*Brooklyn Journal of International Law*
BLR:	*Buffalo Law Review*
CarLR:	*Cardozo Law Review*
CBJ:	*Connecticut Bar Journal*
CEH:	*Central European History*
CKLR:	*Chicago-Kent Law Review*
CLQ:	*Cornell Law Quarterly*
CLR:	*Columbia Law Review*
CR:	*Congressional Record*
CT:	*Chicago Tribune*
DLJ:	*Duke Law Journal*
EHR:	*English Historical Review*
FBAJ:	*Federal Bar Association Journal*
FH:	*Forest History*
FLR:	*Fordham Law Review*
GLJ:	*Georgetown Law Journal*
GPJ:	*Great Plains Journal*
HLR:	*Harvard Law Review*
IaLR:	*Iowa Law Review*
IJE:	*International Journal of Ethics*
ILR:	*Illinois Law Review*
JAH:	*Journal of American History*
JAJS:	*Journal of the American Judicature Society*
JLPUE:	*Journal of Land and Public Utility Economics*
JMH:	*Journal of Modern History*
JPH:	*Journal of Policy History*
JSCH:	*Journal of Supreme Court History*
JSP:	*Journal of Social Philosophy*
LHR:	*Law and History Review*
LLR:	*Louisiana Law Review*
LQR:	*Law Quarterly Review*
LSI:	*Law and Social Inquiry*
MILR:	*Michigan Law Review*
MNLR:	*Minnesota Law Review*

MVHR: *Mississippi Valley Historical Review*
NCLR: *North Carolina Law Review*
NDM: *North Dakota Magazine*
NULR: *Northwestern University Law Review*
NYDN: *New York Daily News*
NYDM: *New York Daily Mirror*
NYH: *New York History*
NYHT: *New York Herald Tribune*
NYT: *New York Times*
NYTr: *New York Tribune*
NYWT: *New York World Telegram*
OHLJ: *Osgoode Hall Law Journal*
PSQ: *Political Science Quarterly*
QJ: *Quarterly Journal*
RP: *Review of Politics*
SAPD: *Studies in American Political Development*
SCR: *Supreme Court Review*
SEP: *Saturday Evening Post*
TMCLR: *Thomas M. Cooley Law Review*
UCLR: *University of Chicago Law Review*
UCiLR: *University of Cincinnati Law Review*
UMLR: *University of Miami Law Review*
UPLR: *University of Pennsylvania Law Review*
USLW: *United States Law Week*
VanLR: *Vanderbilt Law Review*
VLR: *Virginia Law Review*
WES: *Washington Evening Star*
WLR: *Wisconsin Law Review*
WP: *Washington Post*
WS: *Washington Star*
WSJ: *Wall Street Journal*
WVH: *West Virginia History*
WVLQ: *West Virginia Law Quarterly*
YLJ: *Yale Law Journal*
YR: *Yale Review*

Notes

INTRODUCTION

1. Alexis de Tocqueville, *Democracy in America*, trans. Henry Reeve (London: Longman, Green, 1862), 319–20.
2. James Bryce, *The American Commonwealth* (New York: Macmillan Co., 1888), 1:15. This is not to say that in fact Americans lacked a state in the nineteenth century or had only a "weak" one. For some time now, historians have been showing how effectively Americans governed themselves by subsidizing and delegating power to private actors and by using the federal judiciary and national political parties to order social life. Further, Americans used the national bureaucracies they did possess, not simply to deliver the mail, collect customs, distribute public land, and administer veterans' pensions, but also to pursue seemingly unrelated policies, such as regulating sexuality. Stephen Skowronek, *Building a New American State: The Expansion of National Administrative Capacities, 1877-1920* (New York: Cambridge University Press, 1982); William J. Novak, *The People's Welfare: Law and Regulation in Nineteenth-Century America* (Chapel Hill: University of North Carolina Press, 1996); William J. Novak, "The Myth of the 'Weak' American State," *AHR* 115 (2008): 752–72; Brian Balogh, *A Government Out of Sight: The Mystery of National Authority in Nineteenth-Century America* (New York: Cambridge University Press, 2009); Daniel P. Carpenter, *The Forging of Bureaucratic Autonomy: Reputations, Networks, and Policy Innovation in Executive Agencies, 1862-1928* (Princeton, NJ: Princeton University Press, 2001), 65–178; Richard R. John, *Spreading the News: The American Postal System from Franklin to Morse* (Cambridge, MA: Harvard University Press, 1995); Theda Skocpol, *Protecting Soldiers and Mothers: The Political Origins of Social Policy in the United States* (Cambridge, MA: Harvard University Press, 1992), 102–51; Kristin A. Collins, "'Petitions Without Number': Widows' Petitions and the

Early Nineteenth-Century Origins of Public Marriage-Based Entitlements," *LHR* 31 (2013): 1–60; Gautham Rao, "Administering Entitlement: Governance, Public Healthcare, and the Early American State," *LSI* 37 (2012): 627–56; Jerry L. Mashaw, *Creating the Administrative Constitution: The Lost One Hundred Years of American Administrative Law* (New Haven, CT: Yale University Press, 2012); Michele Landis Dauber, *The Sympathetic State: Disaster Relief and the Origins of the American Welfare State* (Chicago: University of Chicago Press, 2012). Only in the early twentieth century, however, did the prerogative power of administrators take on the appearance of a general and alarming fact of political life. James Willard Hurst, *The Growth of American Law: The Law Makers* (Boston: Little, Brown, 1950), 399–400.

3. William E. Leuchtenburg, *The FDR Years: On Roosevelt and His Legacy* (New York: Columbia University Press, 1995), 283–305.
4. George Sutherland, "Private Rights and Government Control," *ABAR* 40 (1917): 204; Felix Frankfurter, "The Task of Administrative Law," *UPLR* 75 (1927): 617–18.
5. Alonzo L. Hamby, *For the Survival of Democracy: Franklin Roosevelt and the World Crisis of the 1930s* (New York: Free Press, 2004).
6. *Politics*, Aristotle, trans. Benjamin Jowett (New York: Modern Library, 1943), 163; see Brian Z. Tamanaha, *On the Rule of Law: History, Politics, Theory* (New York: Cambridge University Press, 2004); Richard H. Fallon, Jr., "'The Rule of Law' as a Concept in Constitutional Discourse," *CLR* 97 (1997): 1–56; Richard A. Epstein, *Design for Liberty: Private Property, Public Administration, and the Rule of Law* (Cambridge, MA: Harvard University Press, 2011), 10–30.
7. Prohibitions del Roy, 12 Coke's Reports 63, 77 Eng. Rep. 1342 (1607).
8. Morton J. Horwitz, *The Transformation of American Law, 1870-1960: The Crisis of Legal Orthodoxy* (New York: Oxford University Press, 1992), 9–31; Elizabeth Mensch, "The History of Mainstream Legal Thought," in *The Politics of Law: A Progressive Critique*, 3d ed. David Kairys (New York: Pantheon, 1998), 23–53.
9. Cass R. Sunstein, "The Office of Information and Regulatory Affairs: Myths and Realities," *HLR* 126 (2013): 1838–78; Jonathan Turley, "The Rise of the Fourth Branch," *WP*, May 26, 2013, B1, B4–B5.
10. "The Constitution or Frame of Government for the Commonwealth of Massachusetts," part 1, section 30 (1780), in Neil H. Cogan, *Contexts of the Constitution: A Documentary Collection on Principles of American Constitutional Law* (New York: Foundation Press, 1999), 52. See also Dr. Bonham's Case, 8 Coke's Rep. 114, 77 Eng. Rep. 638 (1610); Montesquieu, *The Spirit of Laws* (Amherst, NY: Prometheus Books, 2002), 151–62.
11. Transcript of Proceedings before the Attorney General's Committee on Administrative Procedure (Division No. 2), July 10, 1940, 29, box 2, entry 385, DOJ Records.

12. National Industrial Recovery Act, Pub. L. No. 73-67, §3 (a), 68 Stat. 196 (1933).
13. [Charles Evans Hughes,] "Important Work of Uncle Sam's Lawyers," *ABAJ* 17 (1931): 237–38.
14. St. Joseph Stock Yards Co. v. United States, 298 U.S. 38, 51-52 (1936) (Hughes, C.J.).
15. The leading work documenting—and demystifying—this practice was John Dickinson's *Administrative Justice and the Supremacy of Law in the United States* (Cambridge, MA: Harvard University Press, 1927). See also Reuel E. Schiller, "The Era of Deference: Courts, Expertise, and the Emergence of New Deal Administrative Law," *MILR* 106 (2007): 399–441; and, on the vagaries of judicial interpretations of reproduction cost, Louis D. Brandeis to Felix Frankfurter, January 28, 1930, in *"Half Brother, Half Son": The Letters of Louis D. Brandeis to Felix Frankfurter*, ed. Melvin I. Urofsky and David W. Levy (Norman: University of Oklahoma Press, 1991), 409.
16. Robert L. Hale, "Does the Ghost of *Smyth v. Ames* Still Walk?" *HLR* 55 (1942): 1116–40; Bernard Schwartz, "Does the Ghost of *Crowell v. Benson* Still Walk?" *UPLR* 98 (1949): 163–82.
17. Thus, as William J. Novak has argued, law was never simply "an obstruction, a brake, an inertial force, a structural impediment, an ideological hindrance, an exceptionalist constitutional barrier to the development of a modern regulatory and administrative welfare state in the United States." It also was a blueprint for building a liberal kind of "central regulatory welfare state." William J. Novak, "The Legal Origins of the Modern American State," in *Looking Back at Law's Century*, ed. Austin Sarat, Bryant Garth, and Robert A. Kagan (Ithaca, NY: Cornell University Press, 2002), 250–51.
18. Tocqueville, *Democracy in America*, 321–31; Skowronek, *Building a New American State*, 31–34.
19. Herbert Croly, *The Promise of American Life* (New York: Macmillan Co., 1909), 136.
20. Ronen Shamir, *Managing Legal Uncertainty: Elite Lawyers in the New Deal* (Durham, NC: Duke University Press, 1995); Nicholas S. Zeppos, "The Legal Profession and the Development of Administrative Law," *CKLR* 72 (1997): 1119–57.
21. Thus, my account joins the growing literature illuminating conservative thought in the shadow of New Deal liberalism. Kim Phillips-Fein, "Conservatism: A State of the Field," *JAH* 98 (2011): 737–39; see Matthew Avery Sutton, "Was FDR the Antichrist? The Birth of Fundamentalist Antiliberalism in a Global Age," in ibid., 98 (2012): 1052–74; Kim Phillips-Fein, *Invisible Hands: The Making of the Conservative Movement from the New Deal to Reagan* (New York: W. W. Norton, 2009); James T. Sparrow, *Warfare State: World War II Americans and the Age of Big Government* (New York: Oxford University Press, 2011), 78–112; Aaron L. Friedberg, *In the Shadow of the Garrison State: America's Anti-Statism and Its Cold War Grand Strategy* (Princeton, NJ: Princeton University Press, 2000); Barry D.

Karl, *The Uneasy State: The United States from 1915 to 1945* (Chicago: University of Chicago Press, 1983); Ellis W. Hawley, "The New Deal State and the Anti-Bureaucratic Tradition," in *The New Deal and Its Legacy: Critique and Reappraisal*, ed. Robert Eden (Westport, CT: Greenwood Press, 1989), 77–92.

22. Robert T. Swaine, "Impact of Big Business on the Profession: An Answer to Critics of the Modern Bar," *ABAJ* 35 (1949): 89–92, 168–71. My account of the American legal profession's engagement with the administrative state is consistent with Terence C. Halliday and Lucien Karpik's depiction of lawyers as advocates of political liberalism, including the "moderate state." See their "Politics Matter: A Comparative Theory of Lawyers in the Making of Political Liberalism," in *Lawyers and the Rise of Western Political Liberalism: Europe and North America from the Eighteenth to Twentieth Centuries*, ed. Terence C. Halliday and Lucien Karpik (New York: Oxford University Press, 1997), 20–34.
23. Donald R. Brand, *Corporatism and the Rule of Law: A Study of the National Recovery Administration* (Ithaca, NY: Cornell University Press, 1988); Colin Gordon, *New Deals: Business, Labor, and Politics in America, 1920-1935* (New York: Cambridge University Press, 1994), 166–203; James Q. Whitman, "Of Corporatism, Fascism and the First New Deal," *AJCL* 39 (1991): 747–78.
24. "Hughes Urges Bar Aid Law Reforms," *NYT*, September 30, 1931, 22.
25. See Barry Cushman, "The Hughes Court and Constitutional Consultation," *JSCH* 1 (1998): 79–11; Daniel J. Gifford, "The New Deal Regulatory Model: A History of Criticisms and Refinements," *MNLR* 68 (1983): 307–9; Paul L. Murphy, *The Constitution in Crisis Times, 1918-1969* (New York: Harper & Row, 1972), 129.
26. Although it now must be supplemented with subsequently published work, the best entrée into the literature is Laura Kalman, "The Constitution, the Supreme Court, and the New Deal," *AHR* 110 (2005): 1052–80. See also William E. Leuchtenburg, "Comment on Laura Kalman's Article," ibid.: 1081–93; William E. Leuchtenburg, *The Supreme Court Reborn: The Constitutional Revolution in the Age of Roosevelt* (New York: Oxford University Press, 1995); Jeff Shesol, *Supreme Power: Franklin Roosevelt vs. The Supreme Court* (New York: W. W. Norton, 2010); Michael E. Parrish, "The Hughes Court, the Great Depression, and the Historians," *Historian* 40 (1978): 286–308; Michael E. Parrish, *The Hughes Court: Justices, Rulings, and Legacy* (Santa Barbara, CA: ABC-CLIO, 2002), 158–60; G. Edward White, *The Constitution and the New Deal* (Cambridge, MA: Harvard University Press, 2000); Barry Cushman, *Rethinking the New Deal Court: The Structure of a Constitutional Revolution* (New York: Oxford University Press, 1998); Richard D. Friedman, "Switching Time and Other Thought Experiments: The Hughes Court and Constitutional Transformation," *UPLR* 142 (1994): 1891–984.
27. Leuchtenburg, *Supreme Court Reborn*, 156–60; Sidney M. Milkis, *The President and the Parties: The Transformation of the American Party System since the New Deal* (New York: Oxford University Press, 1993), 74–124.

28. Theodore J. Lowi, *The End of Liberalism: Ideology, Policy, and the Crisis of Public Authority* (New York: W. W. Norton, 1969), 125–56; Joanna L. Grisinger, *The Unwieldy American State: Administrative Politics Since the New Deal* (New York: Cambridge University Press, 2012).
29. This is the historian Tony Badger's paraphrase, in "The Lessons of the New Deal: Did Obama Learn the Right Ones?" *History* 97 (2012): 103. See also Dick Armey and Matt Kibbe, *Give Us Liberty: A Tea Party Manifesto* (New York: William Morrow, 2010), 71; Theda Skocpol and Vanessa Williamson, *The Tea Party and the Remaking of Republican Conservatism* (New York: Oxford University Press, 2012), 81; Dana Milbank, *Tears of a Clown: Glen Beck and the Tea Bagging of America* (New York: Doubleday, 2010), 127–37. For contemporaneous objections to the New Deal on individualistic grounds, see James Holt, "The New Deal and the American Anti-Statist Tradition," in *The New Deal: The National Experience*, ed. John Braeman, Robert H. Bremner, and David Brody (Columbus: Ohio State University Press, 1975), 27–49.
30. Douglas H. Ginsburg, "Delegation Running Riot," *Regulation* 18 (1995): 83–84.

CHAPTER 1

1. Ernst Freund, *The Police Power: Public Policy and Constitutional Rights* (Chicago: Callahan, 1904); see Daniel T. Rodgers, *Contested Truths: Keywords in American Politics since Independence* (New York: Basic Books, 1987), 151.
2. Daniel T. Rodgers, *Atlantic Crossings: Social Politics in a Progressive Age* (Cambridge, MA: Belknap Press, 1998), 2.
3. Friedrich A. Hayek, *The Road to Serfdom* (Chicago: University of Chicago Press, 1944), 80; Friedrich Julius Stahl, *Die Philosophie des Rechts*, 3rd ed. (1856), 2:88.
4. Paul D. Carrington, "Ernst Freund," *American National Biography*, ed. John A. Garraty and Mark C. Carnes (New York: Oxford University Press, 1999), 8:470–72. Freund received a doctoral degree in law from the University of Heidelberg in 1884. Later that year, he enrolled as a nongraduate in the Columbia Law School, according to records in the Office of the Registrar at Columbia University. Jillian Cuellar to Daniel R. Ernst, October 30, 2008; *Columbia University Alumni Register, 1754-1931* (New York: Columbia University Press, 1932), 297, 1092.
5. Jane Addams, "The Friend and Guide of Social Workers," in University of Chicago, *A Vesper Service Devoted to the Memory of Ernst Freund, 1864-1932* (n.p., n.d.), 44, box 58, Wigmore MSS; Michael E. Parrish, *Felix Frankfurter and His Times* (New York: Free Press, 1982), 72–75, 81–128; William M. Wiecek, "The Legal Foundations of Domestic Anticommunism: The Background of *Dennis* v. *United States*," *SCR* 2001 (2001): 390–91.
6. Felix Frankfurter and J. Forrester Davison, *Cases and Other Materials on Administrative Law* (Chicago: Commerce Clearing House, 1932), v; Ernst Freund,

review of Frankfurter and Davison, *Cases and Other Materials on Administrative Law, HLR* 46 (1932): 167–68.

7. Parrish, *Frankfurter*, 27–61; Felix Frankfurter to Morris R. Cohen, May 17, 1914, reel 27, FF-LC MSS.
8. Pound to Freund, October 21, 1913, reel 6, Pound MSS; Freund, *Cases on Administrative Law: Selected from Decisions of English and American Courts* (St. Paul, MN: West Publishing Co., 1911), 1.
9. Kenneth F. Ledford, *From General Estate to Special Interest: German Lawyers 1878-1933* (New York: Cambridge University Press, 1996), 7–8. I am indebted to Professor Ledford for his scholarship and advice on the *Rechtsstaat* in Germany.
10. Eric Hahn, "Rudolf Gneist and the Prussian *Rechtsstaat,* 1862-78," *JMH* 49 (1977): D1363–64, D1366.
11. Kenneth F. Ledford, "Formalizing the Rule of Law in Prussia: The Supreme Administrative Law Court, 1876-1914," *CEH* 37 (2004): 203–24. See also Martina Künnecke, *Tradition and Change in Administrative Law: An Anglo-German Comparison* (Berlin: Springer, 2007), 24–25.
12. I found little on Freund's legal education in his papers at the University of Chicago. Published accounts have him studying law at the University of Berlin and Heidelberg University. He once explained that by moving from one university to another, German law students could "study Roman law with Jhering, Constitutional law with Gneist, and the History of the American Constitution with Von Holst," but he did not state that he had studied with any of them. Association of American Law Schools, *Handbook and Proceedings of the Thirty-First Annual Meeting,* 1931: 163; Ernst Freund, "The Study of Law in Germany," *The Counselor* 1 (1891): 133–34. On Freund's early scholarship, see Daniel R. Ernst, "Ernst Freund, Felix Frankfurter, and the American *Rechtsstaat*: A Transatlantic Shipwreck, 1894-1932," *SAPD* 23 (2009): 177 n. 45.
13. Arthur W. Macmahon, "Frank J. Goodnow," *Dictionary of American Biography*, supp. 1–2 (New York: Charles Scribner's Sons, 1958), 250; Frank J. Goodnow, *Comparative Administrative Law: An Analysis of the Administrative Systems, National and Local, of the United States, England, France and Germany* (New York: G.P. Putnam's Sons, 1893), vi; Ernst Freund, "The Law of the Administration in America," *PSQ* 9 (1894): 405; see also Ernst Freund, "Historical Survey," in *The Growth of American Administrative Law* (St. Louis, MO: Thomas Law Book Co., 1923), 40.
14. Freund, "Law of the Administration in America," 406–9.
15. Ibid., 421.
16. Hahn, "Gneist and the Prussian *Rechtsstaat,*" D1366; Freund, "Historical Survey," 9–10; Ernst Freund, "The Substitution of Rule for Discretion in Public Law," *APSR* 9 (1915): 670.
17. Freund, "Discussion," *Proceedings of the American Political Science Association* 6 (1909): 60. For his part, Goodnow deplored American lawyers' preference for

appeals from administrators to common-law courts. "We can do no better than endeavor to beat it into the heads of the legal profession that notwithstanding our boasted protection of private rights in this country, those rights are as a matter of fact much less protected against administrative action than they are under the system of administrative courts in vogue upon the continent of Europe," he told a gathering of political scientists (ibid., 64).

18. Freund, "Law of the Administration in America," 419, 425.
19. Act of April 30, 1892, 1892 N.Y. Laws, ch. 401, §18; People v. Grant, 126 N.Y. 473, 27 N.E. 964 (1891); Act of March 23, 1896, 1896 N.Y. Laws, ch. 112, §§17, 23, 24; see Freund, *Administrative Powers over Persons and Property: A Comparative Survey* (Chicago: University of Chicago Press, 1928), 492–93, 502.
20. Freund, "Historical Survey," 23; see also Freund, *Police Power*, 196, 677; Freund, *Cases on Administrative Law*, 70; Freund, "Substitution of Rule for Discretion," 670; Ernst Freund, "An Inquiry into Administrative Law and Practice: Memorandum Preliminary to a Survey of Statutory Administrative Powers to Determine Private Rights" (confidential proof [1923]), 55; Ernst Freund, "Licensing," *Encyclopedia of the Social Sciences* (New York: Macmillan, 1933), 9:447.
21. Freund, "Substitution of Rule for Discretion," 666; Ernst Freund, "The Substitution of Rule for Discretion in Public Law," *IJE* 25 (1914): 100–101.
22. Freund, "Historical Survey," 23.
23. Ernst Freund, "The Problem of Intelligent Legislation," *Proceedings of the American Political Science Association* 4 (1907): 70–71, 79; see Maurice T. Van Hecke, "Ernst Freund as a Teacher of Legislation," *UCLR* 1 (1933): 92–94; Arthur H. Kent, "The Work of Ernst Freund in the Field of Legislation" (ibid., 94–96).
24. Ernst Freund, "The Correlation of Work for Higher Degrees in Graduate Schools and Law Schools," *ILR* 11 (1916): 307; Ernst Freund, *Standards of American Legislation: An Estimate of Restrictive and Constructive Factors* (Chicago: University of Chicago Press, 1917); Freund to Pound, December 21, 1918, reel 6, Pound MSS.
25. Freund, "Substitution of Rule for Discretion" (1914), 100; Freund, "Substitution of Rule for Discretion" (1915), 666–67, 669, 671, 675.
26. Freund, "Substitution of Rule for Discretion" (1915), 669, 670, 675–76.
27. Freund, "Historical Survey," 22–23; Freund, "Substitution of Rule for Discretion" (1914), 102.
28. "Commonwealth Fund," *NYT*, July 17, 1921, 72; Commonwealth Fund, *Second Annual Report of the General Director for the Year 1919-20*; "Samuel Herbert Fisher," in Charles Hitchcock Sherrill, comp., *Yale College Class of '89 Quindecennial* (New York, 1904), 90; "Lion Award Made to George Murray," *NYT*, December 5, 1937, 61; Henry H. Klein, *Dynastic America and Those Who Own It* (New York, 1921), 62–63, 139.
29. Samuel H. Fisher to Max Farrand, September 2, 1919, box 9, and Barry G. Smith to Farrand, April 6, 1925, box 3, Farrand MSS.

30. Stone later spoke to Farrand of "his original proposition" and "our main purpose" in creating the administrative law project. "Administrative Practices: Conferences with Dean Stone," December 7, 1921, box 2, and Harlan Fiske Stone to Farrand, February 5, 1925, box 6, series 23, Commonwealth Fund MSS. Neither Powell nor Parkinson joined the project. See Ernst, "American *Rechtsstaat*," 176.
31. I discuss these writings in Chapter 5.
32. Farrand omitted Stone's warning that if reform was not the result of "scientific scholarship," it would be the product of "the politician and the agitator." Columbia University, *Annual Reports of the President and Treasurer to the Trustees with Accompanying Documents for the Year Ending June 30, 1916* (New York, 1916), 59–60; "Legal Research: Presented to the Directors at a Meeting on 6-26-20," box 3, Commonwealth Fund MSS.
33. Roscoe Pound, "The Pioneers and the Common Law," *WVLQ* 27 (1920): 1–19. We will return to Pound's account of "the formative era of American law" in chapter 5.
34. Farrand, "Legal Research."
35. Ibid.
36. Freund to Frank J. Goodnow, November 11, 1903, box 6, Goodnow MSS; Freund, *Cases on Administrative Law*. See William C. Chase, *The American Law School and the Rise of Administrative Government* (Madison: University of Wisconsin Press, 1982), 72–73.
37. "Preliminary Memorandum Concerning the Plan for an Inquiry into Administrative Practices Affecting Private Rights," box 2, "Meeting of the Legal Research Committee at the Bar Association, Monday, July 11, 1921, at 10 o'clock," box 3, Commonwealth Fund MSS.
38. Evidently, Pound served with misgivings. "I don't like this business—but don't dare get out of it," he explained to Felix Frankfurter. "God knows what they'll do if some of us don't keep in." Handwritten note on Farrand to Frankfurter, August 31, 1921, reel 81, FF-LC MSS.
39. Benjamin Cardozo in *Handbook of the Association of American Law Schools and Proceedings of the Nineteenth Annual Meeting, Held at Chicago, Illinois, December 29-31, 1921*, 119, quoted in N.E.H. Hull, "Restatement and Reform: A New Perspective on the Origins of the American Law Institute," *LHR* 8 (1990): 73.
40. Fisher was also a partner in a major Chicago law firm. "Meeting of the Legal Research Committee"; Robert S. LaForte, "Walter Lowrie Fisher," *American National Biography* (New York: Oxford University Press, 1999), 8:21–23; Alan B. Gould, "'Trouble Portfolio' to Constructive Conservation: Secretary of the Interior Walter L. Fisher, 1911-1913," *FH* 16 (1973): 4–12; Maureen A. Flanagan, *Charter Reform in Chicago* (Carbondale: Southern Illinois University Press, 1987), 45; Oscar Kraines, *The World and Ideas of Ernst Freund: The Search for General Principles of Legislation and Administrative Law* (Tuscaloosa: University of Alabama Press, 1964), 4, 130–32. Farrand asked Charles Evans Hughes to serve, but Hughes declined in light of

his impending appointment as secretary of state. He became a member of the Legal Research Committee in 1926. Farrand to Charles Evans Hughes, October 21, 1926, and Hughes to Farrand, November 6, 1926, box 2, Hughes-Columbia MSS.

41. George Welwood Murray to Farrand, August 26, 1921, box 1, and Farrand to Murray, August 23, 1921, Commonwealth Fund MSS. Murray considered intervening when Sharfman criticized a railroad reorganization in which he had a part, but Learned Hand, appointed to the Legal Research Committee in 1930, talked him out of it. Murray to Hand, February 14, 1935, box 125, and Hand to Murray, February 18, 1935, box 58, Hand MSS.
42. Harold Laski to Oliver Wendell Holmes, Jr., September 5, 1917, quoted in Parrish, *Frankfurter*, 82; see ibid., 22, 26–128.
43. Freund to Farrand, November 1, 1921, box 2, Commonwealth Fund MSS.
44. [Ernst Freund] "Suggestions of a Working Plan for the Proposed Inquiry into Administrative Law and Practice under the Auspices of the Commonwealth Fund," 5–6, n.d., box 2, Commonwealth Fund MSS.
45. Freund to Farrand, December 5, 1921, box 2, Commonwealth Fund MSS.
46. Freund, *Jurisprudence and Legislation* (n.p., [1904]), 1, 2.
47. Morris R. Cohen, "A Critical Sketch of Legal Philosophy in America," in *Law: A Century of Progress, 1835-1935*, ed. Alison Reppy (New York: New York University Press, 1937), 2:316–17; Freund, "Suggestions of a Working Plan," 13.
48. Frankfurter to Freund, December 10, 1921, reel 82, FF-LC MSS.
49. Farrand to Frankfurter, December 14, 22, 1921, reel 81, FF-LC MSS; Farrand to Freund, December 7, 1921, box 2, Commonwealth Fund MSS.
50. "Administrative Practices: On Friday, December 30, 1921," n.d., box 2, Freund to James Parker Hall, January 4, 1922, Commonwealth Fund MSS; "The Three Days Conference Developed the Following," n.d., box 5, Freund-E MSS.
51. Felix Frankfurter, "Memo of Conference at Chicago, Dec. 31, 1921 and January 1st, 1922," n.d., reel 81, FF-LC MSS; Freund, "Memorandum regarding meeting at New Haven, May 11/22, and conferences in Baltimore and Washington May 13, 15 and 16," n.d., box 5, Freund-E MSS. On Frankfurter's graduate seminar in administrative law, see Frankfurter to William D. Guthrie, December 22, 1922, reel 18, part 13, FF-HLS MSS.
52. Frankfurter to Farrand, January 4, 1922, box 2, Commonwealth Fund MSS; Frankfurter to Farrand, February 14, 1924, reel 82, FF-LC MSS.
53. Freund, "Comment on Frankfurter's Letter of Jan. 4," n.d., box 5, Freund-E MSS.
54. Freund to Frankfurter, May 19, July 5, 1922, reel 81, FF-LC MSS.
55. Edwin Wilhite Patterson, *The Insurance Commissioner in the United States: A Study in Administrative Law and Practice* (Cambridge, MA: Harvard University Press, 1927); William C. Van Vleck, *The Administrative Control of Aliens: A Study in Administrative Law and Procedure* (New York: Commonwealth Fund, 1927). Bontecou's failure to complete her study after the Commonwealth Fund invested

$16,000 in it apparently poisoned the Fund's relations with Frankfurter after 1930. Barry C. Smith, "Report to the Legal Research Committee," May 2, 1931, and Smith to Hand, May 20, 1932, box 125, Hand MSS.

56. I. L. Sharfman to Frankfurter, April 8, 1930, reel 82, FF-LC MSS; Max Lowenthal to Frankfurter, April 13, 1930, and Barry C. Smith, "Interview with Mr. I. L. Sharfman," April 24, 1930, box 6, Commonwealth Fund MSS.
57. "Gerard C. Henderson, Lawyer, Dies at 36," *NYT*, September 1, 1927, 23; *HLR* 41 (1927): 69–70; Gerard C. Henderson to Frankfurter, n.d., reel 40, FF-LC MSS; Parrish, *Frankfurter*, 108, 120; Merlo Pusey, *Eugene Meyer* (New York: Knopf, 1974), 142, 178.
58. Henderson to Frankfurter, September 15, 1923, reel 40, FF-LC MSS; Frankfurter to Farrand, October 4, 1923, box 6, Commonwealth Fund MSS.
59. Marc Winerman and William E. Kovacic, "Outpost Years for a Start-up Agency: The FTC from 1921-1925," *AnLJ* 77 (2010): 145–203; G. Cullom Davis, "The Transformation of the Federal Trade Commission, 1914-1929," *MVHR* 49 (1962): 437–55.
60. Henderson to Frankfurter, September 7, 1922, reel 40, FF-LC MSS; Henderson to Farrand, February 27, 1924, box 6, Commonwealth Fund MSS; Gerard C. Henderson, *The Federal Trade Commission: A Study in Administrative Law and Procedure* (New Haven, CT: Yale University Press, 1924), 334–37.
61. Walter L. Fisher to Freund, March 13, 1924, box 5, Fisher MSS; Helen M. Deane to Farrand, November 11, 1925; Frankfurter to Farrand, April 29, 1924; Farrand to Deane, March 12, 1925; and Freund to Farrand, October 27, 1924, box 6, Commonwealth Fund MSS.
62. Henderson to Farrand, March 6, 1924, May 12, 1925, and Pound to Farrand, March 13, 1924, Frankfurter to Farrand, April 19, 1923, box 6, Commonwealth Fund MSS; George Rublee, review of Henderson, *The Federal Trade Commission*, *HLR* 38 (1924): 269.
63. James M. Landis to Sam Rayburn, December 13, 1933, box 9, Landis-HLS MSS. Landis invoked Henderson twice in his influential lectures, *The Administrative Process* (1938; New Haven, CT: Yale University Press, 1966), 41, 87. See also Louis L. Jaffe, "Invective and Investigation in Administrative Law," *HLR* 52 (1939): 1244.
64. Frankfurter to Farrand, January 25, 1924, box 6, Commonwealth Fund MSS. Frankfurter would similarly aggrandize on behalf of the "physiological study of administrative law in action," even as he bowed to "the pioneer scholarship of Frank J. Goodnow and Ernst Freund," in his introduction to Patterson's *Insurance Commissioner in the United States*, xiii, xvii, and "The Task of Administrative Justice," *UPLR* 75 (1927): 614–21.
65. Freund, "Administrative Law and Practice Report for 1924-25," reel 81, FF-LC MSS; Freund to Frankfurter, March 12, 1923, box 5, Freund-E MSS.
66. Freund to Frankfurter, March 7, 1927, box 7, Commonwealth Fund MSS; Freund to Farrand, May 1, 1925, box 2, Commonwealth Fund MSS.

67. William A. Robson, *LQR* 49 (1933): 177.
68. Farrand, "Outline of Points to Take Up with Regard to Freund's Statutory Survey," n.d., box 7, Commonwealth Fund MSS; Pound to Farrand, November 24, 1926, box 3, Commonwealth Fund MSS.
69. Farrand to Frankfurter, February 24, 1927, and Pound to Farrand, March 1, 24, 1927, box 7, Commonwealth Fund MSS.
70. Frankfurter to Freund, March 9, 1927, box 7, Commonwealth Fund MSS; Farrand to Samuel H. Fisher, April 1927, box 1, Commonwealth Fund MSS.
71. Freund, *Administrative Powers*, 59–60, 580–82.
72. Ibid., 98–99, 101, 29.
73. Keller, *Regulating a New Economy*, 62–65; Felix Frankfurter, *The Public and Its Government* (New Haven, CT: Yale University Press, 1930), 81–122.
74. Freund, *Administrative Powers*, 102, 582–83, 59, 581.
75. Farrand, "Outline of Points."
76. Edwin W. Patterson, review of Freund, *Administrative Powers over Persons and Property*, *CLR* 29 (1929): 104, 105, quoting Lochner v. New York, 198 U.S. 45, 74 (1905) (Holmes, J., dissenting).
77. John Dickinson, review of Freund, *Administrative Powers over Persons and Property*, *APSR* 22 (1928): 985.
78. Farrand to Pound, March 26, 1927, box 3, Commonwealth Fund MSS; George Welwood Murray to Edward S. Harkness, June 28, 1927, box 21, Hughes-Columbia MSS.
79. Frankfurter, *Public and Its Government*, 151, 158, 159; Felix Frankfurter, "Gentlemen, we shall consider in this course," September 28, 1914, 4, part 3, reel 21, FF-HLS MSS; student notes of Frankfurter's seminar on administrative law, 49, box 153, Corcoran MSS; Frankfurter and Davison, *Administrative Law*, vii-viii. Similarly, John Henry Wigmore, dean of Northwestern's law school, argued that "the bestowal of administrative discretion, as contrasted with the limitation of power by a meticulous chain-work of inflexible detailed rules, is the best hope for governmental efficiency." John H. Wigmore, "The Dangers of Administrative Discretion," *ILR* 19 (1925): 441.
80. Woodrow Wilson, "Law or Personal Power," *The Public Papers of Woodrow Wilson*, ed. Ray Stannard Baker and William E. Dodd, 6 vols. (New York: Harper Bros., 1925–27), 2:25, 28, quoted in Michael Les Benedict, "Law and Regulation in the Gilded Age and Progressive Era," in *Law as Culture and Culture as Law: Essays in Honor of John Phillip Reid*, ed. Hendrik Hartog and William E. Nelson (Madison, WI: Madison House, 2000), 258–59, 260.
81. Richard L. McCormick, *The Party Period and Public Policy: American Politics from the Age of Jackson to the Progressive Era* (New York: Oxford University Press, 1986), 311–56; Martin Shefter, *Political Parties and the State: The American Historical Experience* (Princeton, NJ: Princeton University Press, 1994), 36–51. Perhaps Freund's own successes in drafting and lobbying for reform legislation explain why he did not

give up on legislatures. Steven J. Diner, *A City and Its Universities: Public Policy in Chicago, 1892-1919* (Chapel Hill: University of North Carolina Press, 1980), 130–31, 138–39, 142, 147, 156, 158, 165; Thomas R. Pegram, *Partisans and Progressives: Private Interest and Public Policy in Illinois, 1870-1922* (Urbana: University of Illinois Press, 1992), 75, 82, 97, 117; Kent, "Work of Ernst Freund," 95–96.

82. McCormick, *Party Period and Public Policy*, 305–6; Richard Olney to Charles E. Perkins, December 26, 1892, reel 47, Olney MSS.
83. Bruce W. Dearstyne, "Regulation in the Progressive Era: The New York Public Service Commission," *NYH* 58 (1977): 331–47; Martin J. Schiesl, *The Politics of Efficiency: Municipal Administration and Reform in America, 1800-1920* (Berkeley: University of California Press, 1977), 190–91.
84. Louis L. Jaffe, "The Illusion of Ideal Administration," *HLR* 86 (1973): 1185; Kenneth Culp Davis, *Administrative Law* (St. Paul, MN: West Publishing Co., 1951), 38.
85. Felix Frankfurter, review of *The Growth of American Administrative Law*, *HLR* 37 (1924): 640–41.

CHAPTER 2

1. *The Autobiographical Notes of Charles Evans Hughes*, ed. David J. Danelski and Joseph S. Tulchin (Cambridge, MA: Harvard University Press, 1973), 141.
2. "Hughes Sees 'Test' in Federal Boards," *NYT*, October 31, 1930, 33. I learned of this source from Richard D. Friedman's "Charles Evans Hughes as Chief Justice, 1930–1941" (PhD diss., Oxford University, 1979), ch. 4, p. 4.
3. Charles Evans Hughes, "Speech before the Elmira Chamber of Commerce, May 3, 1907," in *Addresses of Charles Evans Hughes, 1906-1916*, 2nd ed. (New York: Putnam's Sons, 1916), 187.
4. Ibid., 186.
5. Harold Greville Hanbury, *The Vinerian Chair and Legal Education* (Oxford: Basil Blackwell, 1958): 100; Felix Frankfurter, "Foreword," *YLJ* 47 (1938): 517; see Richard A. Cosgrove, *The Rule of Law: Albert Venn Dicey, Victorian Jurist* (Chapel Hill: University of North Carolina Press, 1980), 66–102; H. W. Arthurs, "Rethinking Administrative Law: A Slightly Dicey Business," *OHLJ* 17 (1979): 1–45.
6. Albert Venn Dicey, *Lectures Introductory to the Study of the Law of the Constitution* (London: Macmillan, 1885), 172, 177–78, 208, 215–16.
7. Dicey, *Law of the Constitution*, 187, 189–90, 199–200.
8. Prohibitions del Roy, 12 Coke's Reports 63, 77 Eng. Rep. 1342 (1607). See Roland G. Usher, "James I and Sir Edward Coke," *EHR* 18 (1903): 664–75; John Baker, "The Common Lawyers and the Chancery: 1616," in *Law, Liberty, and Parliament: Selected Essays on the Writings of Sir Edward Coke* (Indianapolis, IN: Liberty Fund, 2004), 255–56.
9. Dicey, *Law of the Constitution*, 204, 205, 207–8.

10. Felix Frankfurter, "Foreword: Courts and Administrative Law: The Experience of English Housing Legislation," *HLR* 49 (1936): 427. The Harvard law professor Bruce Wyman summarized Dicey on the *droit administratif* in the opening pages of *Principles of the Administrative Law Governing the Relations of Public Officers* (St. Paul, MN: Keefe-Davidson Co., 1903), 1–2; see also John Dickinson, "Administrative Law and the Fear of Bureaucracy—I," *ABAJ* 14 (1928): 514.
11. Elihu Root, "Individual Liberty and the Responsibility of the Bar," January 15, 1916, *Addresses on Government and Citizenship*, ed. Robert Bacon and James Brown Scott (Cambridge, MA: Harvard University Press, 1916), 516.
12. *CR* 51 (July 30, 1914): 12985–86; George Sutherland, "Private Rights and Government Control," *ABAR* 40 (1917): 204–7.
13. Quoted in Alexander M. Bickel and Benno C. Schmidt, Jr., *The Judiciary and Responsible Government, 1910-1921* (New York: Macmillan, 1984), 619. Bickel found the quotation in an unsigned memorandum in Louis Brandeis's file on *Ohio Valley Water Co.* v. *Ben Avon Borough*, 253 U.S. 287 (1920), and attributed it to Acheson, Brandeis's only legal secretary that term.
14. Robert H. Jackson, "The Administrative Process," *JSP* 5 (1940): 146–47.
15. G. Edward White, "Allocating Power between Agencies and Courts: The Legacy of Justice Brandeis," *DLJ* 1974 (1974): 213–15.
16. John J. Burns to Dean Acheson, April 16, 1940, box 2, Acheson MSS.
17. Charles Evans Hughes, "The Shrine of the Common Law," in *The Pathway of Peace: Representative Addresses during His Term as Secretary of State (1921-1925)* (New York: Harper & Brothers, 1925), 208–9. On this occasion, not simply the venue (Westminster Hall), but also presidential candidate Robert La Follette's recent attacks on judicial review spurred Hughes to Diceyan heights. See William G. Ross, *A Muted Fury: Populists, Progressives and Labor Unions Confront the Courts, 1890–1937* (Princeton, NJ: Princeton University Press, 1994), 193–217, 254–84.
18. Daniel T. Rodgers, "Living without Labels," *LHR* 24 (2006): 176–77.
19. "The Reminiscences of John Lord O'Brian" (1952), 331, COHC; Hughes, *Autobiographical Notes*, xiii, 26; Merlo J. Pusey, *Charles Evans Hughes* (New York: Macmillan, 1951), 1:70–73, 81–82, 116.
20. William R. Castle, Jr., quoted in Pusey, *Hughes*, 2:610; Edwin McElwain, "The Business of the Supreme Court as Conducted by Chief Justice Hughes," *HLR* 63 (1949): 9; Burton J. Hendrick, "Governor Hughes," *McClure's Magazine* 30 (1908): 527.
21. [Charles Evans Hughes,] "Important Work of Uncle Sam's Lawyers," *ABAJ* 17 (1931): 237, quoting George Santayana, *Character and Opinion in the United States* (New York: Charles Scribner's Sons, 1920), 117-18.
22. "Charles Evans Hughes," *American Lawyer* 16 (October 1906): 470; see James F. Simon, *FDR and Chief Justice Hughes: The President, the Supreme Court, and the Epic Battle over the New Deal* (New York: Simon & Schuster, 2012), 26–38; Pusey,

Hughes, 1:132–68, 221; Jonathan Levy, *Freaks of Fortune: The Emerging World of Capitalism and Risk in America* (Cambridge, MA: Harvard University Press, 2012), 286–88.

23. In the same spirit, in July 1906, two Harvard law professors urged that rate regulation, the "conservative" way to control railroads "for the good of the whole people," be given a fair trial "that we may not be driven to the radical alternative of public ownership." Joseph Henry Beale and Bruce Wyman, *The Law of Railroad Rate Regulation with Special Reference to American Legislation* (Boston: William J. Nagel, 1907), iv–v. On Hughes's gubernatorial nomination and campaign, see Robert F. Wesser, *Charles Evans Hughes: Politics and Reform in New York, 1905-1910* (Ithaca, NY: Cornell University Press, 1967), 70–101; Hendrick, "Governor Hughes," 536.
24. John Lord O'Brian, "Charles Evans Hughes as Governor," *ABAJ* 27 (1941): 413.
25. "Governor Hughes Flays John B. Stanchfield," *Elmira Daily Advertiser*, May 4, 1907, 1.
26. Hughes, "Speech before the Elmira Chamber of Commerce," 179–80 (emphasis supplied).
27. *Revised Record of the Constitutional Convention of the State of New York, April Sixth to September Tenth, 1915* (Albany, NY, 1916), 3:3101–2.
28. Hughes, "Speech before the Elmira Chamber of Commerce," 185–87.
29. Ibid., 186; Charles Evans Hughes, "Speech at the Banquet of the Utica Chamber of Commerce, April 1, 1907," *Addresses*, 154–55, 157.
30. Some caveats are in order. Until the first decades of the twentieth century, administrative law existed not as a recognized legal category but as "a hodgepodge of different statutes and common-law doctrines." Reuel E. Schiller, "The Era of Deference: Courts, Expertise, and the Emergence of New Deal Administrative Law," *MILR* 106 (2007): 407. Further, even Dicey would have required full judicial review only when private rights were at stake. Because much administrative action, such as the distribution of public lands, involved "public" benefits, courts could and did refuse to review bureaucrats' decisions regarding them. Even in cases involving private rights, courts might engage in more deferential review when a statute so provided or when review was by the writ of certiorari, which was available in state but not federal courts. The law professor Thomas Merrill concludes that these instances were islands of deference in "a sea of de novo review," but the matter remains controversial. Thomas W. Merrill, "Article III, Agency Adjudication, and the Origins of the Appellate Review Model of Administrative Law," *CLR* 111 (2011): 949; cf. Ann Woolhandler, "Judicial Deference to Administrative Action: A Revisionist History," *AdLR* 43 (1991): 197–245; Jerry L. Mashaw, "Rethinking Judicial Review of Administrative Action: A Nineteenth Century Perspective," *CarLR* 32 (2001): 2245–48; Jerry L. Mashaw, *Creating the Administrative Constitution: The Lost One Hundred Years of Administrative Law* (New Haven, CT: Yale University Press, 2012), 65–78, 112–14, 136–37, 210–18, 245–49.

31. Ernst Freund, *Administrative Powers over Persons and Property* (Chicago: University of Chicago Press, 1928), 556; Woolhandler, "Judicial Deference," 207–8.
32. Roscoe Pound, "Justice according to Law," *CLR* 14 (1914): 12–13; Felix Frankfurter, Administrative law notes, 80–81, box 153, Corcoran MSS.
33. ICC, *Eleventh Annual Report* (1897): 31, 51; *CR* 40 (May 15, 1906): 6889; ICC v. Alabama Midland Railway Co., 168 U.S. 144, 176 (1897) (Harlan, J., dissenting).
34. The Hepburn Act also empowered the commission to fix a just and reasonable maximum rate for the future. This overturned *ICC v. Cincinnati, New Orleans & Texas Pacific Railway Co.*, 167 U.S. 479 (1897), which had limited the commission to the "judicial" function of declaring an existing rate unreasonable.
35. *CR* 40 (February 28, 1906): 3118 (Joseph B. Foraker), quoted in White, "Legacy of Justice Brandeis," 202.
36. *CR* 40 (May 15, 1906): 6685–86, quoted in Merrill, "Appellate Review Model," 958. See Robert Harrison, *Congress, Progressive Reform, and the New American State* (New York: Cambridge University Press, 2004), 58–70.
37. ICC v. Illinois Central Railroad Co., 215 U.S. 452, 470 (1910). See Robert B. Highsaw, *Edward Douglass White: Defender of the Conservative Faith* (Baton Rouge: Louisiana State University Press, 1981), 98–100.
38. ICC v. Union Pacific Railroad Co., 222 U.S. 541, 547 (1912); ICC v. Louisville & Nashville Railroad Co., 227 U.S. 88, 91–92 (1913).
39. *Union Pacific*, 222 U.S. at 547.
40. *Louisville & Nashville*, 227 U.S. at 93–94.
41. *Union Pacific*, 222 U.S. at 547–48. See also Atchison, Topeka & Santa Fe Railway Co. v. United States, 232 U.S. 199, 220–21 (1914) (Lamar, J.). "Scintilla of proof" was a reference to a standard that strictly limited trial judges' ability to direct verdicts. Robert Wyness Millar, *Civil Procedure of the Trial Court in Historical Perspective* (New York: Law Center of the New York University, 1952), 307.
42. Charles Evans Hughes, "Some Aspects of the Development of American Law: An Address before the New York State Bar Association, January 14, 1916," *Addresses*, 335–37, 358–59.
43. Minnesota Rate Cases, 230 U.S. 352 (1913); see also Missouri Rate Cases, 230 U.S. 474 (1913); Allen v. St. Louis, Iron Mountain & Southern Railway Co., 230 U.S. 553 (1913); Chesapeake & Ohio Railway Co. v. Conley, 230 U.S. 513 (1913); Louisville & Nashville Railroad Co. v. Garrett, 231 U.S. 298 (1913).
44. Justice Joseph McKenna concurred without writing separately.
45. Pusey, *Hughes*, 1:304–7. Pitney's comment was on the draft of Hughes's opinion in *Allen*, reproduced on reel 135, Hughes-LC MSS.
46. *Minnesota Rate Cases*, 230 U.S. at 433, quoting San Diego Land & Town Co. v. Jasper, 189 U.S. 439, 446 (1903).
47. John H. Gray and Jack Levin, *The Valuation and Regulation of Public Utilities* (New York: Harper & Brother, 1933), 74.

48. *Minnesota Rate Cases*, 230 U.S. at 433, 434, 450–51. I discuss the *Smyth* doctrine at greater length below.
49. *Id.* at 434, 452–53, 456–57, 466. See Bickel and Schmidt, *Judiciary and Responsible Government*, 254–64.
50. For an expansive understanding of jurisdictional facts, see Bruce Wyman, "Jurisdictional Limitations upon Commissions," *HLR* 27 (1913): 545–69; William C. Chase, *The American Law School and the Rise of Administrative Government* (Madison: University of Wisconsin Press, 1982), 91–94.
51. ICC v. Northern Pacific Railway Co., 216 U.S. 538, 543–44 (1910).
52. Garrett, 231 U.S. at 311–14.
53. E. J. Babcock, *Report of the Geological Survey of North Dakota* (Grand Forks, ND: Herald, 1901), 78; see Alver W. Carlson, "Lignite Coal as an Enabling Factor in the Settlement of Western North Dakota," *GPJ* 11 (1972): 145–53; "Mineral Resources of North Dakota," *NDM* 1 (September 18, 1906): 13–16; Earle J. Babcock, "The Economic Utilization of Lignite Coal," *QJ* 1 (1911): 193–213.
54. Brief for Defendant in Error, 42–46, 5–8, Northern Pacific Railway Co. v. North Dakota, 236 U.S. 585 (1915), *Supreme Court Records and Briefs.*
55. Hughes, "Veto of the Two-Cent Fare Bill," June 11, 1907, in *Addresses,* 195; Allen v. St. Louis, Iron Mountain & Southern Railway Co., 230 U.S. 553 (1913). See Barry Friedman, "The Story of *Ex parte Young*: Once Controversial, Now Canon," in *Federal Courts Stories*, ed. Vicki C. Jackson and Judith Resnik (New York: Foundation Press, 2010), 259–64.
56. Northern Pacific Railway Co. v. North Dakota, 236 U.S. 585, 597 (1915).
57. *Id.* at 599, 598.
58. Morton Keller, *Regulating a New Economy: Public Policy and Economic Change in America, 1900-1933* (Cambridge, MA: Harvard University Press, 1990), 43–65.
59. Morton Keller, *America's Three Regimes: A New Political History* (New York: Oxford University Press, 2007), 192, 190. See David M. Kennedy, *Over Here: The First World War and American Society* (New York: Oxford University Press, 2004); Ajay K. Mehrotra, *Making the Modern American Fiscal State: Law, Politics, and the Rise of Progressive Taxation, 1877-1929* (New York: Cambridge University Press, 2013), 293–348.
60. "The Busy Barrister," *NYTr*, August 19, 1917, D6; Charles E. Hughes, "War Powers and the Constitution," *ABAR* 40 (1917): 240, 247, 241, 232; see Pusey, *Hughes*, 2:367–75.
61. Charles Evans Hughes, "The Republic after the War," *ALR* 53 (1919): 674–75.
62. "End War Policies Now, Says Hughes," *NYT*, December 1, 1918, 19; see Pusey, *Hughes*, 1:375–78.
63. Hughes, "Republic after the War," 670–71.
64. Charles Evans Hughes, "Some Observations on Legal Education and Democratic Progress," *Two Addresses Delivered before the Alumni of the Harvard Law*

School at Cambridge, June 21, 1920 (Boston: Harvard Law School Association [1920]), 32–33.

65. Hughes, "Republic after the War," 672; Hughes, "Some Observations," 33.
66. On the ICC's trial examiners, see Lloyd D. Musolf, *Federal Examiners and the Conflict of Law and Administration* (1953; Westport, CT: Greenwood Press, 1979), 47–52; I. L. Sharfman, *The Interstate Commerce Commission: A Study in Administrative Law and Procedure* (New York: Commonwealth Fund, 1937), 4:73–74.
67. Hughes, "Some Observations," 33; Learned Hand to George Welwood Murray, June 2, 1931, box 125, Hand MSS; Henry L. Stimson to John Foster Dulles, December 2, 1938, reel 3, Dulles MSS; "Remarks of the Honorable Thomas D. Thacher, former Solicitor General of the United States, at the dinner of the American Judicature Society, Washington, D.C., Wednesday Evening, May 9th, 1934," box 62, Hand MSS. See Felix Frankfurter, "The Business of the Supreme Court of the United States," *HLR* 39 (1926): 589–93; J. Gilmer Kroner, "The United States Board of Tax Appeals," *ABAJ* 11 (1925): 642–44. I have not discovered Hughes's opinion of the US Commerce Court, on which, during its short life, specially appointed Article III judges heard appeals from the ICC. See Frankfurter, "Business of the Supreme Court," 549–615.
68. Hughes, "Republic after the War," 671–72.
69. Max Farrand to Charles Evans Hughes, October 21, 1926; Hughes to Farrand, November 6, 1926, box 2; and Minutes of the Legal Research Committee, May 12, 1928, box 21, Hughes-Columbia MSS. As I discuss in chapter 3, Hughes would himself pass judgment on these programs in *Crowell v. Benson*, 285 U.S. 222 (1932); *St. Joseph Stock Yards Co. v. United States*, 298 U.S. 28 (1936); and *Morgan v. United States*, 298 U.S. 468 (1936). The knotty issue of expatriation presented Secretary of State Hughes with the chance to act on his views of administrative procedure. Under existing law, a naturalized citizen who left the United States to reside overseas could be declared to have lacked the requisite intent to become a permanent citizen of the United States or, alternately, to have voluntarily renounced his American citizenship. Hughes might have left the determination of these facts to consular officials overseas, but he knew that these administrators would be quick to resolve the case against the "international chamaeleon," who often embroiled American diplomats in "vexatious controversies with foreign governments." Rather than let the officer assume "the prerogative of a court of justice," Hughes ordered the file sent to the department's chief legal advisor, the able and scholarly Charles Cheney Hyde. Perhaps Hyde was thinking of expatriation when he wrote of Hughes, "Bureaucracy was repulsive to him; and to his mind it assumed a hideous form whenever it enabled or encouraged administrative officers to invade the right of the individual to law itself." Richard W. Flourney, Jr., "Naturalization and Expatriation," *YLJ* 31 (1922): 852, 866; Charles Cheney Hyde, "Charles Evans Hughes: Secretary of State, March 4, 1921 to March

4, 1925," in *The American Secretaries of State and Their Diplomacy*, ed. Samuel Flagg Bemis (New York: A. A. Knopf, 1958), 10:397–98. See Patrick Weil, *The Sovereign Citizen: Denaturalization and the Origins of the American Republic* (Philadelphia: University of Pennsylvania Press, 2012), 83–91.

70. Hughes, *Autobiographical Notes*, 285.
71. Brooklyn Borough Gas Co. v. Public Service Commission, *Public Utilities Reports* 1918F: 335–68; see Public Service Commission v. Brooklyn Borough Gas Co., 189 A.D. 62, 178 N.Y.S. 93 (1919).
72. "The City of New York is threatened with a condition of chaos," November 6, 1919, Julius M. Mayer to Merchants Association of New York, October 21, 1919, box 20, Hughes-Columbia MSS; "Hughes Gets No Fee for Transit Inquiry," *NYT*, November 14, 1919, 19.
73. "Freight Rate Case Set for Argument," *NYT*, May 16, 1926, E14; "Protests New Haven's Valuation," *WSJ*, May 18, 1926, 7; United States v. Los Angeles & Salt Lake Railroad Co., 273 U.S. 299 (1927); Gilchrist v. Interborough Rapid Transit Co., 279 U.S. 159 (1929).
74. Charles Evans Hughes, *The Supreme Court of the United States* (New York: Columbia University Press, 1928), 216–20, 223–24.
75. Hughes, "Shrine of the Common Law," 211. Stephen A. Siegel shows how an economic critique made salient the judges' exercise of discretion in "Understanding the *Lochner* Era: Lessons from the Controversy over Railroad and Utility Rate Regulation," *DLJ* 70 (1984): 232–59.
76. See Barbara H. Fried, *The Progressive Assault on Laissez Faire: Robert Hale and the First Law and Economics Movement* (Cambridge, MA: Harvard University Press, 1998), 3, 160–204.
77. Robert L. Hale, "The Supreme Court's Ambiguous Use of 'Value' in Rate Cases," *CLR* 18 (1918): 210–13; Robert L. Hale, "The 'Fair Value' Merry-Go-Round, 1898 to 1938: A Forty-Year Journey from Rates-Based-on-Value to Value-Based-on-Rates," *ILR* 33 (1939): 521–27; Robert L. Hale, "Does the Ghost of *Smyth v. Ames* Still Walk?" *HLR* 55 (1942): 1122–29.
78. Southwestern Bell Telephone Co. v. Public Service Commission, 262 U.S. 276 (1923).
79. Robert L. Hale, review of *The Validity of Rate Regulations*, by Robert P. Reeder, *PSQ* 29 (1914): 518; Robert Lee Hale to Louis D. Brandeis, June 4, 1916, box 1, Hale MSS; Robert L. Hale, "The Supreme Court's Ambiguous Use of 'Value' in Rate Cases," *CLR* 18 (1918): 229.
80. Ohio Valley Water Co. v. Ben Avon Borough, 253 U.S. 287 (1920); see Bickel and Schmidt, *Judiciary and Responsible Government*, 611–30; Schiller, "Era of Deference," 400–403.
81. Robert L. Hale, "Rate Making and the Revision of the Property Concept," *CLR* 22 (1922): 216; see also Robert L. Hale, "The 'Physical Value' Fallacy in Rate Cases," *YLJ* 30 (1921): 710–31.

82. Gerard C. Henderson, "Railway Valuation and the Courts," *HLR* 33 (1920): 1051; Ernst Freund, "The Right to a Judicial Review in Rate Controversies," *WVLQ* 27 (1921): 211. Freund criticized the *Smyth* doctrine even though he feared that "the consumer, the passenger, the shipper, the wage earner, [and] the 'small man' in general" would use ratemaking as "a weapon to gain economic advantage." Ernst Freund, "Commission Powers and Public Utilities," *ABAJ* 9 (1923): 288, 286; see also Ernst Freund to Robert S. Lovett, n.d., box 2, Freund-E MSS; Robert S. Lovett, *The Railroad Problem: Comments on Certain Methods Suggested for Solving It* (New York, 1919), 29.
83. Donald R. Richberg, "A Permanent Basis for Rate Regulation," *YLJ* 31 (1922): 263; John Dickinson, *Administrative Justice and the Supremacy of Law in the United States* (Cambridge, MA: Harvard University Press, 1927), 202; Thomas Reed Powell, "Protecting Property and Liberty, 1922-1924," *PSQ* 40 (1925): 406–07.
84. "Notes on Cases," 51, box 153, Corcoran MSS; Ray A. Brown, "The Functions of Courts and Commissions in Public Utility Rate Regulation," *HLR* 38 (1924): 141–79; Frederick K. Beutel, "Due Process in Valuation of Local Utilities," *MNLR* 13 (1929): 409–38; Felix Frankfurter, *The Public and Its Government* (New Haven, CT: Yale University Press, 1930), 101–7.
85. Consolidated Gas Company of New York v. Newton, 267 F. 231, 236–37 (1920); see [Robert L. Hale,] "Public Utility Valuations, the 'Unearned Increment' and the Depreciated Dollar," *CLR* 21 (1921): 168.
86. *Southwestern Bell*, 262 U.S. at 307, 306, 292, 289 (Brandeis, J., dissenting). See Melvyn Urofsky, *Louis D. Brandeis: A Life* (New York: Pantheon Books, 2009), 613–14.
87. Brown, "Functions of Courts and Commissions," 167.
88. Edward W. Everett to Newton D. Baker, December 12, 1933, box 20, Baker MSS.
89. Beutel, "Due Process in Valuation," 423–27; Frankfurter, *Public and Its Government*, 95–101, 121; "Recommendation for a Memorial to Congress on the Power of Federal Courts with Respect to Regulation of Public Utility Rates," January 27, 1930, *Public Papers and Addresses of Franklin D. Roosevelt* (New York: Random House, 1938), 1:235. On the jurisdiction-denying bill, see Edward A. Purcell, Jr., *Brandeis and the Progressive Constitution:* Erie, *the Judicial Power, and the Politics of the Federal Courts in Twentieth-Century America* (New Haven, CT: Yale University Press, 2000), 23–26.
90. Houston, East & West Texas Railway Co. v. United States, 234 U.S. 342 (1914); "Hughes Attacks Anti-Packer Order," *NYT*, October 5, 1926, 39; United States v. Trenton Potteries Co., 273 U.S. 392 (1927); "Federal Oil Curb Opposed by Hughes," *NYT*, May 8, 1926, 8; "Hughes Argues WGY Has a Property Right," *NYT*, December 4, 1928, 33; *CR* 72 (February 10, 11, 1930): 3373, 3450. See William G. Ross, *The Chief Justiceship of Charles Evans Hughes, 1930-1941* (Columbia: University of South Carolina Press, 2007), 10–16.

91. United Railways & Electric Co. v. West, 280 U.S. 234 (1930); *CR* 72 (February 11, 13, 1930): 3449, 3553, 3564, 3569, 3587.
92. Simon, *FDR and Chief Justice Hughes*, 179; Ross, *Chief Justiceship*, 15–16.

CHAPTER 3

1. "Hughes Urges Bar Aid Law Reforms," *NYT*, September 30, 1931, 22; "Secured Liberties Sought by Hughes," ibid., June 22, 1937, 21; see Merlo J. Pusey, *Charles Evans Hughes* (New York: Macmillan Co., 1951), 2:626. I am indebted to Richard D. Friedman, "Charles Evans Hughes as Chief Justice, 1930-1941" (PhD diss., Oxford University, 1979), ch. 4, p. 4, for references to these articles.
2. Franklin D. Roosevelt, address at Oglethorpe University in Atlanta, Georgia, May 22, 1932, http://www.presidency.ucsb.edu/ws/?pid=88410, visited July 25, 2013.
3. [Charles Evans Hughes,] "Important Work of Uncle Sam's Lawyers," *ABAJ* 17 (1931): 238.
4. Petition for a Writ of Certiorari to the United States Circuit Court of Appeals for the Fifth Circuit, February 12, 1931, Transcript of Record, Crowell v. Benson, 31–86, 285 U.S. 22 (1932), *U.S. Supreme Court Records and Briefs, 1832-1978* (Gale Cengage).
5. *Id.* at 83–84.
6. Benson v. Crowell, 33 F.2d 137 (S.D. Ala. 1929); Crowell v. Benson, 45 F.2d 66, 69–70 (5th Cir. 1930).
7. Crowell v. Benson, 285 U.S. 22, 46–47, 54, 57 (1932).
8. *Id.* at 54 n. 17. See "Judicial Review of Rate Orders of Administrative Boards: A Reexamination," *HLR* 50 (1936): 87 n. 68, 92; "Judicial Review of Administrative Findings: Crowell v. Benson," *YLJ* 41 (1932): 1047; John Dickinson, "*Crowell v. Benson*: Judicial Review of Administrative Determinations of Questions of 'Constitutional Fact,'" *UPLR* 80 (1932): 1055–82.
9. Brief for Petitioner, 25, Crowell v. Benson, 285 U.S. 222 (1932), *Supreme Court Records and Briefs*. The realization that Hughes proposed not just weight-of-the-evidence but de novo review explains why at least two justices switched their votes after conference, at which only Brandeis voted to reverse. Justice Butler's sketchy notes of the deliberations indicate that Hughes said that the courts had to determine the "question of m[aster] & [s]ervant *vel non*" themselves, but they do not indicate that Hughes said that the question had to be considered de novo. Justices Stone and Roberts defected after receiving Hughes's draft opinion. "If a right to retry the question of jurisdiction on new evidence is accorded the employer," Roberts objected, "he may of course absent himself entirely from the proceeding before the deputy commissioner, wait until an award is made, and then go into court and submit his evidence under a bill of equity." Butler Docket Book, 1931 Term; Owen J. Roberts to Brandeis, January 11, 1932, and Stone to Brandeis, February 19, 1932, reel 58, Brandeis MSS. I do

not know whether Oliver Wendell Holmes, Jr., who resigned before *Crowell* was announced, also abandoned Hughes. Brandeis to Frankfurter, January 10, 1932, in *"Half Brother, Half Son": The Letters of Louis D. Brandeis to Felix Frankfurter*, ed. Melvin I. Urofsky and David W. Levy (Norman: University of Oklahoma Press, 1991), 472.

10. Frankfurter to Harlan Fiske Stone, February 29, 1932, box 13, Stone MSS; *Crowell*, 285 U.S. at 54 n. 17.
11. *Crowell*, 285 U.S. at 54–56; Mark Tushnet, "The Story of *Crowell*: Grounding the Administrative State," in *Federal Courts Stories*, ed. Vicki C. Jackson and Judith Resnik (New York: Foundation Press, 2010), 359–88. See also Bernard Schwartz, "Does the Ghost of *Crowell v. Benson* Still Walk?" *UPLR* 98 (1949): 169–70; G. Edward White, "Allocating Power between Agencies and Courts: The Legacy of Justice Brandeis," *DLJ* 1974 (1974): 228.
12. In a draft, it seems Hughes followed the lower courts in holding that the trial judge had to retry the entire dispute. Apparently, after Brandeis objected, Hughes agreed (in Roberts's words) to "amend his opinion so as to limit the character of the trial in the district court to the two questions which he deems fundamental jurisdictional questions." Roberts to Brandeis, January 11, 1932, reel 58, Brandeis MSS. As published, Hughes's opinion required a retrial only of the facts upon which an administrator's jurisdiction depended. "The essential independence of the exercise of the judicial power of the United States in the enforcement of constitutional rights," Hughes wrote, "requires that the federal court should determine *such an issue* upon its own record and the facts elicited before it." Crowell v. Benson, 285 U.S. at 63–64 (emphasis supplied).
13. *Crowell*, 285 U.S. at 51, 65.
14. Smith v. Illinois Bell Telephone Company, 282 U.S. 133 (1930).
15. The federalism issue also explains why in *Florida v. United States*, 282 U.S. 194 (1931), Hughes reprimanded the ICC for failing to make a finding that certain intrastate shipments unjustly discriminated against interstate commerce, and why, in *Crowell*, Hughes identified navigability as a jurisdictional fact.
16. McCardle v. Indianapolis Water Co., 272 U.S. 400 (1926); Robert L. Hale, "Does the Ghost of *Smyth v. Ames* Still Walk?" *HLR* 55 (1942): 1121. See also Dexter Merriam Skeezer and Stacy May, *The Public Control of Business* (New York: Harper & Brothers, 1930), 165–70.
17. Los Angeles Gas & Electric Co. v. Railroad Commission, 289 U.S. 287, 304–08 (1933). Not surprisingly, Butler dissented. Other victories for state public utility commissions were *Wabash Valley Electric Company v. Young*, 287 U. S. 488 (1933) (Sutherland, J.), and *Clark's Ferry Bridge Co. v. Public Service Commission*, 291 U.S. 227 (1934) (Hughes, C.J.).
18. Lindheimer v. Illinois Bell Telephone Company, 292 U.S. 151, 175, 162–64 (1934).
19. Hale to Charles E. Hughes, September 3, 1934, box 2, Hale MSS; see Robert L. Hale, "The New Supreme Court Test of Confiscatory Rates," *JLPUE* 9 (1934): 307–13;

Robert L. Hale, "Conflicting Judicial Criteria of Utility Rates: The Need for a Judicial Restatement," *CLR* 38 (1938): 972–74.

20. Nebbia v. New York, 291 U.S. 502, 532 (1934); Robert L. Hale, "The Constitution and the Price System: Some Reflections on *Nebbia v. New York*," *CLR* 34 (1934): 425.
21. "Finality of Administrative Findings of Fact since *Crowell v. Benson*," *VLR* 24 (1938): 653–61; Federal Radio Commission v. Nelson Brothers Bond & Mortgage Co., 289 U.S. 266, 277 (1933); Voehl v. Indemnity Insurance Co. of North America, 288 U.S. 162 (1933).
22. National Industrial Recovery Act, Pub. L. No. 73–67, 68 Stat. 197 (1933); Frankfurter to Hugh S. Johnson, May 18, 1933, cited in Nelson Lloyd Dawson, *Louis D. Brandeis, Felix Frankfurter, and the New Deal* (Hamden, CT: Archon Books, 1980), 64; Reminiscences of Jerome N. Frank, 1950-52, April 18, 1950, 26–29, COHC; Reminiscences of Frances Perkins, 1951-55, 5:18, ibid.
23. Charles E. Wyzanski, Jr., to Learned Hand, May 17, 1933, box 27; Wyzanski, to Frankfurter, May 24, 1933, box 1; and Wyzanski to Maude J. and Charles E. Wyzanski, May 16, 1933, box 22, Wyzanski-MHS MSS.
24. Wyzanski to Maude J. and Charles E. Wyzanski, June 4, 1933, box 22, Wyzanski-MHS MSS.
25. "Hughes Urges Bar Aid Law Reforms," *NYT.*
26. Frankfurter advised the New Deal's lawyers to avoid a court test until after their agencies had thus squared themselves with the Court's precedents. Reminiscences of Jerome N. Frank, April 18, 1950, 86–87, COHC; Thomas Austern to Frankfurter, May 1, 1935, reel 12, FF-LC MSS; see "The Supreme Court on Administrative Construction as a Guide in the Interpretation of Statutes," *HLR* 40 (1926): 469–72.
27. The philosopher Horace Kallen, for example, thought NIRA might "lead us toward fascism." Horace M. Kallen to Robert F. Wagner, June 14, 1933, box 220, Wagner MSS.
28. On corporatism and the NRA, see Donald R. Brand, *Corporatism and the Rule of Law: A Study of the National Recovery Administration* (Ithaca, NY: Cornell University Press, 1988), 18–20; James Q. Whitman, "Of Corporatism, Fascism and the First New Deal," *AJCL* 39 (1991): 766–75.
29. Zechariah Chafee, Jr., to Harold M. Stephens, July 30, 1933, box 11, Stephens MSS.
30. "Johnson Says NRA Relies on Industry," *NYT*, October 19, 1933, 10. Notwithstanding his admiration for Mussolini, as two observers wrote, Johnson probably was influenced less "by the whirlpool of ideas afloat" in the Great Depression (including fascism) than by his earlier work for the War Industries Board, which "left him gaping in open-mouthed admiration at the glorious spirit of service moving the American businessman." Lewis L. Lorwin and A. F. Hinrichs, *National Economic and Social Planning* (Washington, DC: US Government Printing Office, 1935), 71; cf. Whitman, "Of Corporatism," 747–78.

31. Lorwin and Hinrichs, *National Economic and Social Planning*, 85; Adlai E. Stevenson, Jr., quoted in Peter H. Irons, *The New Deal Lawyers* (Princeton, NJ: Princeton University Press, 1982), 134.
32. Charles H. Weston, "Memorandum re National Industrial Recovery Act (H.R. 5755)," June 5, 1933, box 247, and Stephens to Chafee, July 12, 1933, box 11, Stephens MSS; Donald R. Richberg to Stephens, July 22, 1933, box 1, entry 48, and Dudley Cates to Hugh S. Johnson, August 18, 1933, box 6, entry 20, preliminary inventory 44, NRA Records; Wyzanski to Learned Hand, May 17, 1933, box 27, Wyzanski-MHS MSS.
33. Moses S. Huberman to Golden Bell, December 13, 1934, and Harold M. Stephens, Carl McFarland, and Moses S. Huberman to Homer S. Cummings, September 22, 1934, box 15270, entry 114, DOJ Records; cf. Irons, *New Deal Lawyers*, 70–71.
34. Panama Refining Co. v. Ryan, 293 U.S. 388, 405–11 (1935).
35. "NRA Orders Are Attacked in High Court," *WP*, December 11, 1934, 1; Stephens to Erwin Griswold, January 7, 1935, box 16, Stephens MSS.
36. "Code Records Hit by Supreme Court," *NYT*, December 12, 1934, 27.
37. "Opposing Arguments in the NIRA Oil Cases," *USLW*, December 11, 1934, 3; Paul Freund to Frankfurter, December 11, 1934, reel 34, FF-LC.
38. *Panama Refining Co.*, 293 U.S. at 418, 430–33. Frankfurter professed to be "really troubled" by "the unabashed way" in which the majority "made 'findings' in the case of delegated power to the President a constitutional requirement." Frankfurter to Wyzanski, January 22, 1935, box 26, Wyzanski-MHS MSS.
39. George K. Ray and Harvey Wienke, "Hot Oil on the Uncharted Seas of Delegated Powers," *ILR* 29 (1935): 1035. Congress enacted a constitutional version of section 9 (c) soon after the decision. Act of February 22, 1935, ch. 18, 49 Stat. 30.
40. *The Secret Diary of Harold L. Ickes: The First Thousand Days, 1933-1936* (New York: Simon & Schuster, 1953), 1:273.
41. Milton Katz to Blackwell Smith, January 6, 1935, box 15, entry 51, preliminary inventory 44, NRA Records.
42. Peter Seitz to L. M. C. Smith, February 14, 1935, box 3, entry 51, preliminary inventory 44, NRA Records; Abe Feller to Carl McFarland, January 18, 1935, box 1, McFarland MSS; John J. Abt to Arthur C. Bachrach, Victor Rotnem, and Monroe Oppenheimer, January 17, 1935, box 929, entry 1, AAA Records.
43. Gregory Hankin to A. G. McKnight, January 8, 1935, box 1, entry 7, inventory A1, NRA Records.
44. L. M. C. Smith to Philip E. Buck et al., January 22, 1935, box 1, entry 7, and L. M. C. Smith, "Outline of Matters on which Legal Division is Preparing Studies and Revisions in Light of Possible Renewal of NRA," April 5, 1935, box 2, entry 8, inventory A1, NRA Records; Arthur C. Bachrach to John J. Abt, January 18, 1935, box 2, entry 1, preliminary inventory NC-144, AAA Records.
45. Reed to Frankfurter, May 7, 1935, reel 94, FF-LC; see "Reed Opens Case in Test on Wages," *WP*, May 3, 1935, 1.

46. Frankfurter to Reed, May 4, 1935, reel 94, FF-LC.
47. Schechter Poultry Corp. v. United States, 295 U.S. 495, 539–40 (1935).
48. *Id.* at 538, 535, 539, 537.
49. Wyzanski to Learned Hand, November 5, 1935, box 27, Wyzanski-MHS MSS.
50. *Schechter*, 295 U.S. at 546–51.
51. "Conference with Justice Brandeis at his request in the ante-room of the Clerk's office, at 2 P.M., May 27, 1935," box 20, Cohen MSS.
52. Wyzanski to Maude J. Wyzanski, August 2, 1935, box 22, Wyzanski-MHS MSS; see William E. Leuchtenburg, *The Supreme Court Reborn: The Constitutional Revolution in the Age of Roosevelt* (New York: Oxford University Press, 1995), 52–81; Robert H. Jackson, *That Man: An Insider's Portrait of Franklin D. Roosevelt*, ed. John Q. Barrett (New York: Oxford University Press, 2003), 19; Robert H. Jackson, *The Struggle for Judicial Supremacy: A Study of a Crisis in American Power Politics* (New York: Vintage Books, 1941), 109.
53. Quoted in Jeff Shesol, *Supreme Power: Franklin Roosevelt vs. The Supreme Court* (New York: W. W. Norton, 2010), 149; see also Leuchtenburg, *Supreme Court Reborn*, 85–90.
54. [Hughes,] "Important Work," 237.
55. William Lasser, *Benjamin V. Cohen: Architect of the New Deal* (New Haven, CT: Yale University Press, 2002), 65–85; Michael E. Parrish, *Securities Regulation and the New Deal* (New Haven, CT: Yale University Press, 1970), 42–72; Ralph F. de Bedts, *The New Deal's SEC* (New York: Columbia University Press, 1964), 30–55.
56. John Worth Kern IV, "Thomas Gardiner Corcoran and the New Deal, 1932-1940" (senior thesis, Princeton University, April 16, 1980), box 637, Corcoran MSS; see also Benjamin V. Cohen, interview by Ruth Lieban, February-April 1970, AJC OH; Joseph L. Rauh, Jr., interview by Katie Louchheim, January 4, 1982, box 73, Louchheim MSS; Joseph L. Rauh, interview by Niel M. Johnson, June 21, 1989, HST OH; The Reminiscences of Gordon Evans Dean, 1959, 92, COHC; Joseph P. Lash, *Dealers and Dreamers: A New Look at the New Deal* (New York: Doubleday, 1988), 137–214; Lasser, *Cohen*, 86–149; George E. Paulsen, *A Living Wage for the Forgotten Man: The Quest for Fair Labor Standards, 1933-1941* (Selinsgrove, PA: Susquehanna University Press, 1996), 75–79.
57. "New Deal and Related Record of Leon H. Keyserling," June 1975, box 12, Cohen MSS; Kenneth M. Casebeer, "Holder of the Pen: An Interview with Leon Keyserling on Drafting the Wagner Act," *UMLR* 42 (1987): 303, 306–7, 313, 321–22, 342, 359; Philip Levy, interview by Judith H. Byne, March 15, 1969, 1–2, 52–53, NLRB OH.
58. Erwin N. Griswold, *Ould Fields, New Corne: The Personal Memoirs of a Twentieth Century Lawyer* (St. Paul, MN: West Publishing Co., 1992), 68, 80, 107–9; "Editorial Board," *HLR* 37 (1923): 133; Michael E. Parrish, *Felix Frankfurter and His Times: The Reform Years* (New York: Free Press, 1982), 223; Wyzanski to Maude

J. and Charles E. Wyzanski, July 19, 1933, box 22, and Wyzanski to A. N. Hand, September 15, 1933, box 26, Wyzanski-MHS MSS.

59. The holdovers were Hammond Chaffetz and Charles Weston; the new hire was Moses S. Huberman. "Personnel, Antitrust Division," December 1932, John Lord O'Brian to William D. Mitchell, February 21, 1933; Stephens to Homer S. Cummings, July 31, 1933, box 241; and Stephens to Frankfurter, September 16, 20, 1933, box 14, Stephens MSS. On Stephens, see Daniel R. Ernst, "State, Party, and Harold M. Stephens: The Utahn Origins of an Anti-New Dealer," *Western Legal History* 14 (2001): 123–57; Daniel R. Ernst, "Dicey's Disciple on the D.C. Circuit: Judge Harold Stephens and Administrative Law Reform, 1933-1940," *GLJ* 90 (2002): 787–812; Philip Levy to Calvert Magruder, n.d., box 1, Levy MSS.

60. "A. H. Feller, Ill 2 Weeks, Eludes Wife's Efforts to Prevent Suicide," *NYT*, November 14, 1952, 1; Harvard Law School, *Announcement*, 1932-33: 4, 1933-34: 4; A. H. Feller to Carl McFarland, January 18, May 31, 1935, box 1, McFarland MSS; Robert L. Stern, "Review of Findings of Administrators, Judges and Juries: A Comparative Analysis," *HLR* 58 (1944): 70–124; Robert L. Stern, "The Commerce Clause and the National Economy, 1933-1946," *HLR* 59 (1946): 645–93, 883–947.

61. Irons, *New Deal Lawyers*, 81; John D. Fassett, *New Deal Justice: The Life of Stanley Reed of Kentucky* (New York: Vantage Press, 1994), 83–84.

62. Paul A. Freund, interview by Katie Louchheim, n.d., box 73, Louchheim MSS; Frankfurter to Thomas G. Corcoran, March 27, 1933, box 638, Corcoran MSS. For Freund's role in drafting a substitute for NIRA, see Thomas H. Eliot to Wyzanski, May 31, 1935, box 24, Wyzanski-MHS MSS; Reed and Stephens to FDR, May 31, 1935, box 183, Freund-P MSS.

63. Charles E. Wyzanski, Jr., interview by Harlan B. Phillips, July 12-13, 1954, 193–94, COHC.

64. The courts usually treated the two formulations as identical. The Social Security Act did not acquire the language until 1939. See E. Blythe Stason, "'Substantial Evidence' in Administrative Law," *UPLR* 89 (1941): 1027–28; Bituminous Coal Conservation Act of 1935, §6 (b), 49 Stat. 1003–04. On the adoption of the language in the FTC Act, see Marc Winerman, "The Origins of the FTC: Concentration, Cooperation, Control and Competition," *AnLJ* 71 (2003): 83–84.

65. In addition, section 9 (a) of the Securities Act prevented respondents from ambushing the administrators by raising legal issues and facts for the first time in court. The same language appeared in the Securities Exchange Act of 1934 and the NLRA from its earliest drafts. Securities Act of 1933, §9 (a), 48 Stat. 80; Securities Exchange Act of 1934, §25 (a), 48 Stat. 901–02; National Labor Relations Act, §10 (e), 49 Stat. 454–55; Labor Disputes Act: Title III, §303 (d), Second Draft, February 19, 1934, box 23, Wyzanski-MHS MSS.

66. Milton Handler, interview by Judith H. Byne, April 15, 1970, 19, 23; Levy, interview, 40, 73; Senate Committee on Education and Labor, *To Create a National Labor Board*, 73d Cong., 2d sess., 1934, 31, 36–37.

67. National Harness Manufacturers Association v. FTC, 268 F. 705, 707 (6th Cir. 1920), quoted in Philip Levy to Calvert Magruder, April 24, 1935, box 1, Levy MSS.
68. House Committee on Appropriations, *Department of Justice Appropriation Bill for 1936*, 74th Cong. 1st sess., 1935, 121–24; National Labor Relations Act, §10 (b) (e) (f), 49 Stat. 454 (July 5, 1935).
69. Thomas I. Emerson, interview by Judith H. Byne, March 13, 1971, 47, NLRB OH; see Thomas I. Emerson, *Young Lawyer for the New Deal: An Insider's Memoir of the Roosevelt Years* (Savage, MD: Rowman & Littlefield, 1991), 34–35; *The Making of the New Deal: The Insiders Speak*, ed. Katie Louchheim (Cambridge, MA: Harvard University Press, 1983), 209.
70. Bituminous Coal Conservation Act of 1935, 49 Stat. 991; see "The Bituminous Coal Conservation Act of 1935," *YLJ* 45 (1935): 303.
71. Robert L. Stern, "Memorandum in Explanation of Revision of the Guffey Coal Bill," n.d., Harold M. Stephens, Carl McFarland, A. H. Feller, and Robert L. Stern to Stanley Reed, June 6, 1935, box 183, Freund-P MSS. Philip Levy considered the labor provisions "a hopeless muddle." The Labor Department lawyer Thomas Eliot called the bill "a piece of legislative villainy undisguised," and Wyzanski told Lewis, Warrum, and Roosevelt that it was obviously unconstitutional. "I. Substantive Defects of the Labor Provisions of the Guffey Bill," n.d., box 1, Levy MSS; Thomas H. Eliot to Wyzanski, June 8, 1935 box 24, and Wyzanski to Maude J. Wyzanski, July 16, August 2, 1935, box 22, Wyzanski-MHS MSS.
72. "A Bill to Regulate Competition in Interstate Commerce in Bituminous Coal," n.d., box 183, Freund-P MSS; Stern, "Commerce Clause and the National Economy," 667. See Thomas C. Longin, "Coal, Congress and the Courts: The Bituminous Coal Industry and the New Deal," *WVH* 35 (1974): 107–13; James P. Johnson, *The Politics of Soft Coal* (Urbana: University of Illinois Press, 1979), 220–24; Barry Cushman, *Rethinking the New Deal Court: The Structure of a Constitutional Revolution* (New York: Oxford University Press, 1998), 159–61.
73. Memorandum of Conversation with Brandeis, May 20, 1936, box 38, FF-LC, in Richard D. Friedman, "Switching Time and Other Thought Experiments: The Hughes Court and Constitutional Transformation," *UPLR* 142 (1994): 1962–63.
74. "A Personal View of Justice Benjamin N. Cardozo: Recollections of Four Cardozo Law Clerks," *CarLR* 1 (1979): 9.
75. Here Hughes was respecting the "norm of consensus" that prevailed under his predecessors and broke down under his successor. Robert Post, "The Supreme Court Opinion as Institutional Practice: Dissent, Legal Scholarship, and Decisionmaking in the Taft Court," *MNLR* 85 (2001): 1331–55; Pamela C. Corley, Amy Steigerwalt, and Artemus Ward, "Revisiting the Roosevelt Court: The Critical Juncture from Consensus to Dissensus," *JSCH* 38 (2013): 20–50.
76. Jones v. Securities & Exchange Commission, 298 U.S. 1, 19, 23–24, 28 (1936); James M. Landis to Frankfurter, March 11, 1936, box 10, Landis-LC MSS; Frankfurter to Stone, April 7, 1936, box 13, Stone MSS. My source for Hughes's change of vote after conference is Charles E. Wyzanski's report to his mother of a conversation

with Thomas Harris, Stone's clerk in the 1935 Term. Harris told Wyzanski that "the Chief Justice at conference voted with the 3 liberals in the SEC case (*Jones v. SEC*), the case involving excess valuation of railroads (*Great Northern*) and the case involving the commodities clause of the Hepburn Act (*Elgin, Joliet R. v. US*), but when he found he was in the minority, he shied away from a 5–4 decision which would accentuate popular doubts about the infallibility of the Sup. Ct." Wyzanski to Maude J. Wyzanski, October 18, 1936, box 22, Wyzanski-MHS MSS.

77. Stone, "Memorandum Re; No. 401," February 4, 1936, box 13, Stone MSS.

78. Ibid.; Wyzanski to Maude J. Wyzanski, October 18, 1936, box 22, Wyzanski-MHS MSS; United States v. Butler, 297 U.S. 1 (1936). After *Butler* was announced, rumors circulated that Hughes had been "willing to go either way in the AAA case" and that he had changed his original vote, but Stone's memorandum indicates otherwise. Further, Wyzanski observed that if Hughes had voted in conference with the dissenters in *Butler*, he ought to have also joined them in opposing the review of a challenge to a rice processing tax in November 1935. Perhaps that earlier vote was why, as Wyzanski had it from Stone's clerk, "Stone knew how the court stood as far back as Nov[ember,] which was before AAA was argued." *Secret Diary of Harold L. Ickes*, 1:535–36; Drew Pearson and Robert S. Allen, *The Nine Old Men* (Garden City, NY: Doubleday, Doran & Co., 1936), 44; Wyzanski to Maude J. Wyzanski, January 11, 1936, box 22, Wyzanski-MHS MSS; Rickert Rice Mills, Inc. v. Fontenot, cert. granted, 296 U.S. 569 (1935), decided, 297 U.S. 110 (1936).

79. Wyzanski to Maude J. Wyzanski, October 18, 1936, box 22, Wyzanski-MHS MSS.

80. Carter v. Carter Coal Co., 298 U.S. at 304, 310, 315 (1936).

81. *Id.* at 317–23 (Hughes, C.J., concurring). Cardozo, writing for himself, Brandeis and Stone, declared the price-fixing provisions constitutional and believed the labor provisions were not properly before the Court. *Id.* at 325–31, 333 (Cardozo, J., dissenting).

82. *Id.* at 317-19 (Hughes, C.J., concurring). Cf. Barry Cushman, "Continuity and Change in Commerce Clause Jurisprudence," *ARLR* 55 (2003): 1033–34; Richard D. Friedman, "Charting the Course of Commerce Clause Challenge," ibid., 1077–83; Barry Cushman, "Small Differences?" ibid., 1120–29.

83. Adkins v. Children's Hospital, 261 U.S. 525 (1923); Lasser, *Cohen*, 53–61; Vivien Hart, *Bound by Our Constitution: Women, Workers, and the Minimum Wage* (Princeton, NJ: Princeton University Press, 1994), 135–45.

84. Morehead v. New York ex rel. Tipaldo, 298 U.S. 587, 619–21 (1936) (Hughes, C.J., dissenting).

85. This charge appeared in an untitled address, commencing "The Chief Justice in opening his speech," box 296, Norris MSS. It was written after the term ended on June 1, 1936. A handwritten marginal note identified it as "Memo from Tom Corcoran."

86. St. Joseph Stock Yards Co. v. United States, 11 F. Supp. 322, 328 (W.D. Mo. 1935).

87. Brandeis, memorandum, May 30, 1930, in *"Half Brother, Half Son,"* 431; see Friedman, "Charles Evans Hughes," ch. 4, pp. 17–20.
88. St. Joseph Stock Yards Co. v. United States, 298 U.S. 38, 51–52 (1936).
89. Frankfurter, Memorandum of Conversation with Brandeis, May 20, 1936, reel 17, FF-LC MSS.
90. *St Joseph Stock Yards*, 298 U.S. at 53–54. *Baltimore & Ohio Railroad Co. v. United States*, 298 U.S. 349, 368–69 (1936), showed that the ban on new evidence was not absolute.
91. *Id.* at 66–67; Mark Tushnet, "Administrative Law in the 1930s: The Supreme Court's Accommodation of Progressive Legal Theory," *DLJ* 60 (2011): 1602.
92. Stone to Helen Stone Willard, June 2, 1936, quoted in Shesol, *Supreme Power*, 221; West Coast Hotel Co. v. Parrish, 300 U.S. 397 (1937); NLRB v. Jones & Laughlin Steel Corp., 301 U.S. 1 (1937); Steward Machine Company v. Davis, 301 U.S. 548 (1937); Wyzanski to Maude J. Wyzanski, January 6, 1936, box 22, Wyzanski-MHS MSS.
93. The Corcoran quote is Ickes's paraphrase and appears in the May 22, 1937, entry in *Secret Diary of Harold L. Ickes*, 1:145. On the court-packing plan, see Leuchtenburg, *Supreme Court Reborn*, 82–162; William E. Leuchtenburg, "Charles Evans Hughes: The Center Holds," *NCLR* 83 (2005): 1196–98; Marian C. McKenna, *Franklin Roosevelt and the Great Constitutional War: The Court-Packing Crisis of 1937* (New York: Fordham University Press, 2002); Shesol, *Supreme Power*; James F. Simon, *FDR and Chief Justice Hughes: The President, the Supreme Court, and the Epic Battle over the New Deal* (New York: Simon & Schuster, 2012), 299–342.
94. W. H. Griffin to Franklin D. Roosevelt, June 3, 1935, box 184, Freund-P MSS. See also Daniel J. Gifford, "The New Deal Regulatory Model: A History of Criticisms and Refinements," *MNLR* 68 (1983): 307–9.
95. Burton K. Wheeler and Paul F. Healy, *Yankee from the West: The Candid, Turbulent Life Story of the Yankee-Born U.S. Senator from Montana* (New York: Doubleday, 1962), 249, quoted in Cushman, *Rethinking*, 36.
96. Edward L. Carter and Edward E. Adams, "Justice Owen J. Roberts on 1937," *Green Bag* 15 (2012): 384, http://www.greenbag.org/v15n4/v15n4_articles_carter_adams.pdf.
97. Stanley Reed, Memorandum for the Attorney General, April 22, 1937, quoted in Leuchtenburg, *Supreme Court Reborn*, 318 n. 100. For the doubters, see Emerson, *Young Lawyer*, 77, 80; James A. Gross, *The Making of the National Labor Relations Board: A Study in Economics, Politics, and the Law* (Albany: State University of New York Press, 1974), 198–204; Wyzanski to Maude J. Wyzanski, May 16, 19, 23, 1936, box 22, Wyzanski-MHS MSS. When the New Deal at last tackled wages and hours in the Fair Labor Standards Act of 1938, Hughes thought the statute "a border line case" but decided not to write separately. Hughes to Stone, January 27, 1941, box 66, Stone MSS; see United States v. Darby, 312 U.S. 100 (1941); Opp Cotton Mills, Inc. v. Administrator, 312 U.S. 126 (1941).

98. The NLRA required a finding that proscribed conduct was "in commerce, or burdening or obstructing commerce or the free flow of commerce, or having led or tending to lead to a labor dispute burdening or obstructing commerce or the free flow of commerce." National Labor Relations Act, §10(e), 49 Stat. 454–55. As Attorney General Francis Biddle noted, in a passage that Hughes quoted approvingly, the constitutionality of such a statute "was not new ground for the author of the *Minnesota Rate Cases*." Francis Biddle, "Foreword," *CLR* 41 (1941): 1157–58, quoted in *The Autobiographical Notes of Charles Evans Hughes*, ed. David J. Danelski and Joseph S. Tulchin (Cambridge, MA: Harvard University Press, 1973), 313.
99. Department of Justice lawyers also saw the FTC Act as a safe harbor when drafting a replacement for NIRA and a substitute for the Guffey Act. "A Bill to Amend the Act entitled 'An Act to Create a Federal Trade Commission" and "A Bill to Regulate Competition in Interstate Commerce in Bituminous Coal," box 183, Freund-P MSS.
100. NLRB v. Jones & Laughlin Steel Corp., 301 U.S. 1, 31, 34–41, 43–47 (1937).
101. For Douglas, see *Democracy and Finance: The Addresses and Public Statements of William O. Douglas as Member and Chairman of the Securities and Exchange Commission* (New Haven, CT: Yale University Press, 1940), 243–47; Philip John Cooper, "Justice Douglas and Administrative Law" (PhD diss., Syracuse University, 1978), 246–59.
102. Consolidated Edison Co. v. NLRB, 305 U.S. 197, 229 (1938); NLRB v. Columbian Enameling & Stamping Co., 306 U.S. 292, 300 (1939); NLRB v. Foote Brothers Gear & Machine Corp., 311 U.S. 620 (1940); NLRB v. Link-Belt Co., 311 U.S. 584, 597 (1941); "Nos. 235 & 236," box 57, Douglas MSS. See James A. Gross, *The Reshaping of the National Labor Relations Board: A Study in Economics, Politics, and the Law* (Albany: State University of New York Press, 1981), 82–83; Rayman Louis Solomon, "Politics, Law and Federal Regulation: The United States Court of Appeals for the Seventh Circuit, 1900-1948" (PhD diss., University of Chicago, 1986), 186–96. Even more deferential decisions suggested that judges could stop reading the record once they found sufficient evidence to support the board's order. NLRB v. Waterman Steamship Corp., 309 U.S. 206 (1940); NLRB v. Bradford Dyeing Association, 310 U.S. 318 (1940).
103. "Finality of Administrative Findings," 655; Shields v. Utah Idaho Central Railroad Co., 305 U.S. 177 (1938). I am indebted to Friedman, "Charles Evans Hughes," ch. 4, p. 12, for the reference to *Shields*. *United States v. Appalachian Electric Power Company*, 311 U.S. 377 (1940), upheld the Federal Power Commission's determination after a de novo review of the record that a stretch of river was navigable. The government's lawyers had asked the lower courts to overturn *Crowell*. Although the lawyers still thought this the right way to dispose of the case, they did "not seek" such a holding in the Supreme Court. *Id.* at 402 n. 7. Hughes did not participate.

104. Railroad Commission v. Pacific Gas & Electric Co., 302 U.S. 388, 395–98 (1938). This chafing of an old wound provoked Butler to protest that the Court was overturning settled precedent. "Generally, speaking, at least, our decisions of yesterday ought to be the law of today," he sniffed. *Id.* at 418 (Butler, J., dissenting).
105. McCart v. Indianapolis Water Co., 302 U.S. 419, 423–41 (Black, J., dissenting). See Alpheus T. Mason, *Harlan Fiske Stone: Pillar of the Law* (New York: Viking Press, 1956), 468; Marquis W. Childs, "The Supreme Court To-Day," *Harper's Magazine* 176 (1938): 586; Roger K. Newman, *Hugo Black: A Biography* (New York: Pantheon Books, 1994), 273–74.
106. Frankfurter to Carl F. Wheat, October 22, 1937, box 250, Corcoran MSS; Driscoll v. Edison Light & Power Co., 307 U.S. 104, 122 (1939) (Frankfurter, J., concurring).
107. Hale, "Ghost," 1129–40; Barbara H. Fried, *The Progressive Assault on Laissez Faire: Robert Hale and the First Law and Economics Movement* (Cambridge, MA: Harvard University Press, 1998), 188–89.
108. Milton Katz to Edwin B. George, March 8, 1939, box 12, Katz MSS.
109. Laura Kalman, *Abe Fortas: A Biography* (New Haven, CT: Yale University Press, 1990), 130.
110. Charles E. Hughes to Charles E. Hughes, Jr., September 22, 1927, box 3, Hughes-Columbia MSS; "Address of Chief Justice Hughes," *ABAJ* 21 (1935): 341.
111. Arthur W. Macmahon and John D. Millett, *Federal Administrators: A Biographical Approach to the Problem of Departmental Management* (New York: Columbia University Press, 1939), 319–20; Transcript of the Proceedings before the Attorney General's Committee on Administrative Procedure, June 28, 1940, 86–87 (Thomas T. Cooke), box 1, entry 385, DOJ Records.
112. Howard D. Dozier, "Memorandum for Mr. Wilson, Department of Justice," January 12, 1937, "F. O. Morgan et al v. United States et al.," June 6, 1936, box 11256, entry 114AC, DOJ Records; Appellants' Brief, 85, Morgan v. United States, 304 U.S. 1 (1938) (*Morgan II*).
113. Dozier, "Memorandum for Mr. Wilson"; A. W. Miller to G. N. Dagger, January 12, 1937, and J. R. Mohler to Dagger, January 12, 1937, box 11256, entry 114AC, DOJ Records; Robert H. Jackson, "Morgan v. United States," 720, box 258, Jackson MSS; "F. O. Morgan et al. v. United States et al."; Transcript of the Proceedings, 87 (Cooke).
114. Wendell Berge to Seth Thomas, June 22, 1936, box 11255, entry 114AC, DOJ Records; Morgan v. United States, 298 U.S. 468 (1936) (*Morgan I*).
115. Argument on Behalf of the Petitioner, March 10, 11, 1938, box 84, Jackson MSS; Butler Docket Book, 1937 Term, 404.
116. *Morgan II*, 304 U.S. at 18, 19, 22 (1938). Black dissented without opinion.
117. "The Kansas City Commission Rate Case: A Radio Talk by Henry A Wallace," April 28, 1938, Wallace to Hughes, May 3, 1938; Hughes to Wallace, May 6, 1938, box 2835, entry 17, USDA Records. For the USDA's revision of its procedures

after *Morgan I*, see Wendell Berge to Thurman W. Arnold, May 17, 1938, box 11255, entry 114AC, DOJ Records.

118. "Secretary Wallace Explains Kansas City Rate Decision," *NYT*, May 8, 1938, 72; Wallace to Sherman Minton, May 9, 1938, *CR* 83 (May 11, 1938): 1922–23 (Appendix).
119. "Address of Justice Hughes at Law Institute," *NYT*, May 13, 1938, 8.
120. "Fair Play for the Citizen," May 16, 1938, *The Editorials of David Lawrence* (Washington, DC: U.S. News & World Report, 1970), 2:48; Howard C. Dunseith to Wallace, May 25, 1938, box 2835, James B. McCreary to Wallace, May 14, 1938; H. M. Sinclair to Wallace, May 19, 1938, box 2774, entry 17, USDA Records.
121. David Lawrence, "Hughes Ruling Gets Quick Action," newspaper clipping, enclosed in Roscoe Pound to O. R. McGuire, May 3, 1938, reel 109, Pound MSS; Allen Throop to SEC, April 27, 1938, box 16, and Office of the General Counsel to the Commission, May 3, 1938, box 29, entry 172, UD WW inventory, SEC Records; Mastin G. White to Henry A. Wallace, May 11, 1939, box 11256, entry 114AC, DOJ Records.
122. Thomas I. Emerson to Review Staff, October 29, 1939, box 6, entry 378, DOJ Records; Gross, *Reshaping*, 30–33; Milton Handler, "The Morgan Case and the National Labor Relations Board," *Labor Law Comments*, no. 5 (October 1938); Walter Gellhorn and Seymour L. Linfield, "Politics and Labor Relations: An Appraisal of Criticisms of NLRB Procedure," *CLR* 39 (1939): 382 n. 97; *Morgan II*, 304 U.S. at 22; FCC, *Fifth Annual Report* (Washington, DC: U.S. Government Printing Office, 1940), 10–11; "Memorandum in re Fair Hearing," May 18, 1940, box 222, BCD Records; "Conference of the Attorney General's Committee on Administrative Procedure," April 27, 1940, 1, 11, box 4, entry 376, DOJ Records. The drafters of new deportation procedures for the Bureau of Immigration also debated the implications of *Morgan II*. John A. McIntire to Marshall E. Dimock, October 19, 1939, box 7, Dimock MSS.
123. Wyzanski to Cummings, September 29, 1938, box 69, Cummings MSS.
124. Warner W. Gardner to James W. Morris, January 21, 1939, box 4402, entry 112, DOJ Records; Joanna Grisinger, "Law in Action: The Attorney General's Committee on Administrative Procedure," *JPH* 20 (2008): 379–418.
125. Daniel T. Rodgers, "Living without Labels," *LHR* 24 (2006): 176–77; see Herbert Croly, *The Promise of American Life* (New York: Macmillan Co. 1909), 360.

CHAPTER 4

1. J. Warren Madden, interview by Judith Byne Seidman, October 29, 1968, 40, NLRB OH (Madden, Cornell Interview).
2. Morgan v. United States 304 U.S. 1, 22 (1938); "Address of Justice Hughes at Law Institute," *NYT*, May 13, 1938, 8.

3. [John Carter Franklin,] *The New Dealers* (New York: Literary Guild, 1934), 270; see Stephen Skowronek, *Building a New American State: The Expansion of National Administrative Capacities* (New York: Cambridge University Press, 1982); G. Cullom Davis, "The Transformation of the Federal Trade Commission, 1914-1929," *MVHR* 49 (1962): 437–55.
4. David Plotke, *Building a Democratic Order: Reshaping American Liberalism in the 1930s and 1940s* (New York: Cambridge University Press, 1996), 157; Martin Shefter, *Political Parties and the State: The American Historical Experience* (Princeton, NJ: Princeton University Press, 1994), 82–83.
5. Kenneth S. Davis, *FDR: The New Deal Years* (New York: Random House, 1986), 631; William E. Leuchtenburg, *Franklin D. Roosevelt and the New Deal, 1932-1940* (New York: Harper & Row, 1963), 266–70; James A. Gross, *The Reshaping of the National Labor Relations Board: A Study in Economics, Politics, and the Law* (Albany: State University of New York Press, 1981), 68–71; James T. Patterson, *Congressional Conservatism and the New Deal: The Growth of the Conservative Coalition in Congress, 1933-1939* (Lexington: University of Kentucky Press, 1967), 2, 316–18; Jason Scott Smith, *Building New Deal Liberalism: The Political Economy of Public Works, 1933-1956* (New York: Cambridge University Press, 2006), 160–78.
6. Wilbert Losson Hindman, Jr., "The New York Constitutional Convention of 1938: The Constituent Process and Interest Activity" (PhD diss., University of Michigan, 1940), 18; Robert P. Ingalls, *Herbert H. Lehman and New York's Little New Deal* (New York: New York University Press, 1975).
7. Judith Stein, "The Birth of Liberal Republicanism in New York State, 1932-1939" (PhD diss., Yale University, 1968), 19–21.
8. "Robert E. Whalen, Albany Attorney," *NYT*, August 13, 1951, 17; "Ochlocracy Here Is Feared," ibid., November 7, 1941, 22.
9. Ingalls, *Lehman*, 88, 254; Hindman, "Constitutional Convention," 18; "Job No. 2," *Time* 20 (September 5, 1932): 12.
10. Stein, "Birth of Liberal Republicanism," 176–78; Ingalls, *Lehman*, 88, 254; Hindman, "Constitutional Convention," 19.
11. Sheila Stern, "The American Labor Party, 1936-1944" (MA thesis, University of Chicago, 1964), 32–35, 63–64; Robert Frederick Carter, "Pressure from the Left: The American Labor Party, 1936-1954" (PhD diss., Syracuse University, 1965), 8–17, 93–96; Warren Moscow, *Politics in the Empire State* (New York: Alfred A. Knopf, 1948), 105–8; Jin Hee Kim, "Labor Law and Labor Policy in New York State, 1920s-1930s" (PhD diss., Binghamton University–State University of New York, 1999), 264–67.
12. Barton quoted in Stein, "Birth of Liberal Republicanism," 205.
13. In New York County, where most of the state's largest law firms were located, 55 percent of all lawyers practiced individually in 1934. A national estimate in 1948 found that 61 percent of American lawyers practiced individually. Committee on Professional Economics of the New York County Lawyers' Association, *Survey of*

the Legal Profession in New York County (New York, 1936), 11–12; Fred B. Weil, ed., *The 1967 Lawyer Statistical Report* (Chicago: American Bar Foundation, 1968), 18.

14. Charles E. Wyzanski, Jr., to Homer S. Cummings, September 29, 1938, box 69, Cummings MSS; Hindman, "Constitutional Convention," 51; see also Vernon A. O'Rourke and Douglas W. Campbell, *Constitution-Making in a Democracy: Theory and Practice in New York State* (Baltimore: Johns Hopkins Press, 1943), 163–64.
15. H. M. Stevens, "New York's Famous Lawyers," *Harper's Weekly*, July 29, 1911, 17.
16. Wayne K. Hobson, "Symbol of the New Profession: Emergence of the Large Law Firm, 1870-1915," in *The New High Priests: Lawyers in Post-Civil War America*, ed. Gerard W. Gawalt (Westport, CT: Greenwood Press, 1984), 3–28; Robert W. Gordon, "'The Ideal and the Actual in the Law': Fantasies and Practices of New York City Lawyers, 1870-1910," in ibid., 51–74; Michael J. Powell, *From Patrician to Professional Elite: The Transformation of the New York City Bar Association* (New York: Russell Sage, 1988), 3–44.
17. "Find Service Boards Haven't Easy Tasks," *NYT*, December 17, 1911; Merlo J. Pusey, *Charles Evans Hughes* (New York: Columbia University Press, 1963), 1:203; see Bruce W. Dearstyne, "Regulation in the Progressive Era: The New York Public Service Commission," *NYH* 58 (1977): 331–47.
18. "To Limit Powers of Commissioners," *NYT*, July 20, 1915, 9; "Makes Tenure Sure for Service Boards," *NYT*, July 25, 1915, 13; Elihu Root, "Public Service by the Bar," *ABAR* 41 (1916): 368–69.
19. O'Rourke and Campbell, *Constitution-Making*, 62–68.
20. "Politics Ruling," *NYT*, August 20, 1938, 2; O'Rourke and Campbell, *Constitution-Making*, 79; Fearon quoted in O'Rourke and Campbell, *Constitution-Making*, 71; Hindman, "Constitutional Convention," 40–44.
21. Ernest D. Leet to Roscoe Pound, March 30, 1938, part 1, reel 34, Pound MSS; "Arthur Eugene Sutherland, Jr., 1902-1973," *Contemporary Authors Online* (Gale, 2002), visited October 6, 2012; Erwin N. Griswold, "Arthur E. Sutherland," *HLR* 86 (1973): 933–35.
22. NYSBA, *Administrative Law in New York* (Albany, 1940), 224; Leet to Pound, March 30, 1938. In 1939 Robert Jackson described Leet as "a young man who was in my office and who had two or three just such [unhappy] experiences [with administrative tribunals], and he never forgave them, and he is crusading to destroy them, and I don't blame him very much." Conference of the Attorney General's Committee on Administrative Procedure, March 16, 1939, box 3, entry 376, DOJ Records.
23. Leet to William A. Searle, March 28, 1938, reel 34, part 1, Pound MSS; Ernest D. Leet, "Address on Some Proposed Changes to the Constitution of New York State, Delivered before the Council of the Federation of Bar Associations of Western New York," *BDLJ*, December 21, 1937, 1, 3, 4, and December 22, 1937, 1, 3.
24. Leet sent excerpts from Jaffe's draft to NYSBA president Joseph Rosch on March 30, 1938; see reel 34, part 1, Pound MSS; see also Leet to Pound, April

28, 1938, box 3, Committee Correspondence Hearings, Minutes and Proposals Files, NYSCC Records. For the published version of Jaffe's report, see New York State Constitutional Convention Committee, *Problems Relating to Judicial Administration and Organization* (Albany, 1938), 781–845.

25. NYSBA, *Administrative Law*, 7, 112, 141, 189, 224–25.
26. *Revised Record of the Constitutional Convention of the State of New York* (Albany, NY, 1938), 3:2064–65 ("*Revised Record*").
27. Ibid.
28. Resolution Adopted at the Meeting of the Executive Committee of the Bar Association, January 5, 1938, reel 77, FF-LC MSS. I discuss Pound and the ABA's Special Committee on Administrative Law in the next chapter.
29. Henry L. Stimson to Felix Frankfurter, March 8, April 13, 1938, John Foster Dulles to Frankfurter, April 18, 1938, reel 77, FF-LC MSS; see John Foster Dulles, "Administrative Law: An Address Given on January 14, 1939, at Langdell Hall, Cambridge," reel 59, "Joint Report of the Committees on Administrative Law and on Federal Legislation on S. 915 (76th Congress) introduced by Mr. Logan," May 2, 1939, reel 4, Dulles MSS; John Foster Dulles, "Administrative Law," *ABAJ* 25 (1939): 275–82, 352–53.
30. "Statement of John Foster Dulles before the Attorney General's Committee on Administrative Procedure," July 12, 1940, reel 59, Dulles MSS.
31. Hindman, "Constitutional Convention," 50, 74–75; Stein, "Birth of Liberal Republicanism," 185, 189–93; O'Rourke and Campbell, *Constitution-Making*, 115, 205–6.
32. *Food For Forums* (February 1938): 17-18; *Constitutional Convention Almanac, 1938* (New York: New York Times, 1938), 7–9.
33. Leet to Searle, March 28, 1938; NYSBA, *Administrative Law*, 8, 114–35, 188–90; Leet to Pound, June 8, 1938, reel 34, part 1, Pound MSS.
34. NYSBA, *Administrative Law*, 8–11, 149–55, 161–62, 192–93; O. R. McGuire to Homer S. Cummings, May 12, 1938, box 4401, entry 112, DOJ Records. I discuss the ABA's bill in the next chapter.
35. Dulles to Charles B. Sears, June 23, 1938, reel 3, Dulles MSS; *Revised Record*, 3:2058–59.
36. Frankfurter to Dulles, June 27, 1938, Dulles to Frankfurter, June 28, 1938, reel 3, Dulles MSS.
37. Leet to Pound, May 19, 1938, reel 34, part 1, diary, June 14, 1938, reel 42, part 2, Pound MSS; "Urges Court Reviews on Official Decisions," *NYT*, June 15, 1938, 12; "Report of the Special Committee on Administrative Law," *ABAR* 63 (1938): 346–51; Minutes, June 14, 22, 1938, Judiciary Committee, box 2, NYSCC Records.
38. "Bureaucracy Issue Splits Committee," *NYT*, July 20, 1938, 9; "Report of the Committee on the Judiciary," Document No. 8, *Journal and Documents of the Constitutional Convention of the State of New York* (Albany, NY, 1938); *Revised Record*, 3:2041; Hindman, "Constitutional Convention," 313–14.

39. Report of the Committee on Administrative Agencies and Tribunals, *ABAR* 63 (1938): 625, 627, 631; Warren Tubbs to Sears, July 18, 1938, box 3, NYSCC Records; NYSBA, *Proceedings*, 1939: 193–94.
40. NYSBA, *Administrative Law*, 159–60, 208; "Judiciary Section Seen as Menacing All State Boards," *NYT*, August 14, 1938, 2; *Revised Record*, 3:2069–70.
41. *Revised Record*, 3:2088.
42. "Anti-Bureaucracy Clause," *NYT*, August 4, 1938, 6.
43. *Revised Record*, 3:2064, 2091, 2101, 2106.
44. Ibid., 3:2046–50, 2092–100.
45. Ibid., 3:2079–81, 2085–86, 2090. On Fertig, see Hindman, "Constitutional Convention," 57–58; "Maldwin Fertig, Legislator, Dies," *NYT*, July 24, 1972, 30. On the functionalist approach at Yale, see Laura Kalman, *Legal Realism at Yale, 1927-1960* (Chapel Hill, NC: University of North Carolina Press, 1986), and Robert W. Gordon, "Professors and Policymakers: Yale Law School Faculty in the New Deal and After," in *History of the Yale Law School* (New Haven, CT: Yale University Press, 2004), 75–137.
46. *Revised Record*, 3:2110; "Curb on Bureaucracy Is Accepted at Albany after New Deal Fight," *NYT*, August 4, 1938, 1; "Judiciary Section Seen as Menacing All Boards."
47. "Judiciary Section Seen as Menacing All Boards"; *Revised Record*, 4:3073, 3085–86; see Kim, "Labor Law and Labor Policy in New York State," 215–16.
48. "Curbing Bureaucracy," *NYT*, August 15, 1938, 14; "Lehman's Letter on Judiciary Plan," ibid., 2; "La Guardia Hits Reviews," *NYT*, August 5, 1938, 5.
49. *Revised Record*, 4:3076–77, 3083.
50. Ibid., 3087, 3093; Hindman, "Constitutional Convention," 318.
51. Robert F. Wagner, "Proposed N.Y. Constitutional Amendments," enclosed in Wagner to Roosevelt, August 31, 1938, OF 88, FDR; "Court Review Plan Adopted at Albany," *NYT*, August 19, 1938, 20.
52. O'Rourke and Campbell, *Constitution-Making*, 220–22, 230–31; "City Bar Rejects Judiciary Article," *NYT*, October 19, 1938, 4.
53. NYSBA, *Administrative Law*, 155–201, 213–35, 237–54; Frank M. Shea, "Shall Judicial Review Be Written into the Constitution?" *BDLJ*, November 4, 1938, 3, 4. Shea echoed Justice Louis Brandeis, who, in his dissent in *St. Joseph Stock Yards*, asserted that "Responsibility is the great developer of men" and asked, "May it not tend to emasculate or demoralize the ratemaking body if ultimate responsibility is transferred to others?" St. Joseph Stock Yards Co. v. United States, 298 U.S. 38, 92 (1936).
54. O'Rourke and Campbell, *Constitution-Making*, 233; Arthur E. Sutherland, Jr., "Lawmaking by Popular Vote: Some Reflections on the New York Constitution of 1938," *CLQ* 24 (1938): 11; "Bar Asks Review of Agency Orders," *NYT*, July 31, 1938, 14. La Guardia is quoted in Hindman, "Constitutional Convention," 377. For polling data on the Court-packing plan, see Barry Cushman, "Mr. Dooley

and Mr. Gallup: Public Opinion and Constitutional Change in the 1930s," *BLR* 50 (2002): 67–74.

55. Reminiscences of John Lord O'Brian, February-June 1952, 443–44, COHC.
56. "Dewey and Ticket at Odds on Issues," *NYT*, October 15, 1938, 1.
57. Reminiscences of John Lord O'Brian, February-June 1952, 1, 4–5, 8–10, 17–19, COHC; John Lord O'Brian, "Metropolitan Club-May 12, 1966," 5–6, box 57, O'Brian-B MSS.
58. Reminiscences of John Lord O'Brian, February-June 1952, 37–38, 41–47, 52–53, 56–57, 191, COHC; O'Brian, "Metropolitan Club," 8. See John Lord O'Brian, "Charles Evans Hughes as Governor," *ABAJ* 27 (1941): 412–13.
59. Reminiscences of John Lord O'Brian, February-June 1952, 96–97, 108, 136–38, 142–45, 148–49, 167–69, 175, COHC. On Root and the "establishment" tradition he spawned, see Morton Keller, "The First Wise Man," *AL* (December 1999): 109; Alan Brinkley, *Liberalism and Its Discontents* (Cambridge, MA: Harvard University Press, 1998), 164–209.
60. Reminiscences of John Lord O'Brian, February-June 1952, 108–9, 119–23, 328–32, COHC; untitled note, enclosed with John Lord O'Brian to A.R.M., n.d., O'Brian-C&B MSS; "O'Brian of Buffalo Out for Governor," *NYT*, November 28, 1919, 5; "Miller and Wadsworth Win at Saratoga," *NYT*, July 29, 1920, 1; "Solid Delegation Urged by Morris," *NYT*, March 27, 1928, 3; " 'Old Guard' Seeks Man for Governor," *NYT*, February 9, 1934, 20; "Brewster is Boomed for Governorship," *NYT*, July 30, 1936, 6.
61. Reminiscences of John Lord O'Brian, February-June 1952, 132, 223–48, 263–85, 334–40, 465–68, COHC; "Von Rintelen Spent $508,000 in His Plot," *NYT*, May 2, 1917, 5; Michal R. Belknap, "John Lord O'Brian," *American National Biography*, ed. John A. Garraty and Mark C. Carnes (New York: Oxford University Press, 1999),16:584; John Lord O'Brian, "Civil Liberty in War Time," in NYSBA, *Proceedings* 1919: 275–313. See William H. Thomas, Jr., *Unsafe for Democracy: World War I and the U.S. Justice Department's Covert Campaign to Suppress Dissent* (Madison: University of Wisconsin Press, 2008), 27–28, 87, 156, 176–77.
62. Wagner's advisors quoted in J. Joseph Huthmacher, *Senator Robert F. Wagner and the Rise of Urban Liberalism* (New York: Atheneum, 1968), 253.
63. "TVA Case Put Off For O'Brian's Race," *NYT*, October 4, 1938, 34.
64. Press release, "Who Is John Lord O'Brian?" n.d., box 407, Wagner MSS.
65. Philip [Besser Gratz] to O'Brian, November 10, 1938, Noel T. Dowling to O'Brian, November 19, 1938, box 49, O'Brian-B MSS.
66. "O'Brian Offices Here," *NYT*, October 14, 1938, 7; Huthmacher, *Wagner*, 251.
67. "Proceedings of the State of New York Republican State Convention Held at Carnegie Hall, New York City, February 19-20, 1920," 101–2, box 57, O'Brian-B MSS; John Lord O'Brian, "The Menace of Administrative Law," *Maryland State Bar Association Reports* 1920: 156.

68. Remarks of John Lord O'Brian, American Law Institute, May 12, 1939, Personal Notebook, 90–95, box 50, O'Brian-B MSS; see also "O'Brian Decries Control before Law Institute," *NYT*, May 13, 1939, 17.
69. Thurman W. Arnold to Frances Arnold, August 6, 1939, box 10, Arnold MSS; see "Says He Was Offered Stock by White, Weld," *NYT*, July 16, 1936, 34; "Broker Defies SEC in A. O. Smith Case," *NYT*, July 17, 1936, 23.
70. Mastin G. White to J. R. Mohler, November 24, 1936, A. W. Miller to White, July 24, 1936, C. B. Miles to White, January 16, 24, February 10, 1937, box 28, entry 70, USDA Records.
71. "Swift & Co. Protest Federal Hearings," *NYT*, January 16, 1937, 31.
72. John Lord O'Brian, "Petition to Set Aside the Order of the Secretary of Agriculture Dated June 1, 1938," Miles to White, January 24, 1937, Respondent's Statement of Exceptions to Examiner's Actions at the Hearing," box 28, entry 70, USDA Records; Swift & Co. v. Wallace, 105 F.2d 848 (7th Cir. 1939).
73. Henry J. Winters to Benedict Wolf, October 29, 1938, box 406, Wagner MSS.
74. "Report of the Standing Committee on Labor, Employment and Social Security," *ABAR* 63 (1938): 269–70; see also *ABAR* 61 (1936): xxx, and 62 (1937): 30, 708–10.
75. "The G—D---- Labor Board," *Fortune* 18 (October 1938): 52–57, 115–18, 120, 23; Peter Irons, *The New Deal Lawyers* (Princeton, NJ: Princeton University Press, 1982), 243–48; Ronen Shamir, *Managing Legal Uncertainty: Elite Lawyers in the New Deal* (Durham, NC: Duke University Press, 1995), 85–86.
76. Christopher L. Tomlins, *The State and the Unions: Labor Relations, Law, and the Organized Labor Movement in America, 1880-1960* (New York: Cambridge University Press, 1985), 200; Leuchtenburg, *Franklin D. Roosevelt and the New Deal*, 243–44; "400 in Chamber Unanimous in Vote for Inquiry by Congress," *WP*, May 4, 1938, X1.
77. Susan Dunn, *Roosevelt's Purge: How FDR Fought to Change the Democratic Party* (Cambridge, MA: Harvard University Press, 2010). On Burke, see Patterson, *Congressional Conservatism*, 47–49; Smith, *Building New Deal Liberalism*, 160–89.
78. Tomlins, *State and the Unions*, 160–84; Gross, *Reshaping*, 50–68; "State A.F.L. Hits NLRB 'Prejudice,'" *NYT*, August 26, 1938, 1.
79. Gross, *Reshaping*, 35, 72; "Fair Play," *Collier's* 101 (June 25, 1938): 70.
80. "Fight on Measure Due in Next Congress," *NYT*, November 13, 1938, B3; *Revised Record*, 4:2947.
81. Reminiscences of John Lord O'Brian, February-June 1952, 168, 123–24, COHC.
82. Arthur Krock, "In the Nation: The Republican Tactics in New York," *NYT*, October 6, 1938, 22.
83. John Lord O'Brian, Address to the Young Men's Republican Clubs of the Eighth Judicial District, Buffalo, NY, October 15, 1938, 4, 9–11, box 407, Wagner MSS.
84. Frankfurter, recalling O'Brian's part, arranged for him to be offered the NLRB's chairmanship in 1935. Charles E. Wyzanski, Jr., to Ruth W. Rintels, August 19,

1935, box 22, Wyzanski-MHS MSS; Reminiscences of John Lord O'Brian, February-June 1952, 321–22, 456, COHC; "Senatorial Battle Page," *NYDN*, October 19, 1938, 32.

85. O'Brian, "Young Men's Republican Clubs," 5.
86. See, for example, *National Harness Manufacturers Association v. FTC*, 268 F. 705, 707 (6th Cir. 1920).
87. James M. Landis, *The Administrative Process* (1938; New Haven, CT: Yale University Press, 1966), 95, 99.
88. Louis L. Jaffe, interview by Jerold S. Auerbach, July 10 to September 22, 1972, 95, box 38, AJC OH. Other lawyers recalled being told to find facts that lacked an adequate basis in the record. Wallace M. Cohen, interview by Judith Byne, March 21, 1969, Ida Klaus, interview by Judith Byne, February 27, 1969, NLRB OH.
89. O'Brian, "Address to the Young Men's Republican Clubs," 6.
90. Ibid., 6–8.
91. Reminiscences of John Lord O'Brian, February-June 1952, 123–24, COHC.
92. O'Brian's Reply to Questions Asked by Times," *NYT*, October 22, 1938, 2; "O'Brian Asserts Campaign Issue Is Job Security," *NYHT*, October 19, 1938, 3; "As Young Voters of Westchester Hail John Lord O'Brian," *NYT*, October 23, 1938, sec. II, 2; "First Voters League to Form O'Brian Unit," *NYT*, October 24, 1938, 2; "O'Brian Jobs Brigade Launches Campaign to Elect Him," *NYT*, November 3, 1938, 7.
93. "O'Brian Group is Formed," *NYT*, October 22, 1938, 2; "New York's Senatorial Candidates: Mr. Stimson Advances Arguments in Favor of the Election of John Lord O'Brian to Congressional Seat," *NYT*, October 21, 1938, 22.
94. "Lehman Endorses Two New Dealers," *NYDN*, October 23, 1938, 20; *NYHT*, October 24, 1938, 1.
95. Elinore Herrick to Robert F. Wagner, August 6, 1938, box 6, Wagner MSS; Gross, *Reshaping*, 117–20.
96. "Keynote Speech of Senator Robert F. Wagner at New York State Democratic Convention, Rochester, NY," September 29, 1938, "Speech of U.S. Senator Robert F. Wagner at Ratification Meeting, National Democratic Club, New York City," October 14, 1938, "Speech of U.S. Senator Robert F. Wagner at Binghamton," October 20, 1938, "Speech of U.S. Senator Robert F. Wagner at Albany," October 24, 1938, box 2, Keyserling MSS.
97. "Senator Robert F. Wagner," *NYDN*, November 3, 1938, 33; Mark Sullivan, "Wagner and the Sit-Down Strike: Operation of Labor Act Poses Questions of Him as Candidate," *NYHT*, October 23, 1938, sec. II, 2; "Wagner Silent on Challenge," *NYHT*, October 25, 1938, 2.
98. "Wagner Rejects O'Brian's Bid to Debate Campaign Issues," *NYHT*, October 26, 1938, 1; "Text of Senator Wagner's Reply on New Deal," *NYT*, October 26, 1938, 8.

99. "Senator Wagner Turns Tail," *NYHT*, October 26, 1938, 22; "Senator Wagner Stands Pat," *New York World-Telegram*, October 27, 1938, box 6, Wagner MSS; "O'Brian Progress Scares Wagner," *Syracuse Post-Standard*, October 26, 1938, 4; "Where Does Wagner Stand?" *NYDM*, October 24, 1938, 17; "Hiding Under the Bed," *NYDM*, October 29, 1938, 13; "O'Brian Attacks Wagner Job Stand," *NYT*, October 27, 1938, 4.
100. Wagner to the Editor of the *Syracuse Post-Standard*, October 29, 1938, box 405, Wagner MSS; "AFL Joins CIO in Supporting Lehman," *NYDN*, October 2, 1938, 2; "A.L.P. Names Lehman with Wild Ovation," *NYDN*, October 4, 1938, 2; "O'Brian Reaffirms Labor Act Stand," *NYT*, October 31, 1938, 6.
101. "Text of Stimson Letter on Labor Relations Act," *NYT*, November 3, 1938, 19.
102. Victor F. Ridder to Robert E. Dowling, October 13, 1938, box 405, Maurine Mulliner to Simon H. Rifkind, November 1, 1938, Wagner MSS; Reminiscences of John Lord O'Brian, February-June 1952, 447, COHC; "Two Senators," *NYT*, November 1, 1938, 22.
103. Someone in the Wagner camp wrote the title of Bruce Barton's *The Man Nobody Knows* (1925) across the top of the press release, "Who Is John Lord O'Brian?" Box 407, Wagner MSS. For the sleepless nights of Wagner's associates, see Huthmacher, *Wagner*, 251. Al Smith also worried about "the drive against Wagner." James Farley, Memorandum, October 31, 1938, box 85, Cuneo MSS.
104. James Wolfinger, "The Strange Career of Frank Murphy: Conservatives, State-Level Politics, and the End of the New Deal," *Historian* 65 (2002): 377–402.
105. John O'Donnell and Doris Fleeson, "New Deal Control at Stake at the Polls," NYDN, November 6, 1938, 8; *NYT*, November 6, 1938, 33; "Nation Turns Eyes on State Election," *NYT*, November 6, 1938, 33.
106. "Roosevelt will Speak for Ticket at Hyde Park," *NYHT*, October 26, 1938, 8; "Five Million in A.F.L. Want Wagner, Says Green," ibid., November 2, 1938, 12; Diaries and Itineraries, 1933–40, November 2, 1938, PPF FDR.
107. Reminiscences of J. Warren Madden, 1957, 126–29, COHC; Kim, "Labor Law and Labor Policy in New York State," 217–18. After the election, Wagner endorsed the change as well. "Wagner Favors Only 1 Change in Labor Act," *NYT*, April 12, 1939, 2.
108. Reminiscences of J. Warren Madden, 127–28, COHC; Madden, Cornell Interview, 39–42.
109. Reminiscences of J. Warren Madden, 128, COHC; "Presses New Deal," *NYT*, November 5, 1938, 1; "Text of President's Address From Hyde Park on Issues in the Coming Election," *NYT*, November 5, 1938, 5.
110. O'Donnell and Fleeson, "New Deal Control," 8; "O'Brian Chides New Dealers for Reform Errors," *NYHT*, November 6, 1938, 27; "O'Brian Warns False Liberals Curb Liberties," *NYHT* November 7, 1938, 4; "Speech of U.S. Senator Robert F. Wagner at American Labor Party Rally, Madison Square Garden," October 31,

1938, box 2, "Speech of U.S. Senator Robert F. Wagner, Morris High School, The Bronx," November 3, 1938, 3, box 2, Keyserling MSS.

111. *Manual for the Use of the Legislature of the State of New York*, 1933: 912, 1939: 1150–51; Reminiscences of John Lord O'Brian, February-June 1952, 447–48, COHC; "Lehman Plurality Officially 64,004," *NYT*, December 8, 1938, 5.
112. "O'Brian Wires Wagner," *NYT*, November 10, 1938, 11; "The Senatorial Election," *NYT*, November 9, 1938, 22; [Gratz] to O'Brian, November 10, 1938, box 49, O'Brian-B MSS.
113. Joseph Alsop and Robert Kintner, "The Capital Parade," *WES*, November 16, 1938, A11.
114. "President May Delay Test on Choice of Smith," *WP*, January 4, 1939, 3; Gross, *Reshaping*, 89.
115. Leiserson, quoted in Gross, *Reshaping*, 90–91.
116. "Wagner Act Faces a Crisis," *Business Week*, July 13, 1940, 24, quoted in Gross, *Reshaping*, 221; Gross, *Reshaping*, 226–28.
117. Gross, *Reshaping*, 196–97, 229–31, 264; Harry A. Millis and Emily Clark Brown, *From the Wagner Act to Taft-Hartley: A Study of National Labor Policy and Labor Relations* (Chicago: University of Chicago Press, 1950), 56–58, 63–65.
118. Reminiscences of John Lord O'Brian, February-June 1952, 446, COHC.
119. Morgan v. United States, 304 U.S. 1, 22 (1938).

CHAPTER 5

1. Charles E. Wyzanski, Jr., to Homer S. Cummings, September 29, 1938, and Alexander Holtzhoff to Cummings, July 8, 1937, box 69, Cummings MSS; Abe Feller to Frank Murphy, January 19, 1939, and Warner W. Gardner to James W. Morris, January 21, 1939, box 4401, entry 112, DOJ Records.
2. "The Janizariat," *Time* 32 (September 12, 1938): 24.
3. Thus, I join those who are impressed by the continuity in Pound's thinking about the administrative state, including Michael Willrich, *City of Courts: Socializing Justice in Progressive Era Chicago* (New York: Cambridge University Press, 2003), 316–17; William C. Chase, *The American Law School and the Rise of Administrative Government* (Madison: University of Wisconsin Press, 1982), 114; and Joseph Postell, "The Anti-New Deal Progressive: Roscoe Pound's Alternative Administrative State," *RP* 74 (2012): 53–85. Scholars who see Pound as doing an about-face include Morton J. Horwitz, *The Transformation of American Law, 1870-1960: The Crisis of Legal Orthodoxy* (New York: Oxford University Press, 1992), 218–19; David Wigdor, *Roscoe Pound: Philosopher of Law* (Westport, CT: Greenwood Press, 1974), 267; Neil Duxbury, *Patterns of American Jurisprudence* (New York: Oxford University Press, 1995), 152; and John Fabian Witt, *Patriots and Cosmopolitans: Hidden Histories of American Law* (Cambridge,

MA: Harvard University Press, 2007), 223, 227–29, 232, although Witt also detected "a conservative streak running through Pound's thinking on administration and the common law."

4. Jedidiah J. Kroncke, "Roscoe Pound in China: A Lost Precedent for the Liabilities of American Legal Exceptionalism," *BJIL* 38 (2012): 128–33; Witt, *Patriots and Cosmopolitans*, 211–78; Joseph A. Page, "Roscoe Pound, Melvin Belli, and the Personal-Injury Bar: The Tale of an Odd Coupling," *TMCLR* 26 (2009): 637–79.
5. Richard E. Shugrue, "Roscoe Pound, Commissioner," in *The History of Nebraska Law*, ed. Alan G. Gless (Athens: Ohio University Press, 2008), 290–95.
6. Wigdor, *Pound*, 103–22; N. E. H. Hull, *Roscoe Pound and Karl Llewellyn: Searching for an American Jurisprudence* (Chicago: University of Chicago Press, 1997), 36–61; Alan G. Gless, "Pound's Accomplishments," in *History of Nebraska Law*, 295–305.
7. Roscoe Pound, "The Causes of Popular Dissatisfaction with the Administration of Justice," *ABAR* 29 (1906): 395, 405.
8. Wigdor, *Pound*, 123–29; Hull, *Roscoe Pound and Karl Llewellyn*, 63–66.
9. John H. Wigmore, "Roscoe Pound's St. Paul Address of 1906," *JAJS* 20 (1937): 176, 177.
10. Roscoe Pound, "Mechanical Jurisprudence," *CLR* 8 (1908): 605–23; Roscoe Pound, "Liberty of Contract," *YLJ* 18 (1909): 454–87.
11. G. Edward White, "(Nathan) Roscoe Pound," *Dictionary of American Biography* (New York: Charles Scribner's Sons, 1981), supp. 7, p. 626.
12. Roscoe Pound, "Executive Justice," *ALReg* 55 (1907): 137, 145–46.
13. Roscoe Pound, "Justice According to Law," *CLR* 13 (1913): 699.
14. Pound, "Executive Justice," 145.
15. Roscoe Pound, "Justice According to Law," *CLR* 14 (1914): 18.
16. Ibid., 21.
17. Ibid., 18, 12; Roscoe Pound, "The Growth of Administrative Justice," *WLR* 2 (1924): 327.
18. Roscoe Pound, "The Administrative Application of Legal Standards," *ABAR* 1919: 453–54; Pound, "Executive Justice," 145, 139; Roscoe Pound, *The Revival of Personal Government: Address by Professor Roscoe Pound before New Hampshire Bar Association, June 30, 1917* (n.p., n.d.), 15, 16.
19. Pound, "Growth of Administrative Justice," 333; Roscoe Pound, "The Law School," in *Reports of the President and the Treasurer of Harvard College, 1915-16* (Cambridge, MA: Harvard University, 1917), 141.
20. Pound, "Law School," 141.
21. Pound, "Growth of Administrative Justice," 324–25, citing Local Government Board v. Arlidge, [1915] A.C. 120.
22. Roscoe Pound to Morris R. Cohen, May 1, 1914, reel 27, FF-LC MSS. Pound referred to *People v. Stevens*, 203 N.Y. 7, 96 N.E. 114 (1911). On patronage politicians' capture of the New York commission, see Martin Landau, "The New York

Public Service Commission, 1907-1930" (Ph.D. diss., New York University, 1952), 54–68.

23. Pound, *Revival of Personal Government*, 19; Carroll v. Knickerbocker Ice Co., 218 N.Y. 435, 113 N.E. 507 (1916). New York lawyers came to deplore the decision as the font of the extremely deferential "legal residuum" standard for review of agency fact-finding. Robert M. Benjamin, *Administrative Adjudication in the State of New York* (1942; Buffalo, NY: William S. Hein, 2001), 1:181–94.
24. Pound, *Revival of Personal Government*, 21, 22; Pound, "Growth of Administrative Justice," 338; Pound, "Justice According to Law," 14:117.
25. Pound, "Growth of Administrative Justice," 338–39. Pound returned to this argument in *The Formative Era of American Law* (Boston: Little, Brown, 1938), 138–67.
26. Roscoe Pound, "The Legal Profession and the Law," in Oklahoma State Bar Association, *Proceedings*, 1925: 185.
27. "Address of Dean Roscoe Pound," in Utah State Bar Association, *Proceedings*, 1927: 65.
28. Roscoe Pound, "A Foreword to the Pageant of Magna Carta," *ABAJ* 14 (1928): 529.
29. On Pound and the reforms of civil procedure, see Stephen N. Subrin, "How Equity Conquered Common Law: The Federal Rules of Civil Procedure In Historical Perspective," *UPLR* 135 (1987): 944–54, 973; Wigdor, *Pound*, 150; Charles E. Clark to Thurman W. Arnold, January 9, 1930, box 8, Arnold MSS.
30. "Dean Pound Won't Go to Wisconsin," *NYT*, February 3, 1925, 13; "League to Choose New World Court," *NYT*, February 15, 1930, 9; Wigdor, *Pound*, 239–41, 247–48.
31. Roscoe Pound, "The Future of the Common Law," *UCiLR* 7 (1933): 357, 358.
32. Roscoe Pound, "The New Deal in the Courts: A Changing Ideal of Justice," *NYT*, September 9, 1934, XX-3, 10.
33. Quoted in Wigdor, *Pound*, 251.
34. Frankfurter to Learned Hand, December 10, 1931, quoted in Michael E. Parrish, *Felix Frankfurter and His Times: The Reform Years* (New York: Free Press, 1982), 198. On the final years of Pound's deanship, see Laura Kalman, *Legal Realism at Yale, 1927-1960* (Chapel Hill: University of North Carolina Press, 1986), 56–62; Wigdor, *Pound*, 248–54; and James F. Clark, "The Harvard Law School Deanship of Roscoe Pound, 1916-1936" (seminar paper, Harvard Law School, May 7, 1999), 112–44, Special Collections Department, Harvard Law School Library, Cambridge, MA.
35. Conant quoted in Kalman, *Legal Realism at Yale*, 61; Frankfurter to Calvert Magruder, July 25, 1934, quoted in Kalman, *Legal Realism at Yale*, 61; Kyle Graham, "The Refugee Jurist and American Law Schools, 1933-1941," *AJCL* 50 (2002): 789–90.
36. "Pound Will Resign Harvard Law Post," *NYT*, September 25, 1935, 2; Pound to Spier Whitaker, September 8, 1936, quoted in Kalman, *Legal Realism at Yale*, 57.
37. Hull, *Roscoe Pound and Karl Llewellyn*, 173.

38. Karl N. Llewellyn, *The Bramble Bush: On Our Law and Its Study* (New York, 1930), 3; Karl N. Llewellyn, "A Realistic Jurisprudence: The Next Step," *CLR* 30 (1930): 435 n. 3.
39. David A. Skeel, Jr., *Debt's Dominion: A History of Bankruptcy Law in America* (Princeton, NJ: Princeton University Press, 2001), 102–5; Robert T. Swaine, "Reorganization of Corporations: Certain Developments of the Last Decade," *CLR* 27 (1927): 901–32 and *CLR* 28 (1928): 29–63; Reminiscences of Jerome N. Frank, April 11, 1950, 11–13, COHC. On Frank, see Robert Jerome Glennon, *The Iconoclast as Reformer: Jerome Frank's Impact on American Law* (Ithaca, NY: Cornell University Press, 1985), 15–25; Peter Irons, *The New Deal Lawyers* (Princeton, NJ: Princeton University Press, 1982), 119–21; Walter E. Volkomer, *The Passionate Liberal: The Political and Legal Ideas of Jerome Frank* (The Hague: Martinus Nijhoff, 1970), 1–8.
40. Jerome N. Frank, *Law and the Modern Mind* (1930; New York: Coward-McCann, 1935), 207–216, 289–301; Roscoe Pound to Karl N. Llewellyn, March 21, 1931, quoted in Hull, *Roscoe Pound and Karl Llewellyn*, 197; Karl N. Llewellyn, "Some Realism about Realism: A Response to Dean Pound," *HLR* 44 (1931): 1222–64.
41. James F. Simon, *Independent Journey: The Life of William O. Douglas* (New York: Harper & Row, 1980), 80–86, 128–30; Reminiscences of Jerome N. Frank, April 11, 1950, 12, COHC.
42. Robert T. Swaine to Jerome N. Frank, May 5, 9, 12, 1933; Frank to Swaine, May 8, 10, 1933, box 16; and Douglas to Frank, January 3, 1934, box 11, series 2, Frank MSS; Jerome N. Frank, "Some Realistic Reflections on Some Aspects of Corporate Reorganization," *VLR* 19 (1933): 541–70, 698–718; Robert T. Swaine, "Corporate Reorganization under the Federal Bankruptcy Power," *VLR* 19 (1933): 317–33; William O. Douglas and Jerome N. Frank, "Landlords' Claims in Reorganizations," *YLJ* 42 (1933): 1003–50; William O. Douglas, "Protective Committees in Railroad Reorganizations," *HLR* 47 (1934): 565–89; Robert W. Gordon, "Professors and Policymakers: Yale Law School Faculty in the New Deal and After," in *History of the Yale Law School*, ed. Anthony T. Kronman (New Haven, CT: Yale University Press, 2004), 84–117.
43. Roscoe Pound, *Contemporary Juristic Theory* (Claremont, CA: Pomona College, Scripps College, Claremont Colleges, 1940), 38.
44. Pound to O. R. McGuire, September 14, 1938, reel 109, pt. 1, Pound MSS.
45. Roscoe Pound, "Law and the Science of Law in Recent Theories," *ALSR* 7 (1934): 1062, 1059, 1062–63.
46. Jerome Frank, "Realism in Jurisprudence," *ALSR* 7 (1934): 1064, 1065–66. The speech was also published as "Experimental Jurisprudence and the New Deal," *CR* 78 (June 18, 1934): 12412–14.
47. Roscoe Pound, "Visitatorial Jurisdiction over Corporations in Equity," *HLR* 49 (1936): 392.

48. Roscoe Pound, "What is the Common Law?" in *The Future of the Common Law* (Cambridge, MA: Harvard University Press, 1937), 10–11, 19. Pound's failure to rank Nazi Germany or Stalinist Russia ahead of the United States in this regard ought not to pass unremarked.
49. Roscoe Pound, diary, February 5, 1937, reel 42, part 2, Pound MSS; "FDR's Court Plan 'Bluff' and Also 'Stuff,' Says Former Harvard Law Dean," *Honolulu Star-Bulletin*, February 10, 1937, 1; "Dean Pound Returns," *NYT*, September 1, 1937, 10.
50. Roscoe Pound, "The New Feudalism," *ABAJ* 16 (1930): 553.
51. "Report of the Special Committee on Administrative Law," *ABAR* 59 (1934): 546–47. For Caldwell's authorship of the report, see Louis G. Caldwell, "Discussion of McCarran-Sumners Administrative Procedure Bill," *Journal of the Bar Association of the District of Columbia* 12 (1945): 64. On Caldwell at the Federal Radio Commission, see Michael Stamm, *Sound Business: Newspapers, Radio, and the Politics of New Media* (Philadelphia: University of Pennsylvania Press, 2011), 55.
52. Caldwell, "Discussion of McCarran-Sumners," 62–63.
53. Proceedings, House of Delegates, *ABAR* 58 (1933): 203–4; "Report of the Special Committee on Administrative Law," ibid., 408, 415.
54. *CR* 70 (January 3, 1929): 1030–33; George W. Norris to John G. Sargent, January 31, 1929, box 194, Norris MSS; Karl Fenning, "Court of Customs and Patent Office Appeals," *ABAJ* 17 (1931): 323.
55. Ollie Roscoe McGuire to Norris, December 31, 1928, January 27, 1929, box 194, Norris MSS; McGuire to Arthur T. Vanderbilt, October 11, 1937, box 142, Vanderbilt MSS; "Ollie Roscoe McGuire," *Who Was Who in America* (Chicago: Marquis Who's Who, 1968), 4:639; see James M. Beck, *Our Wonderland of Bureaucracy: A Study of the Growth of Bureaucracy in the Federal Government, and Its Destructive Effect Upon the Constitution* (New York: Macmillan Co., 1932), xiv; O. R. McGuire to James M. Beck, January 30, 1933, box 5, Beck MSS.
56. *ABAR* 61 (1936): 221–27, 231–35; William L. Ransom to Arthur T. Vanderbilt, August 17, 1937, box 142, Vanderbilt MSS. See George B. Shepherd, "Fierce Compromise: The Administrative Procedure Act Emerges from New Deal Politics," *NULR* 90 (1996): 1575–77; Ronen Shamir, *Managing Legal Uncertainty: Elite Lawyers in the New Deal* (Durham, NC: Duke University Press, 1995), 110.
57. Appel to Ransom, February 24, 1936, box 142, Vanderbilt MSS; Appel to Stephens, May 28, 1937, box 402, Stephens MSS; Proceedings of the Second Meeting of the House of Delegates of the Legal Profession, Columbus, Ohio, January 5-7, 1937, 283–311, Northwestern University Law Library (Shelfmark KF 325a17h687 1937).
58. McGuire to Baker, January 10, 1937, box 23, Baker MSS; Stephens to Appel, January 18, 1937, box 402, Stephens MSS; Shepherd, "Fierce Compromise," 1582–83.
59. Shepherd, "Fierce Compromise," 1582–83; "Report of the Special Committee on Administrative Law," *ABAR* 62 (1937): 821–30.

60. McGuire to Vanderbilt, April 11, 1937, box 142, Vanderbilt MSS.
61. Evidently, the US Court of Claims was chosen because as an Article I court it could issue advisory opinions; whereas an Article III court, such as the US Court of Appeals, could not.
62. Louis G. Caldwell, "Memorandum Concerning Recommendation No. 5 of the Special Committee on Administrative Law," n.d., enclosed in Louis G. Caldwell to Morris, September 16, 1937, and Appel to Morris, June 2, 1937, box 142, Vanderbilt MSS; Appel to Stephens, May 28, 1937, Appel, "Minority Report of the Special Committee on Administrative Law of the American Bar Association," n.d., box 402, Stephens MSS; Agenda for the Meeting of the Board of Governors, Kansas City, Missouri, September 23, 1937, in ABA, Board of Governors Proceedings, Northwestern University Law Library (Shelfmark KF 325.A17B635 1937); *ABAR* 62 (1937): 262, 272, 275, 286–90, 790; William R. Vallance, "Important Action Taken at Meeting of American Bar Association at Kansas City," *FBAJ* 3 (1937): 96–97. The Georgia delegate was the former governor John M. Slaton, who had effectively ended his political career by commuting Leo Frank's death sentence in 1915. See *ABAJ* 25 (1939): 94.
63. "Excerpt from Transcript of Board of Governors Proceedings, Saturday afternoon, October 2, 1937," reel 108, part 1, Pound MSS. A fuller transcription survives as ABA, Proceedings of the Board of Governors, Kansas City, Mo., September 23–28, 1937, 257a, 258, Northwestern University Law Library (Shelfmark KF 325. a17B637 1937-46).
64. Vanderbilt to Pound, October 5, 1937, reel 109, part 1, Pound MSS.
65. Vanderbilt to Pound, October 14, 1937, box 117, Vanderbilt MSS.
66. Pound to Vanderbilt, May 9, 1938, Pound to Walter F. Dodd, April 18, 1938, reel 109, part 1, Pound MSS. See Wigdor, *Pound*, 139–40, 150.
67. Pound to Vanderbilt, October, 11, 1937, and Pound to McGuire, October 26, 1937, reel 109, part 1, Pound MSS.
68. McGuire to Baker, November 27, 1937, box 23, Baker MSS; Pound to Vanderbilt, April 12, 1938, and Vanderbilt to Pound, December 20, 1937, reel 109, part 1, Pound MSS; Vanderbilt to Pound, December 4, 1937, reel 108, part 1, Pound MSS. See Richard Polenberg, *Reorganizing Roosevelt's Government: The Controversy over Executive Reorganization, 1936-1939* (Cambridge, MA: Harvard University Press, 1966).
69. Pound, diary, April 19–22, 1938, reel 42, part 2, Pound MSS. The credit for discovering that Pound regularly endured his second wife's drunken scenes goes to Owen A. McGillivray, Georgetown University Law Center Class of 2010, who noticed and deciphered Pound's coded references to them in his diary.
70. Pound to Stephens, April 18, 1938, box 402, Stephens MSS; Pound to Vanderbilt, April 21, 30, 1938, reel 109, and James R. Garfield to Pound, April 22, 1938, reel 108, part 1, Pound MSS. Evidently, Dodd was appointed to the committee on the strength of his *Administration of Workmen's Compensation* (New York: Commonwealth

Fund, 1936). Vanderbilt had appointed Robert Maguire to assuage ABA members on the West Coast, who felt they had been denied their share of appointments to important committees. Maguire often appeared before Oregon commissions. Vanderbilt to Robert Maguire, October 12, 1937, box 117, Vanderbilt MSS.

71. Garfield to Pound, April 22, 1938, reel 108; Pound to Vanderbilt, April 30, 1938; and Pound to McGuire, May 5, 1938, reel 109, part 1, Pound MSS.
72. Pound, diary, May 9, 1938, reel 42, part 2, Pound to Vanderbilt, May 9, 1938, reel 109, part 1, Pound MSS; Senate Committee on the Judiciary, *United States Court of Appeals for Administration*, 75th Cong., 3d sess., 1938, 162–67; ABA, Summary of Proceedings of the Board of Governors, Washington, D.C., May 9-13, 1938, ABA MSS.
73. Pound to Olive G. Ricker, May 31, 1938; Pound to McGuire, June 13, 1938; and Pound to Vanderbilt, June 22, 1938, reel 109, part 1, Pound MSS.
74. I certainly was fooled. Daniel R. Ernst, "Dicey's Disciple on the D.C. Circuit: Judge Harold Stephens and Administrative Law Reform, 1933-1940," *GLJ* 90 (2002): 792. See also Wigdor, *Pound*, 267–68; Horwitz, *Transformation of American Law, 1870-1960*, 231; Shepherd, "Fierce Compromise," 1591, 1593.
75. Dodd to Pound, May 21, 1938; Pound to Dodd, May 23, 1938; Pound to Vanderbilt, June 22, 1938; Pound to Robert N. Miller, September 22, 1938; Pound to McGuire, December 12, 1938, reel 109; Pound to Frank, November 7, 1938; Frank to Edgar B. Tolman, November 26, 1938, reel 74, part 1, Pound MSS; Tolman to Frank, December 6, 1938, February 27, 1939, series 3, box 40, Frank MSS.
76. "Present at the Creation: Regulatory Reform before 1946," *AdLR* 38 (1986): 524 (K.C. Davis).
77. "Proposed Act: A Bill to Provide for the More Expeditious Settlement of Disputes with the United States and for Other Purposes," *ABAR* 63 (1938): 364–66.
78. Miller to Pound, December 17, 1937, reel 109, and Garfield to Pound, April 22, 1938, reel 108, part 1, Pound MSS; "Report of the Special Committee on Administrative Law," *ABAR* 63 (1938): 336–37 (Pound Report).
79. Senate Committee, *United States Court of Appeals for Administration*, 171, 174, 178.
80. Pound Report, 343, 361; Senate Committee, *United States Court of Appeals for Administration*, 172, 177. Pound was referring to Edward Coke, *The Fourth Part of the Institutes of the Laws of England* (London: W. Clarke, 1817), *71, or James Bagg's Case, 11 Coke's Reports 93b, 98a, 77 Eng. Rep. 1271, 1277–78 (1615).
81. Pound to Cornelius W. Wickersham, Jr., June 6, 13, 1938, reel 109, part 1, Pound MSS; Senate Committee, *United States Court of Appeals for Administration*, 171.
82. Donald A. Ritchie, *James M. Landis: Dean of the Regulators* (Cambridge, MA: Harvard University Press, 1980), 79–87; James M. Landis, *The Administrative Process* (1938; New Haven, CT: Yale University Press, 1966).
83. Shamir, *Managing Legal Uncertainty*, 131–57; Gordon, "Professors and Policymakers."

84. Pound Report, 343; John D. O'Reilly, Jr., "Administrative Absolutism," *FLR* 7 (1938): 311; Pound to Stephens, July 14, 1942, box 31, Stephens MSS.
85. Pound Report, 339–40, 343. For the proposition that "law is whatever is done officially," Pound cited not Llewellyn but an article by Felix S. Cohen, "Transcendental Nonsense and the Functional Approach," *CLR* 35 (1935): 809, 833, with whom he had only an attenuated connection. See Dalia Tsuk Mitchell, *Architect of Justice: Felix S. Cohen and the Founding of American Legal Pluralism* (Ithaca, NY: Cornell University Press, 2007), 36, 45, 130.
86. The quoted language appears in Roscoe Pound, *Administrative Law* (Pittsburgh, PA: University of Pittsburgh Press, 1942), 4, 3; Roscoe Pound, "Fifty Years of Jurisprudence," *HLR* 51 (1938): 780.
87. Morris R. Cohen to Pound, July 9, September 30, 1938, Pound to Cohen, September 15, 1938, in Lenora Cohen Rosenfield, *Portrait of a Philosopher: Morris R. Cohen in Life and Letters* (New York: Harcourt, Brace & World, 1962), 307–9.
88. Joanna L. Grisinger, *The Unwieldy American State: Administrative Politics Since the New Deal* (New York: Cambridge University Press, 2012), 18–19.
89. Pound Report, 346–51.
90. Ibid., 336, 350. For all Pound's talk of sociology, he retained a botanist's notion of proof through the collection and display of specimens. See Kalman, *Legal Realism at Yale*, 46; Hull, *Roscoe Pound and Karl Llewellyn*, 48–49.
91. Pound Report, 345, 347, 348, 349, 350. For Pound's Republican affiliation, see Hull, *Roscoe Pound and Karl Llewellyn*, 62.
92. Pound Report, 360.
93. Ibid., 347 n. 38, 358 n. 68, citing Tri-State Broadcasting Co. v. FCC, 96 F.2d 564 (D.C. Cir. 1938); Saginaw Broadcasting Co. v. FCC, 96 F.2d 554 (D.C. Cir. 1938); Carl I. Wheat, "The Regulation of Interstate Telephone Rates," *HLR* 51 (1938): 846–83.
94. Pound Report, 346 n. 35, citing Saxton Coal Mining Co. v. National Bituminous Coal Commission, 96 F.2d 517 (D.C. Cir. 1938).
95. Pound Report, 343, quoting James M. Landis, "Business Policy and the Courts," *YR* 27 (1938): 237. See James A. Gross, *The Reshaping of the National Labor Relations Board: A Study in Economics, Politics, and the Law* (Albany: State University of New York Press, 1981), 30–39.
96. Joel Seligman, *The Transformation of Wall Street: A History of the Securities and Exchange Commission and Modern Corporate Finance* (Boston: Houghton Mifflin, 1982), 154, 155, 160, 214.
97. Skeel, *Debt's Dominion*, 113–23.
98. Simon, *Independent Journey*, 144–45; William O. Douglas, *Go East, Young Man: The Autobiography of William O. Douglas* (New York: Random House, 1974), 260.
99. Abe Fortas to William O. Douglas, May 20, 1937, box 6, Douglas MSS.

100. Pound Report, 349. In fact, Pound quoted not Swaine but the Harvard professor Merrick Dodd and omitted Dodd's qualification that the reports were "fair-minded and well-documented briefs to be sure." E. Merrick Dodd, Jr., "The Securities and Exchange Commission's Reform Program for Bankruptcy Reorganizations," *CLR* 38 (1938): 225. Swaine's actual characterization of Douglas's reports was less restrained. He likened them to "the dime store novel of the nineties" and "a modern gangster Hollywood thriller." Robert T. Swaine, "'Democratization' of Corporate Reorganizations," *CLR* 38 (1938): 259.
101. Pound Report, 345, 339, quoting Swaine, "'Democratization' of Corporate Reorganizations," 265, 277–78.
102. Jerome N. Frank, "Corporate Reorganization and the Chandler Act," July 25, 1938, 12–14, http://www.sec.gov/news/speech/1938/072538frank.pdf, visited December 14, 2012; Frank to Pound, November 6, 1938, reel 74, part 1, Pound MSS.
103. Frank, "Corporate Reorganization and the Chandler Act," 14; Transcript, Open Forum on Pending Federal Legislation Involving Reorganizations and Securities," July 25, 1938, 106, Northwestern University Law Library (Shelfmark KF325 A17A437 1938); Frank to Pound, February 3, 1939, reel 74, part 1, Pound MSS; see Irons, *New Deal Lawyers*, 128–32, 156–80.
104. Pound to McGuire, September 14, 1938, reel 109, Pound to Frank, November 1, 1938, reel 74, part 1, Pound MSS.
105. I quote from Roscoe Pound, "Some Implications of Recent Legislation," *Vital Speeches* 5 (November 15, 1938): 91, 93. The address also circulated in mimeo, in *Investment Banking* 9 (November 15, 1938): 24–28, in *United States Investor* 49 (November 5, 1938): 1749–52, and in *WVLQ* 45 (1939): 205–19. An excerpt appeared as "Divus Augustus," *WP*, November 19, 1938, 9. For the bankers' attentiveness, see Alden H. Little to Pound, November 3, 1938, reel 14, part 2, Pound MSS.
106. Frank, "Administrative Flexibility or Industrial Paralysis?" November 9, 1938, http://www.sec.gov/news/speech/1938/110938frank.pdf, visited December 8, 2013, 1–2, 9. Frank joked that Pound was slipping into his "anecdotage." Frank to Frankfurter, September 21, 1938, box 27, series 3, Frank MSS.
107. Frank, "Administrative Flexibility," 12–13.
108. Lane to Frank, November 8, 1938, box 32, series 3, Frank MSS. In contrast, James Landis thought that "RP had it coming to him." Landis to Frank, November 12, 1938, ibid.
109. Jerome N. Frank, "SEC and the Rubber Hose," April 8, 1939, 1, 19–24, 37–38, 45–47, http://www.sec.gov/news/speech/1939/040839frank.pdf, visited October 8, 2012. Again Chester Lane objected. "In a very real sense," Lane reminded Frank, "the threat of stop order proceedings or expulsion proceedings, applied by the staff, can extract involuntary confessions." Lane also wondered "whether the personal denunciation of Dean Pound adds to the forcefulness of the paper." Lane to Frank, March 6, 1939, box 32, series 3, Frank MSS.

110. Pound to Stephens, October 13, 1942, box 31, Stephens MSS; see Roscoe Pound, "Modern Administrative Law," and "A General Summary," in *A Legal Institute on Modern Federal Administrative Law Held at Richmond, Virginia, April 28 and 29, 1939* (Richmond, VA: Richmond Press, 1939), 8–24, 79–92; Roscoe Pound, "Fundamental Principles of Administrative Procedure," November 17, 1939, in ABA Section on Legal Education and Admissions to the Bar, "Practice and Procedure before Administrative Tribunals, November 13-17, 1939," ABA MSS; Pound, *Administrative Law*, 63–65; Roscoe Pound, "The Place of the Judiciary in a Democratic Polity," *ABAJ* 27 (1941): 133–39; Roscoe Pound, "For the 'Minority Report,'" *ABAJ* 27 (1941): 664–78.
111. Jerome Frank, *If Men Were Angels: Some Aspects of Government in a Democracy* (New York: Harper & Brothers, 1942), 163 (emphasis deleted). Frank's claim, ibid., 338, that a reader comparing Pound's early and late writings would rub his eyes and ask, "Can this be the same man?" is the locus classicus for those who argue that Pound's thinking about the administrative state underwent an "about face."
112. Louis L. Jaffe, "Invective and Investigation in Administrative Law," *HLR* 52 (1939): 1236; David Cushman Coyle, "Dean Pound appears to disapprove...," enclosed in Douglas to Frank, December 21, 1940, box 25, series 3, Frank MSS; Louis L. Jaffe, review of *Administrative Law*, by Roscoe Pound, *CLR* 42 (1942): 1382; Kenneth Culp Davis, "Dean Pound and Administrative Law," ibid., 103; Lloyd K. Garrison to Kenneth C. Davis, February 17, 1942, box 53, series 11/1/1, Wisconsin MSS.
113. James T. Patterson, *Congressional Conservatism and the New Deal: The Growth of the Conservative Coalition in Congress, 1933-1939* (Lexington: University of Kentucky Press, 1967); Jason Scott Smith, *Building New Deal Liberalism: The Political Economy of Public Works, 1933-1956* (New York: Cambridge University Press, 2006), 160–80; Sidney M. Milkis, *The President and the Parties: The Transformation of the American Party System since the New Deal* (New York: Oxford University Press, 1993), 52–124, 335–36 n. 40.
114. *Kiplinger's Washington Letter*, August 5, 1939, January 27, May 4, November 23, 1940. The Republican Party's platform in 1940 endorsed the Walter-Logan bill. "Logan-Walter Bill Backers Confident Victory Will Come," *ALL* 2 (September 7, 1940): 7.
115. "President Opposes Curbs on Agencies Under Logan Bill," *NYT*, April 6, 1940, 1, 6; Daniel Scroop, *Mr. Democrat: Jim Farley, the New Deal and the Making of Modern American Politics* (Ann Arbor: University of Michigan Press, 2006), 160–62; John B. Oakes, "Agency Curb Passes House," *NYT*, April 19, 1940, 1; "Walter-Logan Bill Appears Dead for Year," *WP*, November 13, 1940, 3; Hedley Donovan, "Senate Bill Passes Walter-Logan Bill, 27-25," *WP*, November 27, 1940, 1; Shepherd, "Fierce Compromise," 1598–1623.

116. S. Rep. No. 422, 76th Cong., 1st Sess. 5 (1939), quoted in Shepherd, "Fierce Compromise," 1601–02; *CR* 86 (April 17, 1940): 4647, 4531, 4732, 1609, quoted in ibid., 1617.
117. Joseph Alsop and Robert Kintner, "We Shall Make America Over: The Birth of the Brain Trust," *SEP* 211 (October 29, 1938): 79.
118. "Address of Chester T. Lane, General Counsel, Securities and Exchange Commission, before the Chicago Convention of the National Lawyers Guild," February 11, 1939, box 9, entry 376, DOJ Records; "Administrative Law Bill," July 22, 1939, box 11, entry 9, inventory A1, "Comments on Logan Bill-S.915," n.d., box 33, inventory ww, SEC Records.
119. Alfred Jaretzki, Jr., "The Administrative Law Bill: Unsound and Unworkable," *LLR* 2 (1940): 294; "Statement of John Foster Dulles, Attorney General's Committee on Administrative Procedure," July 12, 1940, 5, reel 59, Dulles MSS. The Association of the Bar of the City of New York also opposed the bill. Ernest Lindley, "Much Confusion," *WP*, April 19, 1940, 13.
120. I refer to the Senate Report, as appended to Jaretzki, "Administrative Law Bill," 325–26.
121. Jaretzki, "Administrative Law Bill," 305–7; Association of the Bar of the City of New York, "Joint Report of the Committees on Administrative Law and on Federal Legislation on S.915 (76th Congress) introduced by Mr. Logan and Its Companion Bill by Mr. Cellar," May 2, 1939, 5-7, reel 4, Dulles MSS; Louis G. Caldwell, "Memorandum on Logan-Walter Bill (S. 915 and H.R. 6324)," *CR* 86 (April 18, 1940): A2222–23.
122. Because the D.C. Circuit exercised jurisdiction under Article I as well as Article III, Walter-Logan's drafters thought it could issue advisory opinions. A member of the ABA's inner circle considered it "a court of great learning and dignity," unlike the Court of Claims. Newton D. Baker to McGuire, January 12, 1937, box 23, Baker MSS.
123. "Address of Chester T. Lane"; "Administrative Law Bill," July 20, 1939, box 11, entry 9, inventory A1, SEC Records.
124. See James M. Landis, "Crucial Issues in Administrative Law: The Walter-Logan Bill," *HLR* 53 (1940): 1091–92.
125. Robert E. Healy to Sherman Minton, May 10, 1940, box 29, Rowe MSS; Frank to Henry F. Ashurst, May 6, 1940, box 26, inventory ww, SEC Records.
126. Paul Freund to Henry M. Hart, Jr., December 4, 1940, box 87, Jackson MSS; Chester Lane, "Administrative Law Bill," July 20, 1939, box 11, entry 9, inventory A1, SEC Records.
127. Landis, "Crucial Issues," 1093.
128. Healy to Minton, May 10, 1940, box 29, Rowe MSS; see also Breck P. McAllister, "Administrative Adjudication and Judicial Review," *ILR* 34 (1940): 690–92.
129. "Administrative Law Bill," July 22, 1939, box 11, entry 9, inventory A1, SEC Records; see also Robert L. Stern, "Review of Findings of Administrators, Judges

and Juries: A Comparative Analysis," *HLR* 58 (1944): 87–88; Chester T. Lane and Robert M. Blair-Smith, "The SEC and the 'Expeditious Settlement of Disputes,'" *ILR* 34 (1940): 724; Jaffe, "Invective and Investigation,"1232; Frederick F. Blachly to Meyer Jacobstein, January 9, 1940, box 87, Jackson MSS; Ernest Lindley, "Evidence and Courts," *WP*, May 10, 1940, 17.

130. *CR* 86 (September 23, 1940): 12456 (Edward R. Burke).
131. Pound to Francis E. Walter, May 18, 1939, reel 39, part 3, Pound MSS; Walter Gellhorn, "Memorandum of Conversation with Congressman Walter," June 2, 1939, box 8, entry 376, DOJ Records; "Extension of the Remarks of Hon. George H. Bender," in *CR* 85 (November 3, 1939): A747.
132. Landis, "Crucial Issues."
133. Pound to Burke, May 18, 1940, in *CR* 86 (September 23, 1940): 12456–57; "Logan-Walter Bill Supported by Dean Pound," *ALL* 2 (May 25, 1940): 1. The reference to those who saw administration as a fourth branch of government was a jab at Landis, whom Pound privately described as advocating "an extreme of administrative absolutism." Pound to H. M. Wright, January 30, 1939, reel 109, part 1, Pound MSS; cf. Landis, *Administrative Process*, 47; "Symposium on Administrative Law," *ALSR* 9 (1939): 181.
134. *CR* 86 (November 19, 1940): 13662; Hedley Donovan, "Senate to Get Bill to Curb U.S. Agencies," *WP*, November 20, 1940, 3.
135. Davis, "Dean Pound and Administrative Law," 89; James Edward Brazier, "Who Controls the Administrative State? Congress and the President Adopt the Administrative Procedure Act of 1946 (PhD diss., Michigan State University, 1993), 168–72; "Agencies Not Dismayed by Bill's Passage," *ALL* 2 (November 30, 1940): 3; Roosevelt to Jackson, November 29, 1940, Robert H. Jackson, "Draft Veto Message of Walter-Logan Bill," November 25, 1940, box 91, Jackson MSS; Franklin D. Roosevelt, Veto Message, *CR* 86 (December 18, 1940): 13943. Jackson had spoken against the bill when the ABA's House of Delegates endorsed it in January 1939. Brazier, "Who Controls?" 104–5.
136. Grisinger, *Unwieldy American State*, 77.
137. Garfield to Pound, April 22, 1938, reel 108, part 1, Pound MSS.
138. CR 86 (April 15, 16, 1940): 4534, 4603. The House's investigation of the NLRB in 1939-40 had a similar cast of characters. Ira Katznelson, *Fear Itself: The New Deal and the Origins of Our Time* (New York: Liveright Publishing Corp., 2013), 272–74.
139. Roosevelt, Veto Message, 13943.
140. Arthur T. Vanderbilt, "Legal Education, Bar Organization and Economics," *Annual Survey of American Law* 1942: 966. See Grisinger, *Unwieldy American State*, 14–58.
141. Joseph W. Henderson, "Administrative Procedure," *CBJ* 17 (1943): 237; W. M. Kiplinger, *Washington is* Like *That* (New York: Harper & Brothers, 1942), 311–18.

142. Daniel R. Ernst, "The Ideal and the Actual in the State: Willard Hurst at the Board of Economic Warfare," in *Total War and the Law: The American Home Front in World War II*, ed. Daniel R. Ernst & Victor Jew (Westport, CT: Praeger, 2002), 170.

CHAPTER 6

1. Charles Henry Caffin, in *Handbook of the New Library of Congress*, comp. Herbert Small (Boston: Curtis and Cameron, 1897), 37; Charles Evans Hughes, "Speech before the Elmira Chamber of Commerce, May 3, 1907," in *Addresses of Charles Evans Hughes, 1906-1916*, 2nd ed. (New York: Putnam's Sons, 1916), 181.
2. Caffin, in *Handbook*, 37–38.
3. Dick Armey and Matt Kibbe, *Give Us Liberty: A Tea Party Manifesto* (New York: William Morrow, 2010), 71, 66–67.
4. *Revised Record of the Constitutional Convention of the State of New York, April Sixth to September Tenth, 1915* (Albany, NY: J. B. Lyon, 1916), 3: 302.
5. "Reed Makes Plea for Liberal Aims," *WS*, May 30, 1935, 11.
6. "Hughes Warns of Autocracy in Democracy," *Boston Evening Transcript*, June 21, 1920, 2.
7. Ernst Freund, *Administrative Powers over Persons and Property: A Comparative Survey* (Chicago: University of Chicago Press, 1928), 583.
8. Conference of the Attorney General's Committee on Administrative Procedure, March 16, 1939, 27, 30, box 3, entry 376, DOJ Records; Walter Gellhorn, "Symposium on Procedural Administrative Law: Introduction," *IaLR* 25 (1940): 423.
9. Peter H. Schuck provides an excellent synopsis of methods of "controlling administrative discretion" in *Foundations of Administrative Law*, 2nd ed. (New York: Foundation Press, 2004), 175–82.
10. Probably most found the *Rechtsstaat* ideal in Friedrich Hayek's work rather than in that of the largely forgotten Freund. See, for example, Theodore J. Lowi, *The End of Liberalism: Ideology, Policy, and the Crisis of Public Authority* (New York: W. W. Norton, 1969), 298. Those who looked to Freund included Richard B. Stewart, "The Reformation of American Administrative Law," *HLR* 88 (1975): 1694 n. 118, and William C. Chase, *The American Law School and the Rise of Administrative Government* (Madison: University of Wisconsin Press, 1982), 134–35, 141.
11. Walter Gellhorn, *Federal Administrative Proceedings* (Baltimore: Johns Hopkins Press, 1941), 131; see Reuel E. Schiller, "Enlarging the Administrative Polity: Administrative Law and the Changing Definitions of Pluralism, 1945-1970," *VanLR* 53 (2000): 1389–453.
12. John Schwartz, "Some Ask If Bailout Is Unconstitutional," *NYT*, January 15, 2009, A16; Armey and Kibbe, *Give Us Liberty*, 66, 71, 4; W. Cleon Skousen, *The Five Thousand Year Leap: 28 Great Ideas That Changed the World* (1981; Franklin,

TN: American Documents Publishing, 2009), 173; Sean Wilentz, "Confounding Fathers: The Tea Party's Cold War Roots," *New Yorker*, October 18, 2010, 32–39.

13. Greater Boston Televison Corp. v. FCC, 444 F.2d. 841, 850–51 (D.C. Cir. 1970); see Reuel E. Schiller, "Rulemaking's Promise: Administrative Law and Legal Culture in the 1960s and 1970s," *AdLR* 53 (2001): 1156; Matthew Warren, "Active Judging: Judicial Philosophy and the Development of the Hard Look Doctrine in the D.C. Circuit," *GLJ* 90 (2002): 2599–633.
14. On this point, see Judkins C. Mathews, review of *Creating the Administrative Constitution*, by Jerry L. Mashaw, *LHR* 30 (2012): 1193.
15. Hamdi v. Rumsfeld, 542 U.S. 507, 533 (2004); Rasul v. Bush, 542 U.S. 466 (2004); "Reaffirming the Rule of Law," *NYT*, June 29, 2004, A26; see Louis Fisher, *The Constitution and 9/11: Recurring Threats to America's Freedoms* (Lawrence: University Press of Kansas, 2008), 190–97, 231–34.
16. Carol D. Leonnig, "Court: Ability to Police U.S. Spying Program Limited," *WP*, August 15, 2013, 1; see Justin Crowe, *Building the Judiciary: Law, Courts, and the Politics of Institutional Development* (Princeton, NJ: Princeton University Press, 2013), 263–66.
17. [Charles Evans Hughes,] "Important Work of Uncle Sam's Lawyers," *ABAJ* 17 (1931): 238, 237; Willard Hurst, "The Legal Profession," *Wisconsin Law Review* 1966: 974; James Willard Hurst, *The Growth of American Law: The Law Makers* (Boston: Little, Brown, 1950), 340.
18. Robert W. Gordon, "The American Legal Profession, 1870-2000," in *The Cambridge History of Law in America*, ed. Michael Grossberg and Christopher Tomlins (New York: Cambridge University Press, 2008), 3:112; see Mark Tushnet, "The Rights Revolution in the Twentieth Century," in ibid., 383–85; Mark J. Green, *The Other Government: The Unseen Power of Washington Lawyers* (New York: Grossman Publishers, 1975), 286.
19. Daniel T. Rodgers, *Age of Fracture* (Cambridge, MA: Belknap Press, 2011), 41–76.
20. Martha Derthick and Paul J. Quirk, *The Politics of Deregulation* (Washington, DC: Brookings Institution, 1985); William W. Fisher III, "Legal Theory and Legal Education, 1920-2000," in *Cambridge History of Law in America*, 3:42–45; Cornelius M. Kerwin, *Rulemaking: How Government Agencies Write Law and Make Policy*, 3rd ed. (Washington, DC: CQ Press, 2003), 225–29; "Cost-Benefit Analysis: Over-reliance on a Flawed Approach," http://www.progressivereform.org/costBenefit.cfm, visited August 24, 2013.
21. "People's Rights Ignored," *ALL* 5 (December 21, 1943): 5. On the storm over the OPA's hearing procedures, see Joanna L. Grisinger, *The Unwieldy American State: Administrative Politics Since the New Deal* (New York: Cambridge University Press, 2012), 35–55.
22. Quoted in Meg Jacobs, *Pocketbook Politics: Economic Citizenship in Twentieth-Century America* (Princeton, NJ: Princeton University Press, 2005), 230.

23. Wong Yang Sung v. McGrath, 339 U.S. 33, 46 (1950); Grisinger, *Unwieldy American State*, 83–86, 99–107; Statement of Thurman Arnold before the Subcommittee on Ethics and Morals of the Committee on Labor and Public Welfare, United States Senate, July 6, 1951, 5, box 5, Arnold MSS; Laura Kalman, *Abe Fortas: A Biography* (New Haven, CT: Yale University Press, 1990), 126–51.
24. Martha F. Davis, *Brutal Need: Lawyers and the Welfare Rights Movement, 1960-1973* (New Haven, CT: Yale University Press, 1993); Charles A. Reich, "Individual Rights and Social Welfare: The Emerging Legal Issues," *YLJ* 74 (1965): 1245–57.
25. R. Jeffrey Smith, "Top Military Lawyers Oppose Plan for Special Courts," *WP*, August 3, 2006, A11; Brief of Former United States Diplomats . . . as *Amici Curiae* in Support of the Petitioners at 6, Boumediene v. Bush, 553 U.S. 723 (2008).
26. Armey and Kibbe, *Give Us Liberty*, 71.
27. Quoted in Kate Zernike, *Boiling Mad: Inside Tea Party America* (New York: Times Books, 2010), 9. See also Theda Skocpol and Vanessa Williamson, *The Tea Party and the Remaking of Republican Conservatism* (New York: Oxford University Press, 2012), 104–6, 116–18; Ronald P. Formisano, *The Tea Party: A Brief History* (Baltimore: Johns Hopkins University Press, 2012), 63–80.
28. "Essential Reading: What Would Hayek Have Made of His New Cheerleader?" *The Economist*, June 26, 2010, 78.
29. Flint Hills Tea Party of Kansas, "Our Core Values," http://www.flinthillsteaparty.com/about.html, visited May 23, 2013; Branson (Missouri) Tea Party, https://www.teapartypatriots.org/groups/branson-tea-party, visited May 23, 2013.
30. Raymond (New Hampshire) Area Tea Party, "What We Stand For," http://raymondareateaparty.weebly.com/our-positions.html, visited May 23, 2013; Tea Party Roundup (Laramie, Wyoming), "Values Statement," http://teapartyroundup.com/WhoWeAre.html#whoweare, visited May 23, 2013; Massachusetts Tea Party, "Urgent Stat: Congress Has Been Dismissed!!!" http://massteaparty.org/2012/03/urgent-stat-congress-has-been-dismissed-must-act-now-small-window-before-we-become-a-dictatorship/, visited May 23, 2013; Marilyn M. Barnewall, "How in the Hell Did We Get Here?" December 18, 2011, http://www.tricitiesteaparty.info/?p=833#more-%27, visited May 23, 2013; Alexandra Jaffe, "IRS Targeting Scandal a Political 'Gift from Heaven' for Tea Party Groups," *The Hill*, May 15, 2013, http://thehill.com/homenews/campaign/299765-irs-scandal-a-political-gift-from-heaven-for-tea-party, visited May 23, 2013.

Index